The Media Writer's Guide
Writing for Business and Educational Programs

By
William Van Nostran

Focal Press
Boston   Oxford   Aukland   Johannesburg   Melbourne   New Dehli

Focal Press is an imprint of Butterworth–Heinemann.

 A member of the Reed Elsevier group

 Recognizing the importance of preserving what has been written, Butterworth–Heinemann prints its books on acid-free paper whenever possible.

 Butterworth–Heinemann supports the efforts of American Forests and the Global ReLeaf program in its campaign for the betterment of trees, forests, and our environment.

Library of Congress Cataloging-in-Publication Data
Van Nostran, William.
　The media writer's guide: writing for business and educational programming / by
William Van Nostran.
　　　p.　cm.
　Rev. ed. of: The scriptwriter's handbook. 1989.
　Includes bibliographical references (p.) and index.
　ISBN 0-240-80316-7　(alk. paper)
　1. Television authorship.　2. Industrial television—Authorship.
3. Video recordings—Authorship.　4. Television in education.
5. Mass media—Authorship.　6. Business writing.　　　I. Van Nostran,
William, Scriptwriter's handbook.　II. Title.
PN1992.7.V36　1999
808.2'25—dc21　　　　　　　　　　　　　99-26484
　　　　　　　　　　　　　　　　　　　CIP

British Library Cataloguing-in-Publication Data
A catalogue record for this book is available from the British Library.

The publisher offers special discounts on bulk orders of this book.
For information, please contact:
Manager of Special Sales
Butterworth–Heinemann
225 Wildwood Avenue
Woburn, MA 01801-2041
Tel: 781-904-2500
Fax: 781-904-2620

For information on all Butterworth-Heinemann publications available, contact our World Wide Web home page at:
http://www.focalpress.com

10 9 8 7 6 5 4 3 2 1

Printed in the United States of America

TABLE OF CONTENTS

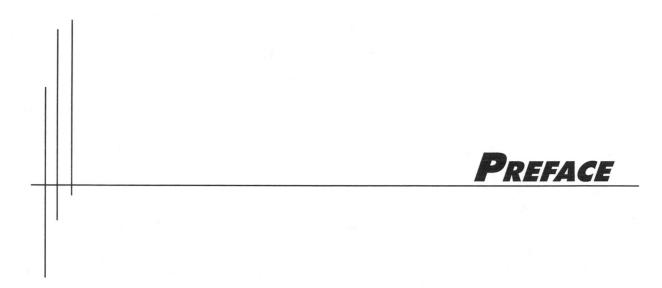

PREFACE

"Don't reinvent the wheel." Among the most well-worn of business cliches, this pragmatic aphorism ranks right up there with "If it ain't broke, don't fix it." In recent years, I've come to believe that, contrary to popular wisdom, there is much to be said for reinventing wheels and reinventing them well—creating wheels not only with spokes but a certain panache. Those who make a living in corporate, educational and organizational media are continually reinventing wheels. It is our raison d'etre. Take this book, for instance. It was "invented" in 1983 as *The Nonbroadcast Television Writer's Handbook*. I long since forgot how I positioned that first version, so I recently went back to a musty copy to refresh my memory. In those days, the use of video as a communication, training, and sales tool by companies, healthcare organizations, government agencies, and educators had been boosted by the ¾ inch U-matic videocassette—a convenient, economical tool for narrowcasting to specialized audiences.

In 1989, an expanded, updated version of the book was published with a much-improved title: *The Scriptwriter's Handbook*. Several technical advances had altered the media landscape. New, smaller consumer-oriented VCR formats as well as the growing acceptance of cable television were beginning to chip away at the dominance of three monolithic broadcast networks as the primary way in which television was experienced in the home.

Corporate communicators could now mail a video program directly to an employee or prospect.

At the same time, between 1983 and 1989, my awareness of the writing process was refined through a variety of experiences: exposure to master teachers of writing such as Donald Murray, Donald Graves, and Lucy McCormick Calkins. My workshop activities expanded to include the creative process, stimulated by folks like David Lyman at the Maine Photographic Workshops, and the so-called creativity mafia, led by luminaries such as Howard Gardner, Donald Perkins and Teresa Amabile, etc. So the late 1980s seemed like a good time to reinvent *The Nonbroadcast Television Writer's Handbook*.

Future Shock

In the late eighties, of course, how was I to know that in just a few short years something called the World Wide Web would come along? That personal computers would become audio and video playback devices? That there would be a new wave of gurus known as the digerati?

Although the writing process portions of *The Scriptwriter's Handbook* were still largely valid, by the late 1990s, the focus on creating Web sites and other interactive media, along with new developments in digital video, made me realize it was time to reinvent the wheel once again. And so the book you are reading came into being.

Part I focuses on adapting a universal writing process to linear media writing and is drawn largely from my previous book. Part II, however, is almost totally new material exploring issues and techniques applicable to interactive digital writing. Production script formats more suited to the challenges of interactive media production, as well as several new interactive writing examples, are included in this version.

Fortunately, my own career took a turn that brought me more intimately into contact with the burgeoning field of interactive digital media, broadening my experience with the form and stimulating my thinking on the subject. I felt more up to discussing the challenges of interactive digital media writing.

And yet, for all the hype surrounding the Technological Revolution leading to the Information Age, the Knowledge Explosion, and Information Superhighway, as a "new media" writer and producer, I often find myself reinventing wheels. Here's a modest example: In the 1970s and 1980s, several of my corporate projects used video as a campus recruiting tool. Today, as an executive producer at VuCom newMedia, I find myself creating interactive digital media tools to persuade the best and the brightest to come work for one of our client companies.

Furthermore, the specific functionality, graphic look, thematic approach, and choice of narrative and musical style for one company's college recruiting CD-ROM will, and must be (at least on the surface), totally distinctive—reflective of that organization's industry, work force, values, and corporate culture. That is what our clients pay us to do—create a media experience that appears to be unique to their organization. Nine times out of ten, however, we probably reinvent an existing wheel, simply changing the hubcap.

I am not denigrating the effort, talent, and craftsmanship required to do this. Working with a diverse pool of clients on wide-ranging subject matter demands writers who are highly observant, quick studies, skilled at divining client needs (the unspoken as well as the highly visible), and who possess the stamina and persistence to look at each project as though it is, indeed, the very first time this challenge has been faced. It is suicidal at the outset of a project to assume we know the solution. Only by working diligently through the research and writing process described in Part I can we hope to reinvent wheels with any sense of originality. Indeed, the most important contribution a writer makes to any project lies in the exercise of imagination.

Media in the 21st Century

As this book goes to publication in early 1999, the rush of adrenaline from a new millennium will surely stimulate many technical advances and enhancements to the way organizations use media to make things happen. Given the many new developments in digital video as both a production tool and broadcast/playback technology, we are poised for dramatic growth in that arena. Likewise, high definition TV (HDTV) and other display technologies may, at last, free producers and viewers from television's fixed three-by-four aspect ratio and offer new creative possibilities for corporate and organizational communicators and trainers.

And, of course, there is now no stopping the growth of the World Wide Web as a major new force in the evolution of corporate advertising, sales, customer service, communications, and training. The personal computer is now a full-fledged multimedia tool with far greater potential for becoming a rich source of information and knowledge—not simply data.

So I harbor no illusion that a decade or so from now there will be good reason to revise, update, and rethink this text once again. By then, however, I will leave it to someone else to reinvent this wheel—spokes and all. In the meantime, I hope this book is useful to students and professionals seeking a proven, pragmatic approach to the evolving and expanding field of media writing in the dawning years of the twenty first century.

ACKNOWLEDGMENTS

"A writer's occupation is one of the loneliest in the world," wrote Rachel Carson, perhaps the most influential environmental writer of the twentieth century. Media writing, by necessity, offers more opportunity for collaboration and interaction than book writing.

Although the actual writing was, indeed, sometimes a lonely occupation, this update to *The Scriptwriter's Handbook* could not have been written without the "crash course" in interactive digital media my job as executive producer at VuCom newMedia afforded me. In particular, Tom Vasko, operations manager at the company's Cleveland office, showed unusual patience in my early months as I came up to speed with the digital media world. Tom also became something of a collaborator on this book, designing the format and contributing artwork and suggestions while transforming my draft documents into desktop publishing files. Once again, he demonstrated great patience, especially in my hectic race to finish.

In addition, my many conversations and projects working with Robert Schulte and Peter Babula, also in VuCom newMedia's Cleveland office, provided new insight into the technical realities of media in a digital domain.

In my days as a freelance corporate media writer in the New York City area, I was fortunate in having a number of colleagues and directors who often improved my scripts in many ways. Among these people are Jim Libby, David Emmerling, Walter Schoenknecht, Chris Howe and Bill Hoppe.

From start to finish, I have worked on this book with not one, but two editors at Focal Press—Tammi Harvey and Terri Jadick. Both combined their professional counsel with liberal amounts of encouragement and understanding.

Finally, my wife, Lynne, and daughters, Kirsten and Kendra, graciously endure my painstaking writing schedule while offering support and refuge from the writer's enforced isolation. From Kendra's graduate studies in Media Ecology at New York University, I became exposed to the writings of media ecologists such as Neil Postman, who has informed many of my recent thoughts on media.

To all these people and to the countless others who have made a difference in my work as a media writer and who have enriched my life, thanks once again.

DEDICATION

FOR LYNNE, KIRSTEN,
AND KENDRA

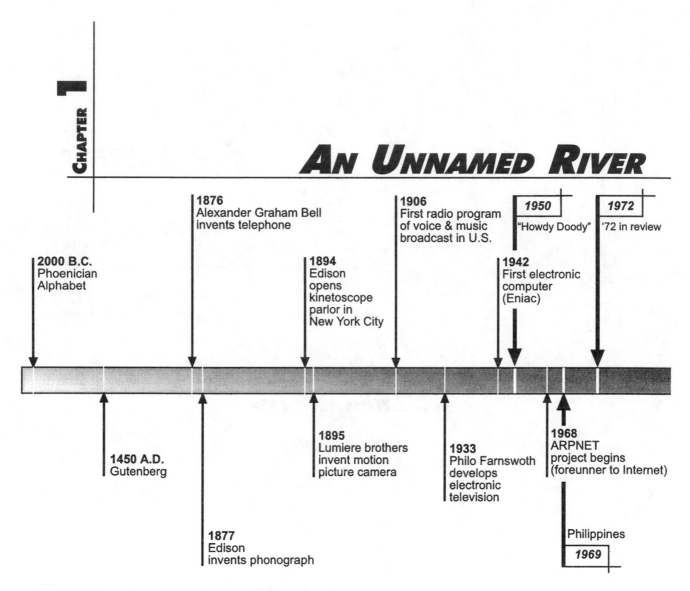

CHAPTER 1

AN UNNAMED RIVER

2000 B.C.
Phoenician
Alphabet

1876
Alexander Graham Bell
invents telephone

1894
Edison
opens
kinetoscope
parlor in
New York City

1906
First radio program
of voice & music
broadcast in U.S.

1950
"Howdy Doody"

1972
'72 in review

1942
First electronic
computer
(Eniac)

1450 A.D.
Gutenberg

1895
Lumiere brothers
invent motion
picture camera

1933
Philo Farnswoth
develops
electronic
television

1968
ARPNET
project begins
(foreunner to Internet)

1877
Edison
invents phonograph

Philippines
1969

Most of the inventions that make today's interactive digital media possible have taken place within the last 150 years.

Writing a book on media likely to be published on the cusp of the twenty first century makes it nearly irresistible to open by gazing into the techno-progress crystal ball and, as so many pundits and politicos of late, prophesize on the unlimited potential of the so-called new media to alter the course of man/womankind for the greater good. If for no better reason than to indulge my creeping crotchetiness, I will resist, or, at least, delay giving in to the urge.

To get a clear picture of where we stand among the ever-changing new media landscape, especially as it relates to corporate, medical,

educational, and other non-entertainment new media applications, I find it equally instructive to stop, do a "one-eighty," and gaze back down the path we have already trod.

That path takes an anecdotal storytelling bent. So the first half-century of this media retrospective is couched in personal recollections—anecdotal incidents drawn from my own media work. I've chosen the following destinations: 1997, 1982, 1972, 1968, 1951, and 1944.

As we travel back in time, pause occasionally to place some of your own life's mile markers into this timeline—putting the breathtaking pace of key technological developments into still more vivid personal perspective.

1997: Full Employment

In the spring of 1997, I joined a Midwestern new media production company as executive producer. The firm, VuCom newMedia, is a "pioneer" in new media applications for business.

features and benefits of the new Wrangler RFA tire for light trucks and utility vehicles.

- interactive laptop PC sales presentations—for companies ranging from CAP Toys to Seegott, a special-chemical distributor.

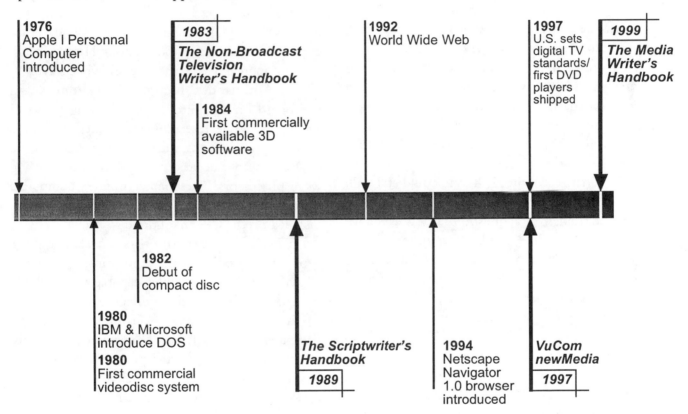

1976
Apple I Personnal Computer introduced

1983
The Non-Broadcast Television Writer's Handbook

1984
First commercially available 3D software

1992
World Wide Web

1997
U.S. sets digital TV standards/ first DVD players shipped

1999
The Media Writer's Handbook

1982
Debut of compact disc

1980
IBM & Microsoft introduce DOS
1980
First commercial videodisc system

The Scriptwriter's Handbook
1989

1994
Netscape Navigator 1.0 browser introduced

VuCom newMedia
1997

My own formative personal media experiences are flagged in bold. Consider how you have been influenced by media experiences.

On joining them, I viewed a range of company projects produced over the past five to six years. Programming such as:

- interactive touch screen presentations using CD-i technology for Saturn dealer showrooms—updated annually for each new model year.

- a Goodyear Tire & Rubber Company CD-ROM used by sales representatives to train local Goodyear dealerships on

- a variety of Internet applications: a Michigan utility that went on-line to improve customer service and build awareness of its product offerings; a regional sporting goods retailer promoting its image, store locations, and trying to build business via the World Wide Web. (One of my first projects was to upgrade the Web site for an upscale northern Michigan golf resort to make it more interactive, with an eye toward on-line reservations and credit card transactions.)

VuCom newMedia was also helping diverse clients create intra- and extranet applications, from desktop training tools to customer service projects.

On joining the company, I was surrounded by youth. Bright, energetic individuals who understood more about computer technology as it related to media than I ever wished to know. As "early adopters" of the technology, they were in an environment of selling and producing not just projects, but also advocating the very *concept* of interactive new media applications for several years. Versed in topics from compression and integration of video into digital materials to programming interactivity for cross-platform applications and using custom designed software for in-house project planning, management, and billing, they often served as a test facility for new software from Macromedia, Adobe, and others.

Engrossed in the field, one could still walk into a work area and overhear people wrestling to clarify such fundamental questions as, "What do we mean by 'new' media?" And, "If traditional video applications involve a mix of elements such as live motion video, computer generated graphics, audio—including music and sound effects—electronically produced visual special effects, and 35mm slides, why don't we call a linear video production a 'multimedia' project?"

Furthermore, in the midst of all this high-tech work, many VuCom clients, including Fortune 500 corporations, were still asking us to produce traditional 35mm speaker support *slides!*

Granted, such presentations invariably consisted of computer-generated images, yet the output was a "plain, old" slide in a plastic mount for display in a Kodak Carrousel™ projector. No computer program to crash here; just bring spare bulbs. A throwback to the dinosaur days of Eastman and Edison!

So there I am, a balding, pot-bellied fifty-ish writer smack dab in the center of the "new media" industry, and the phrase has such little specificity it is a virtually meaningless way to describe the work my younger colleagues and I are doing. To clarify the confusion caused by such fuzzy terminology, let's journey further *back* in time and analyze the forces that created an industry still struggling to define itself.

1982: Waiting for Delivery

Like an expectant father in the pre-Lamaze era, I sit waiting for delivery. My first computer, in reality a dedicated word processor (three heavy cartons requiring a large delivery truck and hand dolly), will weigh in at a few hundred pounds! A far cry from the Pentium-packed 2-pound laptop I write on now and carry with me to work while traveling.

Admittedly, I might have gone a tad overboard on the purchase of the original word processor. While researching content for a video series on productivity, I'd been introduced to the newest tool to spur productivity in the office: Wang word processors. These single-minded computers came with a proprietary word-processing program installed on the CPU hard drive.

One feature of this new corporate productivity tool was that the printing function allowed you to use a printer capable of providing the quality of a typewritten document, as opposed to the telltale dot-matrix look of most early computer printouts. It allowed corporate secretaries to enhance their productivity while improving the quality and appearance of written documents. Well, as soon as I saw what these early machines could do—crunch *words*, not numbers—I wanted one!

It would make my life easier. No more retyping an entire page of a script because I'd screwed up one line of copy.

It would improve my writing! If I read a proposal one last time before sending it off, saw a single sentence that needed clarification, I could do so without retyping at least a page of text.

So I shelled out what was a lot of money (about three to four times the cost of the laptop I now use) and bought one for my fledgling cottage industry.

In 1982, I was waiting delivery of equipment that almost always went to secretaries in large corporations, a telling bit of social commentary.

Then came a brief period in which word processing was further centralized in large typing pools—centers of productivity with input and output measurements.

It was only the previous year, 1981, with IBM's Johnny-come-lately entry into the personal computer market, that PCs began to go mainstream. It took a few more years of technological improvements and the debut of Microsoft Windows 1.0 in 1985 until middle-managers overcame the stigma associated with key-stroking and PCs began appearing on manager's desks. Their acceptance eliminated the word-processing center, forcing managers to "hunt and peck" their way through their own business correspondence. With user-friendly word-processing programs, one need not be a fast, accurate typist to produce error-free documents.

Just then, the doorbell rings, and I sign the bill of lading for my bouncing baby boy—and begin to tear open the crates. He was handsome. But we couldn't play yet. I had to make an appointment for the company's installer to come and set the little bugger up. Seems like eons ago. Yet it was only yesterday.

'72 In Review

In 1972, I was a lot more like the bright, energetic young people at VuCom newMedia a quarter century down the road. I'd taken my first civilian job after a stint in the Air Force during Viet Nam. I'd joined the corporate communications staff of another Ohio firm, Owens-Corning Fiberglas.

One of my first large projects was a video annual report to employees: a review of the year 1972 and a look ahead to top management's expectations for the coming year. The target audience: the company's far-flung field sales force and plant management.

There was no question what to call this medium. It was *television*—pure and not so simple. Producing a professional-looking corporate video in 1972 was an evolving craft. Bear in mind, in 1972, the term "camcorder" had not yet entered America's collective vocabulary. There were no Blockbuster Video outlets.

Corporate video producers were pioneers in 1972. Westward, ho, and all. One thing became clear from the outset: Television was *multimedia* in a big way. The finished program consisted of interviews with the president and key division vice presidents shot on broadcast quality tape (in those days, that meant videotape a full 2 inches wide). These segments included cutaway 16mm film footage shot on location at various Owens-Corning facilities—manufacturing plants, technical center, etcetera. For other topics we wished to document but that didn't merit the expense of a 16mm film shoot, we raided the corporate photo library and inserted 35mm slides. Still other topics (the company had just won a contract to insulate the Alaskan pipeline, for instance) were illustrated with a combination of library film footage and artwork illustrating the pipeline's snake-like route from Point Barrow to Prudhoe Bay.

Editing was done in New York City, at the postproduction facility of the company we'd hired to execute our vision. Editing videotape in 1972, even in the most professional broadcast-quality facility, was primitive by today's standards.

No computer editing here. Tape machine room and edit suite were literally one and the same. Our videotape editor did not get to sit at a console and enter commands via a keyboard. He found "in" and "out" cues manually.

Once he had both the playback and record machine cued properly, he actually physically marked the 2-inch wide tape with magic marker and previewed the edit! That way he could cue to the exact spot again. Or, if the director asked to have a cue moved either way by a second or two—the editor used the markings as a reference point.

But this all seemed a high-tech marvel compared to editing the silent film clips used as insert footage. My memories include the fact that we seemed to be working in a broom closet. Three people, the film editor, the director, and myself, squinting and pointing at a tiny 16mm frame seen through a moviola viewer.

The editor, an elderly, curmudgeonly East

European with remnants of a thick accent, was a good enough film editor but lacking in the client relations department. Working late one night, we were trying to finish the last few sequences. Bear in mind that once edit choices were made, we had only a length of work print quality film which had been physically cut and pasted, and cut and pasted time again—held together by nothing more than a substance which glue-sniffing, pubescent teenage boys would pay lots of money for on the street. Once the director and I would leave to enjoy a nightcap, this poor slob's work had only begun. He would painstakingly recreate this work using the master footage—being so much more careful with it so as not to scratch the emulsion.

Nor did he seem oblivious to the fact that while we would be tipping back a Drambuie, he would still be confined to his cell-like workroom a.k.a. broom closet. Periodically, we would meekly endure one of his "outbursts." He would begin by tossing all the film clips draped around his neck into the air, as he stormed out the room yelling in his broken English, "It's always this way! No respect. The editor is always afterthought. We work like oxen. Well I am oxen no longer. I refuse to work under such conditions!"

Stomping down the hallway to the elevator, he leaped into the next car going up, down, or sideways. Was he gone for good? What had he just done to our production schedule? For the first time in my young life, I understood the power labor could wield over management.

Where he went and what he did once those elevator doors opened again, I can only surmise. Probably it was no more imaginative than stepping out onto the street (if he'd happened to catch a down elevator) or up on the roof (if he'd walked into one headed the opposite direction) for a smoke. After some deep drags on strong European cigarettes, gazing calmly at soft moonbeams, he would actually return to our cubbyhole. Acting as though nothing whatsoever had transpired, he would calmly pick up precisely the correct piece of film footage from the floor and ask, "Now how long did you want this shot to last?"

Ultimately, however, the reason I chose 1972 as one of my media timeline stopping points has little to do with quaint film and video editing techniques or the fact my company was using videotape to communicate such information. What is truly significant about *"72 in Review"* (as it was so imaginatively titled) was neither message, medium, nor editing tools, but rather the *distribution method:* the Sony U-matic ¾-inch videocassette.

Prior to 1972, if a company created a training video to distribute throughout the organization, ½ inch black and white helical scan videotape decks plagued by a host of playback problems was the only option. Video playback was as dicey as playing the slots. Imagine being a sales manager far from corporate headquarters faced with playing a video as part of your quarterly sales meeting.

First, you'd thread the tape manually. You'd hit "play" and start twisting dials to get a solid, clear image. Ten minutes into the program, however, the picture breaks up, then becomes unviewable. The machine's playback heads had clogged! To remedy the situation, the heads had to be cleaned with alcohol on a cotton swab. "Well, let's forget the videotape. Just read the memo from marketing," he might announce before moving to the next, less technically demanding, topic.

But the videocassette eliminated the entire hassle and uncertainty associated with small format video playback. The tape arrived in the mail encased in plastic. If you dropped it you didn't risk seeing tape unwind all over the floor.

Just pop the cassette into the tape deck, hit the Play button and, voila, a full-color video image appears, looking every bit as bright and clear as the broadcast television people were now used to viewing at home. From 1972 forward, corporation after corporation established videocassette networks—putting video playback equipment in branch offices, on factory floors, and in research centers, lunchrooms, and classrooms across the country.

The big three automakers established dealer networks and sent out hours of promotional and sales and service training videos. Retail outlets used video to train employees in everything from running cash registers to how to sell more product. And as hospitals and teaching institutions purchased video equipment, pharmaceutical companies ramped up for video-based physician education and product promotion videos.

By summer of 1972, internal communication groups began producing hours of video on topics ranging from employee benefits to company news, major product announcements, and safety training videos. Business and industry began spending significantly on video equipment for internal production as well as for outside production services.

In just a little more than a decade, the total dollar volume of organizational video had grown to $3.8 billion per year in 1985. With the average corporate video operation producing around 30 programs annually, the total hours of organizational television programming approached 55,000 hours.[1] Trade organizations like the International Television Association (ITVA) were flourishing. An industry had matured. Television was no longer only associated with watching *"Mary Tyler Moore"*, the *"Tonight"* show, major league baseball and made-for-TV movies. The sight of video monitors and VCRs was omnipresent throughout corporate America.

1968, The Philippines

The Philippine Islands are archipelagoes in the South Pacific. During the Vietnam War, two huge U.S. bases were used as strategic supply and command centers. Subic Bay, a naval base situated on the large island of Luzon on the South China Sea, served as Naval Operations Center. In 1968, I was stationed at Clark Air Base, headquarters for the Thirteenth Air Force. Further north and inland, it lies buried in volcanic ash today victim of the 1991 nearby Mount Pinatubo eruption. Air bases in Thailand and Taiwan reported up the chain of command to the Thirteenth Air Force, where I worked in the Public Information Office.

My service time gave me hands-on experience in journalism. Not investigative reporting, of course. More like work done by corporate communicators or public relations firms—put the company line "spin" on the story.

In addition to the Vietnam War, something far more productive was taking place in the military in 1968. Although completely unaware of this activity at the time, it would profoundly affect my future and, indeed, the life of anyone working in corporate communications and education today.

The Department of Defense (DOD) asked RAND to come up with a design for a communications network that could survive a nuclear holocaust. RAND proposed solving this problem with a "distributed, many-to-many" network, one in which the responsibility for relaying information was spread equally among all nodes on the network—"hot potato" routing, it was termed. The concept was simple: link supercomputers at different locations in the nation using leased long-distance lines.

In 1969, while I was still busily writing news releases in the Philippines, the first node on this new network, the DOD's Advanced Research Projects Agency, dubbed ARPAnet, was established in a lab at UCLA. By year's end, the number of nodes on the burgeoning network was up to a whopping four! Even by the time I'd left the Air Force and was working on my first major corporate video project in 1973, the network was only somewhere between 30 to 50 nodes. And no one, save a few DOD insiders and high-tech university computer scientists, knew that this was even going on.

Unbeknownst to the general population, America had begun laying "track" for a new transcontinental communications network known as the Internet! ARPAnet was a wide area network connecting private and public institutions for defense and artificial intelligence research. It proved far more significant in changing human perceptions of time and space than the laying of the transcontinental railroad in 1896. Here was the beginning of a revolutionary communication technology, the World Wide Web.

And yet, in the Philippines where I was living

at the time, English was the primary language among Filipinos because the dialects of their native tongue, Tagalog, varied from one island to another so drastically that someone from the island of Leyte could not comprehend Tagalog as spoken on Luzon!

Spring, 1951 (or thereabouts)

I recall a fine spring day—walking down the big hill, which seemed ever so much bigger as a first- or second-grader than it appears to me now. On this day, however, I seemed to glide down the hill, undistracted by anything that might catch a seven-year-old boy's fancy. Instead, I am hurrying home. Today is the day I've been eagerly anticipating.

While I was in school, watching billowy clouds slip gracefully past the large pane glass windows, sometime while I fidgeted practicing my letters, television arrived in my household.

I'd already seen television. I knew what a treat awaited me at home. I have a distinct image of a small black-and-white cathode-ray tube emanating from what looked like a terribly oversized radio, a glowing electronic image ensconced in a mahogany-like casement with large plastic dials. I didn't know quite what the dials did much less how these black-and-white moving images of the world came to life so magically inside the cabinetry. I just knew it was there. And that it was neat.

There he was—a masked man atop a white steed that stood prone on its haunches and stretched its front hooves toward the sky. I'd seen that TV show at my relatives' home in a working-class Pittsburgh neighborhood. Then on the long drive back to Akron, Ohio, I'd wonder if someday we might get one of those great big magical wooden cabinets of our very own.

When I got to the front door that day, I was ready for every single minute of *"Howdy Doody!"* Life in America would never be the same—no siree, bob!

1944

A Navy destroyer, the USS Smalley has just been christened and is on its maiden voyage, out to the Pacific. Into the uncharted waters of war. My father is aboard, leaving behind a young wife and newborn son. He is one of an entire generation who is in the service during this time of world war—their lives tossed and tumbled by the mighty currents of humanity run amok.

To mold and motivate these raw recruits into a unified fighting machine, new technology is used, and we have the birth of the "Army Training Film." These films used the medium to show young infantrymen how to take their weapon apart, clean it, and reassemble it so it would not fail them in the heat of battle.

And the Armed Forces learned something about using film for training purposes. It worked! Troops at every installation got the same message. The training film was always available. It never spent a week in sick bay. The sight and sound capabilities of the motion picture made it particularly suited for showing *how* to perform a procedure.

In another vein, motivational films put Hollywood's best talent to work producing such classic documentary series as Frank Capra's *Why We Fight* films. These propaganda films, still studied by film students today, put some of America's best and brightest filmmakers to work for the Department of Defense.

During this same era, a group of scientists and mathematicians at the University of Pennsylvania were also hard at work for the Department of Defense. Their assignment was to design and build the world's first large-scale general-purpose electronic computer. When they finished in 1946, the war was winding down, but the computer age was just beginning. Called ENIAC, the prototype for today's laptops included 18,000 vacuum tubes, occupied 15,000 square feet of space, weighed 30 tons and costs $400,000!

Nineteen forty-six was also the year in which RCA built what many considered the Model T of television sets. It was the 630 TS model, a black-and-white set priced at a mere $385. By year's end, RCA had sold 10,000 units. I was almost three years old.

Back to the Present

To those who say linguistics is an arcane study, the murky waters of media terminology in the late '90s shows how vital it is to have precise names for the things of our everyday lives. We would be far better equipped to use so-called multimedia more imaginatively and productively if we could begin to clarify with language the ways in which the computer and audio-visual experiences are being combined.

We are mixing media and computer technology in ways not possible a mere 20 years ago. The pace of technological growth is far outrunning the mind's capacity to comprehend the meaning of these so-called new media.

It's as though we stand at a place where two mighty rivers join to form a third river. To get here, some of us rafted down the rapids of the video river—fed by tributaries such as film, photography, theatre, music, dance and radio. Another group, standing on the opposite bank, came to this point by traversing the equally rapid waters of computer technology, where bits and bytes give the binary world seemingly infinite possibilities. These computer engineers and mathematicians, programmers, interface designers, and pioneering Web masters believed they would surely reach a "promised land" if, like Lewis and Clark, they simply kept moving forward.

Only within the past few years have we begun to see the two rivers winding closer and closer together. Up to that point, we had only caught glimpses of one another through the trees and banks separating the two rivers.

Now we see that the two disciplines, like the rushing, swirling waters of this third riverbed, have become inextricably intertwined. Safe passage down this third river will involve mixing crews—so that the best, most talented rafters from the two rivers bring their expertise to bear to meet the challenges that lie ahead when traversing the uncharted waters of this unnamed river. To say that we know where we're headed is the kind of arrogance that tempts nature and quickly leads to danger.

Footnotes

1. Alan R. Richardson, editor, *Corporate and Organizational Video* (New York: McGraw-Hill, Inc.), 1992, pgs.xvii-xviii.

CHAPTER **2**

NAMING THE RIVER

It is unfortunate that no truly appropriate name has been given to the type of medium spawned by the marriage of the computer with existing audio-visual media and print. Marshall McLuhan's groundbreaking book, *Understanding Media: The Extensions of Man,* would have been quite different if the computer in its present form had been on the scene in the 1960s. The Internet of today is, perhaps, the ultimate "extension of man."

But McLuhan's book was written in a decade when broadcast television seemed the most ubiquitous example of media as extension of man. Yet a basic premise of McLuhan is that *all* media, and he uses the term broadly, function as extensions of man.

"In the electric age, we wear all mankind as our skin,"[1] wrote McLuhan. So sensitive is he to this concept of the electric age that he uses the light bulb to drive home his contention that the effect of media is distinct from the content that they convey. He calls the electric light pure information, a medium without a message unless used to "spell out some verbal ad or name."

McLuhan is more interested in each medium's innate power to change man's environment than the content that comprises the programming. To dramatize the point, he refers to the transforming power of the electric light:

The electric light ended the regime of night and day, of indoors and out-of-doors. But it is when the light encounters already existing patterns of human organization that the hybrid energy is released. Cars can travel all night, ballplayers can play all night and windows can be left out of buildings. In a word, the message of the electric light is total change. It is pure information without any content to restrict its transforming and informing power.[2]

Medium and Message

Today's media writer must master a variety of media as well as content. It is the media writer's challenge to unleash the "transforming and informing power" of media.

Writing imaginatively and appropriately for any medium is difficult enough. The task is compounded when multiple media are involved and integrated with the interactive potential made possible by the marriage of computer and media. Writing about the role of interactivity in computer based training, Gloria Gery calls it "what the computer permits that no other instructional approach can approximate except for a one-on-one Socratic dialogue between an expert and a learner."[3]

The thrust of this book is based on the premise that designing and writing interactive media applications for the technology of today and tomorrow requires a media versatility and dexterity rare among writers. It is analogous to asking a fiction writer to excel in writing poetry, novels, short stories, dramas, and screenplays, and then combining the several genres into an integrated, seamless whole.

Several writers have excelled in more than one genre: Shakespeare was a poet-dramatist. Chekov wrote both great dramas and humorous short stories.

Yet many writers are comfortable in only one literary form. Henry James, master novelist, failed miserably in several attempts at playwriting. Despite his extraordinary facility with words, the theatre was not in his blood.

Master One Medium at a Time

We could dive directly into the topic of writing for today's digital interactive "multimedia." I prefer, however, an approach that begins by recognizing the inherent strengths and weaknesses of each medium available to the multimedia writer in the context of linear applications. By focusing first on the possibilities and potential of each individual medium, the writer is better equipped to make the interactive media experience all it can and should be for the target audience.

This book is organized to encourage multimedia thinking by first learning and applying a media-writing process to the most common *linear* media used today in corporate communication and training:

- Print
- Audio
- Film
- Live performance
- Video

Of these linear media, three are *multi*media in the common sense understanding of the term. Video and film engage both eye and ear. Each fluidly mixes images (still or motion), graphics, and animation that unfold in time and are linked to a sound track that may also include various auditory stimuli: narration, dialogue, music, and sound effects.

Print plays to our sense of sight and is the product of literate societies, requiring such reading skills as knowledge of an alphabet, punctuation, syntax, etcetera. Audio plays to our sense of hearing, and may include narration, dialogue, music, and sound effects. (A mix of all these auditory elements in a single linear presentation does not, however, constitute a multimedia experience since all are perceived by the *ear*.)

A live performance such as a classroom instructor or executive speaker, for example, appeals to both sight and sound (facial expression and gesture, at the very least, complementing oral content). The speaker may integrate additional media into the experience by projecting slides or computer graphics, showing videotape, or having the class listen to ambient sounds.

Digital Interactive Multimedia Experiences

Part II focuses on bringing the types of interactivity available to the corporate media writer when the computer endows linear media with digital random-access capabilities. This media experience involves using a computer to deliver content and provide the man-machine interface required for even the most rudimentary interactivity—a simulated "Socratic dialogue."

This includes information or training delivered over networks, such as the Internet and its intra- and extranet variants. Interactive CD-ROMs and touch-screen kiosks provide other methods for delivering interactive multimedia experiences, offering both greater bandwidth (more on this in Part II) and, as a result, opportunity for multimedia variety and richness than many current networked applications. (To date, however, both CD-ROM and Internet applications rely upon video compression to handle the large amount of data comprising video images. This is changing with digital video disc (DVD) technology.)

The digital information of an interactive multimedia experience may also reside directly on a personal computer hard drive. The PC may be a desktop, a laptop, or freestanding public kiosk.

Digital video currently has multiple meanings: On one hand, analog media such as a Hollywood motion picture can be captured on a DVD for playback using a DVD player. In addition, it is also possible to use digital cameras to acquire footage in digital format. This facilitates all-digital storage, retrieval, post-production, and image manipulation.

All these media, however, save for the live performance, which is a "real life" experience, were created in analog formats. It is only when they needed to be accessed via computers that the translation to the "bits and bytes" of information necessary for digital presentation became an absolute requirement. The 12-inch videodisc of the 1980s is the forerunner of today's compact digital videodisc, or DVD.

The videodisc, widely available and in use for corporate training and kiosk applications in the early 1980s, was the first delivery system for such computer-based training. So far, however, we are focusing on the *distribution* method, which is like saying the same television program may be distributed on broadcast TV, on cable, or as a videocassette.

The features distinguishing a digital presentation from its analog cousin centers on user control of content through the random access capabilities the computer affords. Typically, people interact with a computer by means of a:

- **Keypad**   - **Touchscreen**
- **Mouse**   - **Joystick**

Most recently, voice-activated computer software is opening new windows on the manner in which we interact with computers. So we could add the word "microphone" to the above list.

Figure 2.1: Bandwidth throughput illustrates how a video signal must be compressed for various digital distribution systems.

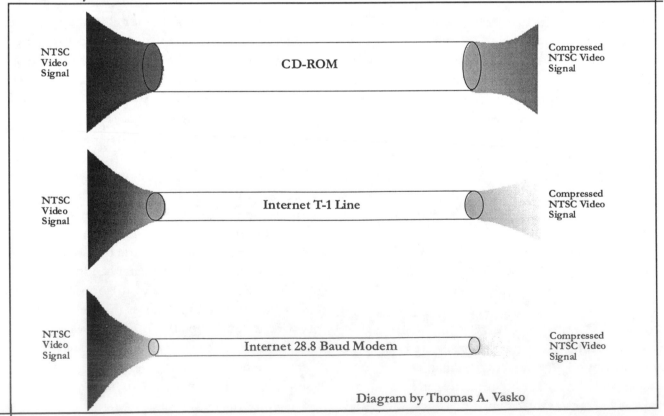

Diagram by Thomas A. Vasko

Bringing interactivity to a media presentation is nothing new. In the '70s and early '80s, it was not at all uncommon for trainers to develop learning packages consisting of a videocassette and a workbook. Generally, the videocassette was used to disseminate information. The print material contained additional reading, exercises, quizzes, case studies, tests, or other activities for the learner to perform—tools for enhancing understanding and retention.

The videotape was rarely intended to view from beginning to end. Rather, the viewer would be instructed periodically to pause or stop the video and go off-line to the workbook, where they would continue the learning experience by reading or answering questions based on material presented in the previous video segment. A crude form of interactivity.

Once it became possible, however, to package all program elements—audio, video, text, graphics, photos, etcetera, as uniform bits and bytes, the entire program could reside together in the digital domain. And the computer could, like Socrates, provide instantaneous feedback to questions or ask still more questions in return.

Furthermore, additional "bits and bytes" could be created to provide various types of random access and branching, permitting users to select their own idiosyncratic path through the material based on their interests, preferences, responses to specific situations, or immediate needs.

Is the Computer a Communication Medium?

The answer, of course, depends on the criteria used to describe a medium. Here is how the dictionary deals with the topic:

> **Media or mediums: 1.** a means for sending information to large numbers of people; **2.** media. The various means used to convey information in a society, including magazines,

newspapers, radio and television: the mass media.[4]

If McLuhan considers the electric light a medium, then the computer, especially the personal computer, has proven an equally illuminating "extension of man." All media used in today's communications environment were initially conceived as tools for "sending information to large numbers of people." From the Phoenician alphabet to Phylo T. Farnsworth and the television picture tube, creators of these technologies have envisioned their use as tools to enhance communication of a message—embodied in symbols (the alphabet) or real-world representations (sight and sound). Even their names suggest their relationship to the physical senses they stimulate:

- **Photograph**
- **Phonograph**
- **Motion picture**
- **Television**

Yet it is oversimplifying to suggest that the inventors of television, radio, motion picture, and so on had a clear vision of the content and uses these media would spawn. They were men of science, not communicators. Edison invented both the phonograph and motion picture (working closely with W.K.L. Dickson on the latter.) Marconi took the ideas of Edison, Nikola Tesla, and others to create radio.

A High-Speed Counting Machine

Returning to Webster, a computer is defined as "a device that computes, esp. an electronic machine that performs high-speed mathematical or logical calculations and assembles, stores, correlates, or otherwise processes and prints data."[5]

The impetus for the computer grew from work on cracking the German encryption code during World War II. (Ironically, the "fathers" of the computer were also the original "hackers.")

The only function a computer can perform

is to count. And it counts only to one. This is achieved by sensing voltage, whether a particular circuit is "on" or "off."

Since the computer merely distinguishes between zeros (off) and ones (on), it counts using a binary number system that is translated into a decimal system: 0=0; 1=1; 10=3; 11=4; 100=5; 101=6; and so on. Each digit in this binary system, each zero or one, is a "bit". Eight together equal a "byte". These calculations are performed by the Central Processing Unit, or CPU.

Entering information into the CPU requires other devices. In the early days, one way to feed large amounts of data into big mainframe computers was by cards with holes punched in various areas to communicate binary information. Each hole in the card corresponded to a zero or one.

Writing this, I'm using a keyboard to input data. With every keystroke, the CPU translates each different key into the series of zeros and ones that stand for an "A," "B," or other alphanumeric input. I also occasionally input information with a mouse. I might also import existing data from a floppy disc or CD-ROM.

For several decades, the computer's primary output was to a printer. There were no graphics to display in color, just numbers and letters.

The first computer screens borrowed from television technology and used cathode-ray tubes (CRTs) for display devices. Initially, these monitors displayed only letters and numbers. Although the computer monitor uses technology similar to television, there are important differences for media producers, graphic artists, and writers.

Display Technologies

Although they seem similar, computer and television monitors do not share identical display technology. The television picture is composed of horizontal scan lines. These lines are scanned from top to bottom, half at a time, every other line. Half the lines are equal to a field, and both halves to a frame. Until high-definition television became commercially available, the number of scan lines

was always the same: 525. And television is always shown at 30 frames per second.

A computer monitor, by contrast, projects dots onto the screen. Each dot is a pixel (picture element), and the more pixels, the sharper the image. Pixel size is known as the dot pitch. The rate at which the screen changes from one image to another is known as the refresh rate. Refresh rates vary from 20 times per second to more than 100 times per second. (Since standard television displays 30 frames per second, a refresh rate of 30 is needed to display normal video.) Other limitations relating to storage and transmission of the enormous number of bits and bytes comprising video images create other problems, which is why videos usually are compressed for computer display.

Computers Go Artsy

With the advent of graphics capabilities and software, the computer becomes a tool for creating graphics as well as storing, sequencing, displaying, and manipulating them. Animation, similar to motion picture or video animation, provides the illusion of graphics that can move.

As Nicholas Negroponte points out in his book, *Being Digital*, "bits commingle effortlessly… …the mixing of audio, video and data all in bit form is called multimedia."[6]

A significant distinction between communication media and the computer is the role software programming plays. Negroponte refers to this as a specialized second type of digital information: "bits about bits" or "a bit that tells you about the other bits."[7] Because of the ability to place content into the shell of software programming, the computer is especially suited for applications allowing the user to have some control over access to information (games, training, Internet searching, etc.), creating the *illusion* that the human has entered into two-way dialogue with the computer. (On the Internet, of course, it is possible to enter into direct dialogue with other individuals, using the computer simply as a "medium" to facilitate the conversation.)

I say "illusion" because on a practical level, computer-based instruction, for instance, is always limited in the variability (and therefore richness) of the dialogue by budgetary and other resource limitations placed upon program designers. The software shell into which content is placed offers only a finite number of possibilities.

Fulfilling the stimulus-response potential of the computer as a communication/training tool, experimenting and creating new forms, that is the imaginative challenge facing all that create such material. To quote Negroponte again: "New information and entertainment services are not waiting on fiber to the home; they are waiting on imagination."[8]

Part II of this book focuses on the challenge of unleashing the interactive imagination.

The computer's incredible and ever growing versatility is one of its unique characteristics as a medium.

The following media charts provide comparative thumbnail sketches of each medium in terms of its historical role of disseminating content. With the invention of moveable type and its resulting ease of duplication and distribution, print becomes the first mass medium.

Figure 2.2 Medium—Print

General Features

Single sensory (sight only)

A highly personal "one-to-one" medium

Extremely portable

Uses the phonetic alphabet (discursive symbols) and, therefore, requires a degree of literacy for full comprehension/appreciation.

Print has a permanency that many other media lack.

Ink squeezed onto dead trees (Nicholas Negroponte's description of the analog nature of print) is, for some reason, easier to read than text on a computer monitor. Writers and editors may create works on computers, but at some stage in the writing process, they almost invariably edit from printouts because it gives a more accurate sense of grammatical and stylistic usage.

Can incorporate other non-motion media such as photography, artwork, graphics, still frames from video, etc., allowing Langer's presentational and discursive imagery to exist side-by-side and enrich the meaning of each.

Strengths

From its inception, the alphabet and an individual's ability to interpret phonetic symbols has proven empowering—to individuals and societies as a whole. The ability to read and write is perhaps the most intellectually liberating force in any culture.

McLuhan writes that "the alphabet meant power and authority..." why nearly all judicial, military, corporate and organizational rules and regulations are committed to print.

Can be created for both a linear and non-linear type of access.

Weaknesses

Ironically, print's major drawback is the necessity for literacy on the part of both sender and receiver. Literacy exists on many levels. The ability to read and write does not guarantee facility, sophistication or versatility in use of the written word.

Paradoxically, although written language is often used to codify and clarify rules, regulations and contractual relationships, it is still open to individual interpretation due to the subtle and detailed discursive richness of language. (As well as making laws open to interpretation, this same richness is what makes Shakespeare a playwright for the ages.)This is why corporate communicators consider delivery of a uniform, consistent message one of the strengths of a video presentation. The video medium's ability to incorporate spoken word (with interpretive vocal inflection) and presentational images make it less open to individual interpretation as it moves through an organization.

Special Considerations for Writer

The degree of literacy of both writer and reader bear significantly on the effectiveness and shared meaning inherent in a written communication.

Although the language of any communication must be geared to the audience, this is especially vital in print communications. Writing for auto mechanics is quite different than writing for automotive engineers.

In today's multimedia environment, facility with the print medium is essential. Business sites on the World Wide Web incorporate a large amount of text. CD-ROM screens incorporate text as well as graphics and visuals.

Figure 2.3: Medium—Television

General Features

Television is a sight and sound *motion* medium.

Uses an electronically created visual image. The picture consists of high-speed electrons, each producing a luminous spot on a cathode-ray tube. A complete image is composed of horizontal scan lines that refresh thirty times every second. Frames per second: 30

Television is still best viewed on a cathode-ray tube screen. It can also be displayed using Liquid Crystal Display (LCD) technology, which permits video to be shown on a laptop computer or projected onto a screen.

Can be viewed in ambient light.

Television can be broadcast live or recorded on videotape, which permits immediate playback.

The pure electronic image (shot, recorded and played back on video equipment) has a live, "happening-now" presence.

Electronic production techniques and post-production digital manipulation of video images offer writers a wide range of special effects, computer-generated graphics and animation techniques.

Sound includes option for stereo and Dolby™ surround sound using digital video disc (DVD) technology.

Strengths

Television and videotape have immediacy. This results from both the live look of the electronic image as well as videotape's instant playback capability. NOTE: When video is digitized and compressed for playback on a computer, some of this "live" quality may be lost depending on the compression technique and configuration of the computer used for playback.

People relate to television in a highly personal way due to years of conditioning as home viewers.

Widespread home VCR ownership provides additional viewing opportunities for producers of corporate or medical content. (Tapes can be sent directly to an employee's home.)

Television easily incorporates other media, such as film, slides or other graphics.

Weaknesses

With typical screen size of 24 inches diagonally, viewing audience size is limited to about 20 people.

Because of traditional small screen size, television is often referred to as a "close-up" medium.

Compared to the 35mm slide or 16mm-film image, the standard TV picture has relatively poor resolution. High definition TV technology will improve this situation.

Typical single-screen video format is in a fixed 3 by 4 aspect ratio.

Special Considerations for Writer

Since video viewing can range from a single person in front of a small screen to large screen projection and even videowalls, the video writer should have an understanding of the program's ultimate viewing environment.

Video production facilities vary widely in terms of equipment and capabilities, the video writer should have an appreciation of the budget and production capabilities of those charged with executing the program. This will have an impact on the program format, use of special effects, animation, etc.

Digital Video Notes

Because there are several ways in which the term "digital video" can be used, it is easy to generate confusion discussing digital video. The following are brief descriptions of current digital video formats.

Digital encoding of analog video—analog videotape can be digitally encoded, translating the visual image on tape to digital form. Typically this is done for two reasons:

1) To facilitate non-linear digital editing in the post-production process. In this case, raw footage is edited in digital form. But the final output generally produces an analog videotape master.

2) To facilitate playback in digital media. Typically, this involves not only encoding, but also compressing video images so they take up less bandwidth. This allows video to be accessed via a computer. The computer or laser disk player may be accessing the video data directly from a hard drive, off a CD-ROM, digital video disk, or via a network.

More recently digital cameras and recording formats are used to capture video signals in a digital format. This is analogous to digital audio recording.

Figure 2.4: Medium—Film

General Features

A photographic medium. Images are captured on film, which must then be processed.

Frames per second: 24 Aspect ratio can vary, but is almost always wider than television's 3-by-4 aspect ratio.

Film is generally projected for viewing; however, film transfers excellently to videotape. So film is frequently transferred to tape for editing and/or viewing.

Strengths

Like video, film is a sight and sound motion medium. Film is a large screen medium—allowing for a breadth and scope that goes beyond small screen TV.

Film production gear is still more portable and better suited to low-light documentary situations than video.

Film has excellent image resolution and contrast ratio; superior to current broadcast TV standard.

Weaknesses

Because it is a photographic image—film lacks the "live" look and immediacy of video's electronic picture. Even when transferred to videotape, film retains its photographic look.

Film does not permit instant playback while shooting. This is because the exposed film requires lab processing and prints to be made adding cost and time to the production process.

Special Considerations for Writer

The writer needs to know whether the film is intended for projection or will be transferred to tape and viewed on a TV or computer screen.

The writer should have a sense of the end use of film. Many TV commercials, music videos and other programs shot on film are actually meant for the video medium. On the other hand, a film that is being shot for one-to-one interaction becomes its special brand of magic.

Figure 2.5 Medium—Audiocassette and other sound recording media

General Features

Single sensory (sound only).

Extremely portable playback capability.

Strengths

The audiocassette's primary advantage for corporate, educational and organizational communication is portability. Sales representatives can play audiocassettes in their car while driving their territory.

With a Walkman™, personal cassettes can be listened to while jogging or engaging in other physical activities.

Relatively speaking, the audiocassette is inexpensive to produce.

Can be a good "one-on-one" tutorial aid, especially for some types of task training when combined with a workbook or job aid to provide the necessary visualization.

Ironically, the medium's greatest strength results from its biggest drawback: because it lacks a visual component, writing for the ear provides tremendous latitude in time and space. Vivid locations and situations can be created with a few words, sound effects and music.

Can be used effectively to communicate content involving human interaction—e.g., sales situations, interviewing techniques, employee counseling, etc.

Can also be used to present an expert on a subject or to provide a motivational platform for executives.

Weaknesses

The main drawback to audiocassettes is that they do not engage the eye. The audiocassette in a classroom environment, for example, leaves listeners free to be visually distracted; concentration may be difficult.

The ability to show while telling is lost with this medium, making it unsuitable for mechanical subjects or other instructional content difficult to convey through words alone (anatomy, for instance). Long segments of uninterrupted narration can become tedious.

Special Considerations for Writer

The writer must be open to the creative possibilities of the audiocassette and write imaginatively for the speaking voice and ear.

Role models, such as early radio dramatic writing or tales from oral cultures such as Native Americans, provide examples of how the lack of a visual component can be turned to good advantage by allowing listeners to create their own mental imagery.

Figure 2.6 Medium—PC-Based Interactive Digital Media

General Features

Combines personal computer technology with text, graphics, animation, audio and, in some formats, full-screen, full-motion video.

Random access capabilities allow user to interact directly with on-screen information, accessing data or information on a "need-to-know" basis.

Non-linear branching capabilities provide program developers opportunity to present content as "scenarios" with multiple outcomes based on path selected by user. You "tell yourself" a story by interacting with the content.

Can incorporate game formats and various testing strategies to meet training goals.

Strengths

High degree of user participation and involvement makes interactive media ideal for training to technical subject matter such as medical, financial, engineering and other complex, abstract subject matter.

Efficient way to communicate and train since each user makes individual choices regarding what information to access and how deeply to explore each topic.

Permits pre- and post-diagnostic testing with capability to track results and send user to appropriate remedial learning components.

Allows program design team to make optimal match between content and media (i.e. use of motion, animation, text, graphics, sound, etc.)

Similarity to video game technology offers opportunity for incorporating entertainment value into program design (edutainment).

Easily installed and adapted to kiosk settings for public access or trade show/convention floor use.

Weaknesses

Additional media and software design, authoring, programming and testing results in longer production lead times than for traditional linear media.

Users require computer hardware with compatible multimedia capabilities and specifications.

Not ideal for large audience display or interaction.

Special Considerations for Writer

Writers must organize content in non-linear, random access modes to capitalize on interactive branching potential.

Need to work with new design tools (flowcharts, etc.) and interact with additional personnel such as software programmers.

Need to know capabilities and limitations of various hardware, delivery systems (Internet, CD-ROM, etc.) and software authoring programs.

Requires flexibility, versatility and imagination to capitalize on full range of available media in various combinations and the potential for differing interactions.

Every Medium Possesses "Magic"

No medium is inherently "better" than another. Each has individual characteristics, strengths, and weaknesses.

The book is still a perfectly good "viewer"; simpler, more flexible, and better suited to linear exposition and detailed argumentation than the computer screen as a text viewer.

On the surface, film and video seem to share fundamental characteristics. But the motion picture's photographic image, big-screen theatricality, and association with theatrical drama and entertainment contrast sharply with television's small screen, live electronic presence, and close-up sense of immediacy. They typically occupy quite different viewing environments.

The "magic" they share, however, is the language of montage—picture storytelling in combination with music, sound effects, narration, and dialogue.

Audio, except for certain very astute broadcasters (such as National Public Radio) and more sophisticated advertising writers and producers, is often underrated and too easily dismissed as a communications tool. Its ability to make listeners focus on the human voice, music, and sound effects and to allow each listener to create an internal visual reality offer a potential for communication that is rarely exploited in industrial or educational media writing. One need only listen to classic comedy albums such as Carl Reiner interviewing the 2,000-year-old man as portrayed by Mel Brooks to appreciate the imaginative power this medium can unleash.

The computer can take on multiple personalities, depending largely on the user's intent of the moment. It can be a high-speed "number-cruncher," flexible graphics design tool, or the optimal self-correcting typewriter. When used as a communications tool, its ability to create the illusion of user-control and one-to-one interaction become its special brand of magic.

Whatever you wish to name this "river" created by the joining of computer technology and audio/visual media, nature has imbued it with certain immutable forces—giving this river its own distinctive personality—unlike any other river.

Yet just as the Mississippi, the Nile, and the Danube rivers have their own "magic", so, too, do various media possess "magic." It is the media writer's job to marry magic with subject matter to reach the target audience to create fully realized media experiences. That's what the rest of this book is about.

Summary

In the past, writers often had the luxury of honing their craft by working in a single medium: television, radio, print, theatre. Over time, specialization conferred a degree of mastery. Today's multimedia capabilities, by contrast, are forcing writers to develop the full range of media-writing muscles. To write for multimedia implies a mastery of all media.

Ironically, like the body builder in a gym, you cannot tone every muscle at once: some exercises focus on abs, others build upper-body strength and so on. Likewise, to develop dexterity and the ability to work fluidly with all media in an interactive mode, the writer must first master the craft of each individual medium, learning what it does best and how to tell a story conveying a message in that medium.

Part I provides a process for tackling linear writing assignments in various sight and sound media. This is where you lay the foundation for the more strenuous workouts that come later.

Footnotes

1. Marshall McLuhan, *Understanding Media: The Extensions of Man* (New York: McGraw-Hill Book Company, 1964), p. 47.
2. Ibid., p. 52.
3. Gloria Gery, *Making CBT Happen* (Tolland, MA: Gery Performance Press, 1987), p. 14.
4. *The American Heritage Desk Dictionary* (Boston, MA: Houghton Mifflin Company, 1981) p. 601.
5. Ibid., p. 214.
6. Nicholas Negroponte, *Being Digital* (New York: Alfred A. Knopf, 1995), p. 18.
7. Ibid., p. 18.
8. Ibid., p. 30.

THE LINEAR SCRIPTWRITING PROCESS

Learning to write good media scripts is more like learning to play the violin than learning to ride a bike. Though frustrating at first, riding a bicycle eventually comes in a joyous flash of balance and coordination. From then on, bike riding is mastered. Years may pass with no practice, but all it takes is a minute or two and one is skillfully riding again.

Mastering the violin is a different story. It takes several years to become good enough to play decently before friends and relatives. Simply to maintain technical proficiency, constant practice and daily repetition is a must. Given musical talent and good instruction, the young violinist may achieve a measure of virtuosity. Yet it will still take constant playing, concertizing, and life experience from the school of hard knocks to become a consummate musician—one whose playing seems to come straight from the heart with little or no effort.

Writing involves the same patient labor and dedication to craftsmanship to develop mastery of form and content. Reading this book will not transform you overnight into an accomplished media writer. That takes an apprenticeship and constant practice.

The chapters in Part I, however, offer an approach to linear media writing assignments grounded in practical experience and coupled with study and research in the teaching of writing. With Part I as a foundation, the second part of this book focuses on interactive digital-media writing. Unless you already possess experience and knowledge of linear media scriptwriting, it will be a mistake to skip to Part II, even if that is your primary interest. The media writing process introduced in Part I is equally valid for interactive-media assignments.

"Catching On..."

Whatever your present stage of evolution as a writer, we are not dealing in a field of absolutes. Each new media writing project poses new problems and challenges. The learning curve for all writers consists of a series of peaks and valleys on the way to competency and craftsmanship. John Gardner put it well in his advice to would-be novelists:

> *If the aspiring writer keeps on writing—writes day after day, month after month—and if he reads very carefully, he will begin to 'catch on.' Catching on is important in the arts, as in athletics. Practical sciences, including the verbal engineering of commercial fiction can be taught and learned. The arts can be taught, up to a point; but except for certain matters of technique, one does not learn the arts, one simply catches on.*
>
> *If my own experience is representative, what one mainly catches on to is the value of painstaking—almost ridiculously painstaking—work.*[1]

For media writers, what one mainly "catches on to" is a way of thinking and working that is process-driven. The goal is to develop a personal writing strategy that combines good creative results with a high level of productivity and consistency. The experienced writer internalizes steps in the scriptwriting process, automatically asking him or herself the appropriate question at the right moment as the process unfolds. As with any creative endeavor, a dialog takes place between the emerging work and the writer. The quality of that dialog determines the quality of the finished work.

A Media Writing Process

Chapters 3 through 8 offer a systematic approach to the problems posed at various stages of the media writing process. This process involves five discrete steps:

Step 1: Assimilation
Chapter 3: Collecting Information for the script
Chapter 4: Organizing Information: Translating research into an Action Plan

Step 2: Rehearsal
Chapter 5: Concept Development

Step 3: Drafting
Chapter 6: The Imaginative Eye
Chapter 7: The Imaginative Ear

Step 4: Revision
Chapter 8: Making the Most of Feedback

Step 5: Editing
Also addressed in Chapter 8

Figure 1.1 illustrates the steps and process. The left side of the diagram lists the techniques and activities the writer performs during that stage of the process.

The right side of the diagram describes specific writing products that result at the conclusion of each phase. At the end of the assimilation phase, for instance, the writer produces an analytical audience profile, objectives, and content outline. Rehearsal results in a creative media treatment. The drafting phase concludes with a complete first-draft script.

These products flow from the techniques or activities the writer engages in during each step of the process. These products are ways of communicating your decisions to others involved in the project: the client, producer, director, software programmer, and the like.

These are the people who read your scripts. (The viewing audience experiences your work only through sights and sounds appearing on screen in a time-based chronology.) Those who actually read your script base production decisions on your documents. They approve expenditures of money, sometimes large expenditures of money, based on the blueprint laid out in your script.

Although many writing products result during each of these steps, the ultimate aim is the finished shooting script—a script the client has approved as meeting the needs of the target audience, a script the subject-matter expert deems technically accurate, the producer uses to confirm the final budget, and the director uses to plan and schedule production.

The Production Script: A Definition

Let's define what we mean by a media script: *"A script is the written description of a chronological sequence of events, describing sounds, pictures, and ideas, using media production terminology."*

The media writer is not so much engaged in arranging words on paper to be experienced directly by a reader (like a poet) as in describing a specific sequence of events destined to become the action seen and heard on screen. The television and film writer use terminology that has significance to the production team: LONG SHOT, MEDIUM SHOT, CLOSE-UP, PAN, TILT, DOLLY, and ZOOM.

Figure 1.1: Steps in the Scriptwriting Process

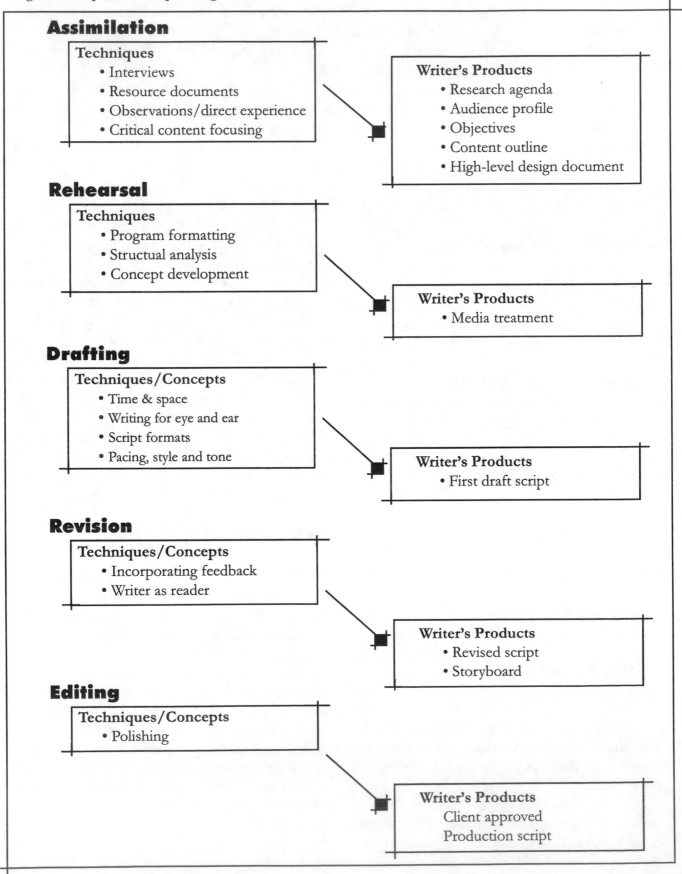

As we'll see later, interactive media writers have an additional set of production related terminology to learn: ROLLOVER, HOT ZONE, PULL DOWN MENU, and the like. (For a complete description of production terminology, see the Glossary.) The best media scripts serve as useful, practical production tools.

Form and Content

Throughout the writing process, the media writer searches for "ways of marrying form and content," as the biographer Leon Edel writes. As Edel puts it, "A writer of lives is allowed the imagination of form but not of fact."[2]

The media writer faces a similar challenge. We are allowed imagination of form but not of fact. The facts, or content of our scripts, lie within the objectives of our clients and the technical knowledge of the subject matter expert. It is our duty, however, to client and audience alike, to imbue the content with an imaginative form based on the characteristics of the chosen medium.

Footnotes

1. John Gardner, *On Becoming a Novelist* (New York: Harper & Row, Publishers, 1983), p. 17.
2. Leon Edel, *Writing Lives* (New York: W. W. Norton & Co., 1984), p. 13

CHAPTER **3**

COLLECTING INFORMATION FOR THE SCRIPT

> "The discipline of the writer is to learn to be still and listen to what his subject has to say to him."
>
> Rachel Carson

In writing workshops, I like to introduce the assimilation process with a short exercise. I ask the group to think of a time when they were personally "invested" in a piece of writing. The writing need not be a script. It could be a poem, a corporate report, even a love letter. Whatever the writing task, it must have been a positive experience, one in which the writing achieved its goal and the writer was pleased by the outcome. I give the class a few moments to jot down reasons why they "connected" with that piece of writing.

Then they must recall a time when they did not connect with a writing effort and the task was difficult, painstaking, and tedious. They were unsatisfied with the result, taking joy only in completing the grim task. The class jots down all the reasons why they found this writing experience a chore.

We discuss their responses, listing them in two columns on a flip chart. Invariably, the successful writing experience is characterized by such assertions as:

"I knew the subject matter cold."
"I enjoyed creative freedom."
"I was able to express what was in my mind."
"I had the full support of the client and subject matter experts."
"The writing flowed effortlessly."
"I knew exactly what the objectives were."

Turning to the second column, typical answers include:

"The objectives were never nailed down."
"I didn't grasp all the details."
"I was trying to satisfy a committee."
"I wasn't allowed to write the material the way I wanted to."
"My boss kept trying to second-guess me."
"I didn't have access to the executives I was writing for."

If you analyze the differences in these writing experiences, two themes emerge. First, successful and satisfying writing experiences require the writer's mastery of the subject matter as well as appreciation of the project's goals and target audience. Second, writers must be permitted reasonable creative freedom to shape the content into a form that corresponds to the writer's inner, creative vision.

Research is more than looking up cold facts or recording the client's perception of the need for the program. Research is an active journey into the heart of a communication challenge or training problem. Research is the writer's "indoctrination." (I write my best scripts when I believe most strongly in the communication's cause.)

The highly imaginative naturalist writer Rachel Carson describes it this way:

> *"The writer must never attempt to impose himself upon his subject. He must not try to mold it according to what his readers or editors want to read. His initial task is to come to know his subject intimately, to understand its every aspect, to let it fill his mind. Then, at some turning point, the subject takes command and the true act of creation begins...*[1]

In short, you must not only collect raw data and information, but also begin the process of being able to think about the subject matter. Only then can the "true act of creation begin." So let's explore research techniques, seeking to do such a thorough job that the subject "fills" the media writer's mind.

Goals of Research

There are three main goals of research:

1. **To determine what the media presentation will be about.**

2. **To collect and assimilate content, personalizing the subject matter.**

3. **To determine the communication environment.**

Many business, medical, and educational media projects involve highly technical, complex subjects. Such topics cannot be researched through publicly available material. It takes access to inside information, which must be pieced together by talking with content specialists. Furthermore, for most informational or training projects, research should go beyond content.

It's equally important to develop an appreciation of your client's total communications or training environment. Insight into the audience's likely attitude toward the topic, the logistics of the viewing or interactive-media environment, and even cultural attitudes within an organization all yield insights that become invaluable once it's time to decide on form and style.

The Core Question

For any media writing, the goal of all research activities is to develop an answer to one fundamental question:

"What do you want to say, to whom, and for what purpose?"

Answers to the core question fall into one of three categories of information:

1. *"What do you want to say..."* provides information relevant to the content of the communication.

2. *"To whom..."* focuses on the audience for the finished program.

3. *"For what purpose..."* gives the writer an understanding of objectives, what the presentation intends to accomplish.

Although research is always the first step in the writing process, specific research activities vary from project to project. A field trip may be essential for one topic and totally inappropriate for the next. Interviews with the target audience may generate valid input for treating some material yet be superfluous in other instances. Furthermore, it's not uncommon to conduct research under deadline pressure. The media writer needs solid research methods—an efficient and flexible system that yields comprehensive data.

In today's high-tech environment, clients are often more preoccupied about media delivery than content and intent. They may be more focused on creating an Internet application or shooting video that can also be integrated into a touch-screen kiosk than thinking about such mundane matters as the core content and rationale for the project. The researcher's most difficult yet most important task often involves shining a bright spotlight on the "why" of the communication when everyone around is fretting over the "how."

The Research Agenda

The research agenda offers a method of coming to grips with the complexities of each assignment. By creating a research agenda, the writer formulates a plan of attack for extracting the hard data and psychological insights needed to proceed to more conceptual work. The research agenda identifies and itemizes specific steps that will be taken to gather input on content, audience, and objectives. It includes activities such as interviews, observations, videotapings, readings, and questionnaires (see Figure 3.1).

Getting an Overview

To formulate a research agenda, the writer needs an overview perspective on the proposed content, audience, and goals. Usually, this information is gained from an initial discussion with the client, possibly a subject-matter expert and, sometimes, a project manager or producer. In this first meeting, you're seeking a big-picture answer to the core question: "What do you want to say, to whom, for what purpose?"

Guard against bogging down in details on content, audience, objectives, or media. Focus on developing a sense of the total scope of the

communications/training project and factors influencing how the target audience and communications environment will influence the task. For now, keep your interview technique exploratory and open-ended. Encourage the client to discuss the rationale for the project as well as the subject matter.

Probe with questions that relate to elements of the core question, beginning with, "What do you want to say?" Fortunately, you'll find the client usually answers in general terms at first. For example:

> "We want to demonstrate that Goldin/Lewis is the best damn firm in the fiercely competitive construction management business."

Resist the temptation to jump into details right away. Ask only those follow-up questions that are essential to comprehend the client's statement of content. If you're called in to develop a media presentation about blood gas analyzers and you haven't the vaguest idea what blood gas analyzers are about, now is the time to find out. But don't press for detailed content. That comes later.

Once you've got the gist of the subject matter, go directly to the next part of the core question:

> "What do you want to say, **to whom**..."

Informational or training media projects are invariably targeted to a specific viewing audience. The composition of that audience, their predisposition to the subject, and the viewing environment all bear significantly on the writer's ultimate media creative strategy. So during this initial meeting, seek a basic understanding of the target audience. The client may tell you...

> "We want to tell our story *to the corporate/institutional buyers of construction management services.* We're already well-known and established with the entrepreneurial developer."

The client has a specific target audience in mind. By focusing on the intended audience, the media writer learns a great deal about the nature of the research and writing assignment. Change the audience, and you face an entirely different communications challenge.

"We want to give *new employees* an overview of what it's like to work at Goldin/Lewis."

Even though the core content may be identical, the nature of the communications or training task changes radically based on the client's intended audience. When the audience consists of sales representatives, for example, the approach to subject matter will be markedly different in content and tone than a similar subject presented to potential customers.

Beware the client who wants to address multiple audiences in a single presentation. This usually results in a program that lacks focus—unless it can be facilitated by the structure of an interactive interface and navigational structure allowing differing audiences to search the content pertinent only to them.

Depending on the writer's familiarity with the target audience, a significant portion of the research agenda may focus on gaining insight into audience attitudes or level of knowledge. Interviews with representative audience members, observation of their work activities, or use of research tools such as attitude surveys are techniques the writer may find helpful for some assignments. However it's accomplished, the writer must construct a valid profile of the target audience—and their receptivity to the message.

But before getting too involved in profiling the audience, complete the overview interview by probing about the purpose, or objective, of the program:

What do you want to say, to whom,
for what purpose?

The answer to this final part of the core question forms the foundation for delineating program objectives. Remember, informational and training media projects are generated by clients who expect some concrete outcome. The writer's work is ultimately measured by the success of the finished program in meeting stated goals.

In general, the most common objectives for media presentations are to inform, to instruct, to demonstrate, to motivate. As electronic commerce becomes more routine on the World Wide Web, the task is often to motivate site visitors to place an order or book a hotel reservation electronically. Frequently, a media project involves multiple objectives. As with the content and the audience, the writer's task in research is to arrive at a specific understanding and agreement with the client on goals. It starts with an overview...

"...the construction business is subject to cyclical ups and downs. When the economy is strong, entrepreneurial developers are very active. But in a soft economy, they tend to pull back. Our goal is *to sell ourselves to corporate buyers of construction management services* to help offset the cyclical nature of the construction business. Corporate building decisions are not so vulnerable to economic cycles."

With a solid overview of the program's content, audience, and objectives, the writer is ready to delve into specifics.

Creating a Research Agenda

The research agenda is a list of people the writer must interview, activities the writer should observe firsthand, and any written documents that will serve as reference material. A research agenda may include any or all of the components shown in Figure 3.1 We'll explore these one at a time.

Content Research

Use of Interviews

Typically, interviews are conducted with subject-matter experts, individuals possessing special knowledge and insight into the "what" of a communication. Occasionally, more than one expert will provide input. Sometimes the client also serves as a subject-matter expert. Whenever possible, interview those who can provide overview material first. That way, you'll develop the proper perspective for interviews with those specialists who fill in the details. The research agenda in Figure 3.2 refers to a sales and marketing project for a major construction management firm.

There are several things to note about this research agenda. First, it's clear that this is the writer's initial research agenda following an overview interview with one of the principals in the construction management firm. The research agenda identifies several additional people to interview—some in person, some by telephone.

Notice how the writer seeks specific points of view from each interview subject.

The right-hand column comments on how each person will contribute to the overall perspective. For this topic, the research agenda includes sites and locations to be visited primarily for observation. The writer's research task is like piecing together a mosaic in which the complete understanding of the whole comes from investigation of individual pieces.

Given the complexity of this research assignment—documenting a construction management firm's projects over several years and identifying the organizational and construction management techniques that distinguish the firm from its competitors—this research agenda is likely to evolve as research progresses. An interview with one individual may lead the writer to others who should also be interviewed.

Interviewing Skills

Successful interviewing involves mental preparation, concentration, listening skills, and an

Figure 3.1: Elements of the Research Agenda

Content research:	• Interviews • Observations	• Readings • Questionnaires/surveys
Audience research:	• Interviews • Observations	• Readings • Questionnaires/surveys
Verifications:	• Objectives and communications environment • Ongoing throughout the research stage	

Definitions

Interviews: discussions you have with content experts or members of the target audience in order to gain their knowledge or insights on the project

Observations: those physical locations or processes you must see to gain knowledge of the visual possibilities inherent in the content

Readings: those sources, often primary ones, that you need as reference material

Questionnaires/Surveys: formal documents the writer prepares to elicit hard data from those involved in the project

Figure 3.2: Sample Research Agenda

Research Agenda

Client: Goldin/Lewis, Inc.
Project: Sales and Marketing Presentation

Personal Interviews:

Arthur Lewis	Since we have spoken previously with Roger Goldin, we'd like to meet first with Arthur, then the "supporting cast," and return to Roger for a final interview at the end.
Gene McDowell	Since McDowell has been the firm's attorney from the beginning, he is in a unique position to comment on the firm's growth and accomplishments.
John Miller and/or Bill Robertson	Envision conducting this interview at a construction site to begin visual potential and production logistics for location shooting.
Hayward Simpson (PR Firm)	Given the public relations applications for the completed film, it may prove beneficial to establish a personal working relationship with Simpson.

Telephone Interviews:

William Link (architect)	Since the Plaza Building is likely to be featured in the presentation, Link might be a good architect to start with. (Should someone from Goldin/ Lewis make an initial contact so our call will be expected?)
Plaza Project contact	You suggested we speak with clients. Who on the Plaza project should we consider the prime contact?
Other Architects?	Without going into "overkill" at this stage, what other architects would you suggest we talk with?
Any addtional clients or subcontractors?	

Site Survey

Construction sites and buildings	Obviously, past accomplishments, current constuction, and drawing board projects are critical to the film. Initial thought should be given to which are featured. These probably should be special cases, extraordinary logistical problems, etcetera. What do you think is most representative of the special construction management expertise you offer clients?
Monday morning staff meeting and office tour	As Roger Goldin suggested, sitting in on a Monday morning staff meeting should provide insight into the operational side of the business, the management style, and what's "on the plate."

Questionnaire

We're preparing a brief questionnaire, which we'd like Roger Goldin and Arthur Lewis to complete independently. We may also ask Gene McDowell and Hayward Simpson to give us some input via the questionnaire as well.

ability to probe with follow-up questions. In preparing interview questions, try to take the audience's point of view. Devil's advocate questioning can be a valuable interview technique:

> "What makes Goldin/Lewis better than older, more established and well-known construction management companies?" or, "How have you maintained control during your growth from a small office to an organization of hundreds in many different cities?"

Such questions are also open-ended, beginning with words like *how*, *what* or *why*. Because they require explanations, not a simple yes or no, open-ended questions are ideal for getting interview subjects talking freely and in detail.

Good interviewers are good listeners. While you will prepare a list of questions in advance, interviews invariably take on a life of their own. The ability to keep probing for complete answers or to pursue a totally unexpected line of questioning will help you extract valuable information from content experts.

Some interviewers take notes. Others prefer audiocassette recordings. I lean toward taking notes, even if I am recording, since I mistrust technology. Furthermore, if you've got only an audio recording, chances are you will have to listen to the entire interview a second time to take notes. So why not work productively and listen critically just once?

Remember that you are serving as a surrogate researcher for the audience. Never feel inhibited about asking the content expert to clarify a fuzzy point. If you don't fully understand the subject, how can you explain it to the audience?

Often, the audience would want to ask the identical question. Pursuing content from the audience's point of view is the only way to write convincingly and make intelligent, informed recommendations about program format, structure, and style.

Observations

The eye is a vital research tool when writing for multisensory media. Eventually, you'll organize visual content for the eye of the audience. While there are, of course, certain abstract or conceptual topics (such as financial presentations, mathematical concepts, etc.) that require the writer to devise an entire visual framework from imagination, more frequently, you'll need to consider the various visual sources you must see to thoroughly research the topic.

In addition to field trips, the writer should not overlook existing artwork, graphics, photographs, slides, film footage, or other visuals that relate to the subject. Such materials may or may not be suitable for integrating into the production, but find out what does exist. Consider those source materials as a way of developing your own visual fluency with the subject.

Sometimes the subject matter demands personal observation, as with the Goldin/Lewis marketing program. Writing about the firm's construction expertise takes firsthand knowledge of projects. The research agenda for Goldin/Lewis eventually took the writer to a variety of construction sites.

Likewise, when writing about a manufacturing process, a new surgical technique, or a new product, it's imperative to gain personal visual knowledge of what is involved. What does the manufacturing process look like? What's involved in the new surgical technique? How does the new product work?

When doing this visual research, focus on the physical characteristics of the process or machinery and how well such visual elements can be translated to the screen. Learn to look for what is not visible as well as the plainly visible. If key elements of a manufacturing process are hidden from view, consider animation as a means of visualizing that process. If you're looking at a manufacturing process in which the finished product is created in clearly visible stages, however, then watch the process with an eye toward location shooting.

A vital consideration in observation research is the correlation between real and screen time. Real-time events often need to be condensed and compressed through editing to create pacing suitable for a viewing experience. A laboratory experiment, for example, may take hours, even days, to accomplish in real time. In researching such a

process, the writer should focus on those discrete steps that are essential to the communication and then fashion an explanation appropriate for screen time.

Sometimes, local color may be an important visual element of the communication. If your subject is an orientation to a college campus, walk the campus with an eye toward potential visual input that will help convey the character of the institution. Interviewing often accompanies this observation. So be prepared to ask questions of those living or working in the environment.

Sometimes it's useful to experience what your audience is ultimately expected to experience. In preparing to write a video training package to teach job-hunting skills to people on welfare, I began by sitting through a weeklong class, learning the same skills from an experienced instructor. My association with the participants during breaks provided valuable insight into the needs of that audience.

Figure 3.3: Direct Observation

Often you have to go and see your subject with your own eyes. Photo by James G. Libby, for *The Lehrer-McGovern Experience*. Used with permission.

A camera can prove invaluable in recording visual sources for your own reference and for pre-production planning sessions with the director. Document your observations with snapshots or instant photographs.

Hand-held consumer camcorders can be valuable research tools as well. Their use need not be limited to simply a preliminary shoot. Dr. Michael Ezzo, former vice president of VuCom newMedia Learning, advises clients to videotape entire classroom training sessions as a tool for evaluating the validity of current training materials.

Experienced instructors often say things like:

> "Ignore what the manual says— once you start working in the field, the best way to handle this situation is to..." or, "In my experience, even though the company's policy is (whatever), I always tell customers" or, "You can skip the next chapter because it's not really relevant to our new accounting system."

Such comments provide valuable insight into how to update or revise company policy as well as training materials. The client, however, must be committed to genuine performance improvement— not just give lip service to training.

Readings

Your research agenda should include a list of written sources. These references can include published documents such as annual reports, product literature, press releases, promotional copy, training manuals, technical bulletins, or benefits booklets. Often, however, the most useful written sources are less formal documents: research reports, internal memos, planning and implementation schedules, field test, reports, or marketing intelligence. Occasionally, the client or content expert plans ahead and has several pertinent documents ready and waiting for the writer. If not, ask! Experience will develop the sense of inquiry needed to uncover these valuable references.

In gathering this material, most writers prefer too much rather than too little. Better to ask for something and not need it than to realize at midnight before the due date that you're missing a vital reference.

Sometimes you will need proprietary, confidential, or otherwise sensitive information as background for understanding your assignment. When sensitive subject matter is involved, business ethics require writers to honor client requests for confidentiality.

Don't overlook the library as a research source. If you're writing on a general or extremely topical subject, the library is a good place to bone up, particularly for initial interviews. I do a lot of pharmaceutical product scripts and always check out library books written for patients suffering from the disease or condition the client's drug is intended to treat.

Additionally, media writers often have access to special business or medical libraries. Corporate headquarters sometimes contain libraries or information centers with a wealth of material pertinent to their industry. Trade associations also produce reams of material and publish periodicals and books and produce videos and other media.

Questionnaires and Surveys

Questionnaires and surveys can elicit information in a more objective way than informal interviews. Not every subject will lend itself to this formal technique, but the writer should always be on the lookout for occasions when a well-designed survey will yield useful information.

The survey continued by listing a variety of projects that might be potential subject matter for shooting. Although more extensive than one would typically develop, the questionnaire proved a valuable tool for focusing research results. Every second must count, especially when producing a linear media presentation.

In the Goldin/Lewis project, scores of people were interviewed inside and outside the firm in an attempt to identify characteristics that made the organization stand out from its competition. To verify our hunches and also make certain we were developing a presentation for the intended audience, the corporate buyer of construction services, we asked Messrs. Goldin and Lewis to complete the questionnaire in Figure 3.4.

Audience Research

When it comes to knowing the audience, staff writers hold a decided edge over the outside consultant or freelancer. The staff person has greater opportunity for daily contact with the people who constitute various segments of the organizational population.

Personal knowledge of the audience is most critical when a communication is likely to meet resistance. One research objective, then, should be to determine the daily dynamics of the communications environment. When you're dealing with a negative communications environment, or when the objective of the communication involves motivation or persuasion, then insight into the audience—their opinions and attitude—is vital. Because an approach that generates enthusiasm in one organization may strike a paternalistic chord in another, the tone of the communication and your motivational appeal becomes increasingly important.

Interviewing representative audience members is one way to develop the psychological insight needed to present content effectively. Go about the selection process in the same manner as for content interviews. Devise a research agenda indicating whom you should talk to and what unique perspective she or he brings to the subject. Be sure to set the proper tone for audience interviews at the outset. When talking with hourly employees, for instance, they will perceive you as a management representative. To generate frank, honest responses, you must gain trust and establish rapport.

Once you sense the subject opening up, you can still play devil's advocate. Seek honesty and spontaneity in these sessions. When the topic is sensitive, abandon note taking or audio recording. You're not after content in these discussions; probe feelings, attitudes, and individual perceptions. Don't lead the subject. A lengthy pause often generates a more telling response than a complex follow-up question. The pause, in itself, is a form of communication. Let it play out.

For some topics, audience observation may be more relevant than interviewing. If the subject involves training in the operation of specific equipment, observe an operator in action, and ask questions as appropriate.

Surveys or questionnaires can also be designed to go to members of a program's target audience and can be a productive way to get a sense of the audience's predisposition toward the communication. Don't overlook the possibility of existing surveys that can augment your research. In new product development, focus groups are often employed to react to the product's concept, features, and benefits. Get a copy of the final results. Many revisions to employee benefits programs are preceded by extensive research to determine the employees' perceptions of the company and its compensation policies. That's great background for understanding the employee audience.

In researching content and audience, keep the client's overall objective in mind. As you develop greater knowledge of the subject and communications task, continue to analyze whether you have sufficient data to meet the client's needs. If not, either more research is required or the objective should be reassessed.

Figure 3.4: Goldin/Lewis Questionnaire

1. Rank the following attributes (from "1" to "10") in order of importance to most *corporate* buyers of construction services.
(1 = Most Important; 10 = Least Important)

_____ Reputation for quality
_____ Reputation for on-time completion
_____ Reputation for subcontractor bidding, negotiations, agreements, and cost control
_____ On-site construction supervision expertise
_____ Capability to provide both construction and interior finishing
_____ Top management involvement
_____ Organizational size and corporate resources
_____ Experience of project managers and middle management
_____ Creativity and problem solving
_____ Aggressiveness, dedication, and commitment
_____ Other (Specify: _____)

2. Rank the same attributes in order of importance to most *building owner/developer* buyers of construction services.

_____ Reputation for quality
_____ Reputation for on-time completion
_____ Reputation for subcontractor bidding, negotiations, agreements, and cost control
_____ On-site construction supervision expertise
_____ Capability to provide both construction and interior finishing
_____ Top management involvement
_____ Organizational size and corporate resources
_____ Experience of project managers and middle management
_____ Creativity and problem solving
_____ Aggressiveness, dedication, and commitment
_____ Other (Specify: _____)

3. With the objectives of your corporate image presentation in mind, evaluate the following potential messages. Select *five* you think are most important, and rank them "1" through "5" with "1" being most important:

_____ "Goldin/Lewis has the construction management experience to solve any complex construction challenge."
_____ "Goldin/Lewis's top management is personally involved in every project."
_____ "The Goldin/Lewis organization consists of a core of highly motivated team members who have direct access to top management."
_____ "Goldin/Lewis people take pride in developing creative solutions to the unique construction problems presented by each client's needs."
_____ "Goldin/Lewis fosters a productive, responsive owner/architect/construction management team relationship."
_____ "Although Goldin/Lewis is a young organization, the combined construction experience of principals and key project managers equals decades of practical experience in every phase of the business."
_____ "Goldin/Lewis is expanding its organizational base through a network of local construction management offices."

_____ "Goldin/Lewis is involved in significant European construction projects."

_____ "Although Goldin/Lewis' growth has been spectacular since its formation, growth has always been carefully controlled, responding to client needs for expertise, service and individual attention."

_____ "Although many projects pose special challenges, the process of construction management involves the application of analytical, almost scientific problem-solving techniques. The same thought process is brought to bear on every project."

_____ Other:

_____

4.   Consider the following list of projects in terms of their significance in the overall presentation:

759 Second Avenue

_____Of major importance; must be included
_____ Important
_____Of some importance
_____ Not important

If you checked "Of major importance" or "Important," describe the one idea or impression the audience should receive from our description of the project:

_____

Plaza Center, Philadelphia

_____ Of major importance; must be included
_____ Important
_____ Of some importance
_____ Not important

If you checked "Of major importance" or "Important," describe the one idea or impression the audience should receive from our description of the project:

_____

_____ Of major importance; must be included
_____ Important
_____ Of some importance
_____ Not important

If you checked "Of major importance" or "Important," describe the one idea or impression the audience should receive from our description of the project:

_____

When is Research Over?

How do you know when research is over? First, once you begin hearing the same answers over and over. When you can predict stock answers to your research questions, you've likely begun to understand the subject—sometimes as thoroughly as the content experts. This is a good sign that you've gone beyond researching as a task and have assimilated the material.

Or eventually you simply run out of questions. During the initial phase of interviewing, answers to each question are likely to suggest new questions. When you've gone down this path to its logical conclusion, you've exhausted your questioning possibilities.

Of course, if you work from a research agenda and keep it updated, you'll know research is over when you complete all the items on the agenda—another reason to adopt this tool. In most cases, you'll know research is completed simply because you've run out of time.

Screenwriter William Goldman wrote about the research he did for the motion picture *Butch Cassidy and the Sundance Kid:*

> *Eventually, I'd done all the research I could bear. I hoped I had a story that would prove coherent, so I sat down and wrote the first draft in 1966.*
>
> *It took four weeks.*
>
> *When someone asks how long it takes to write a screenplay, I'm never sure what to answer. Because I don't think it took four weeks to do Butch. For me, eight years is closer to the truth.*[2]

Granted, it's rare that an informational scriptwriter would be allowed the luxury of eight years to complete the research task. Often, eight hours seems like a luxury. The point is, your research should ultimately allow you to assimilate the subject matter, which is precisely why Goldman *could* produce his first draft screenplay so rapidly.

When your subconscious and conscious minds have ample opportunity to "play" with the material, you'll begin to start "itching to write," the best sign of all the research effort has been productive.

"Boring" Subjects

At seminars I teach, it's not uncommon for someone to ask, "What do you do when you come across a boring subject?" I always get on my soapbox with this retort: "There's no such thing as a boring subject—there's only boring writing."

Your job as writer is to discover ways of making the subject come to life using the medium selected for the project. If the subject bores you, how can you possibly hope to make it interesting to others? The writer's task, as Rachel Carson advised, is "to come to know his subject intimately, to understand its every aspect, to let it fill his mind. Then at some turning point the subject takes command and the true act of creation begins..."[3]

To achieve that degree of intimacy with the subject matter, you must approach the topic with enthusiasm. Good writing springs from sound research and an eagerness to communicate the results of that work.

Footnotes

1. Paul Brooks, *Rachel Carson at Work—The House of Life* (Boston: G. K. Hall & Company, 1985), pp. 1, 2.
2. William Goldman, *Adventures in the Screen Trade* (New York, New York: Warner Books, Inc., 1983), pp. 123-124.
3. Paul Brooks, op. cit.

CHAPTER 4

ORGANIZING INFORMATION: TRANSLATING RESEARCH INTO AN ACTION PLAN

Documents the media writer generates communicate solutions to the communications training problems inherent in the project at key stages of its evolution. These early written products, not yet scripts, are ways of communicating your research results to others involved in the project: the client, producer, director, multimedia programmer, art director, etcetera.

These documents go by many names, including proposal, high-level design document, recommendation, or action plan. Whatever you call it, the assimilation phase of the media writing process should always address at least five items:

- Audience profile
- Viewing environment
- Objectives
- Content outline
- Treatment

For interactive projects, these topics should also be addressed:

- Navigational structure
- User interface
- Media mix

For interactive training programs, it may also be appropriate to delineate learning level, instructional design strategies, tactics, and testing mechanisms at this time.

By organizing research results into a format that establishes parameters for the project, you discover the scope of the project, where you're headed, and how you plan to get there. Just as a shooting script functions as a blueprint for a video crew, the action plan serves as a blueprint for the media writer. It's easier, faster, and far more efficient to generate a first draft script working from a content outline, flow chart, and creative treatment than from a mound of disjointed research findings, random notes, and tape-recorded interviews.

More important, the action plan provides a superb checkpoint of communication between writer and client. It's an ideal method of feeding back research results and verifying your understanding of the program's audience, goals, and content. It's a way of saying to the client: "This is what I heard you say you wanted. Did I hear correctly?" Usually, the client finds areas requiring a slightly different focus, an oversight in content, a shift of emphasis here and there.

The action plan also provides an ideal format for introducing creative ideas in the form of a screen treatment. Once agreed to by the client, the action plan forms a contract between writer and client, a go-ahead to proceed as planned. Finally, the action plan allows the producer and director to respond to the writer's initial ideas. From the content outline and treatment, the director can begin to formulate the program as a production. The producer should be able to budget and schedule the production. If you're a writer working for a production company or agency, these initial documents may constitute your bid package to the client.

In short, the action plan lets client, producer, director, programmer, and others involved in the production know just what the writer has learned from research and where the project is headed substantively and creatively.

This chapter focuses on writing the first four elements of the action plan: audience profile, viewing environment, objectives, and content outline. Only after clarifying these aspects of the project should the writer pursue the conceptual and visual thinking needed to create a media treatment or address user interface and screen design for interactive projects. Issues relating to interactivity and creative concepts must be grounded in a thorough appreciation of audience, objectives, viewing environment and content.

The Audience Profile

Writing an insightful description of the target audience often gets overlooked in the crush of a project. After all, shouldn't the client know the target audience better than the writer? Why expend effort on feeding back what the client already knows?

Clients often want to tell the audience what *they* think the audience needs to hear. The audience's information/training needs may, however, be quite different from the client's perception of reality. Additionally, it's important that you verify your perception of the target audience's attitude toward the viewing experience to make certain you and others on the project are in sync. An analytical audience profile is your way of letting the client know you understand and appreciate the dynamics of the communication environment.

Internal and External Audiences

In the broadest terms, your script will be aimed at either an internal or external audience.

Internal audiences consist of employees, hospital or institution staff members, union members, or members of professional groups. The program to introduce a new product to a national sales force, for example, typifies the internal communication. The writer's point of view focuses on what the sales force needs to know to successfully sell the product.

Introducing the same new product to potential buyers, however, becomes an external communication requiring a different perspective. External audiences are public audiences: customers, patients, government officials, financial analysts. The writer not only conveys information but also portrays an image of the organization to outsiders. That image should be consistent with an organization's overall public relations posture.

Knowing whether you're writing for an internal or external audience provides an initial handle on the perspective to take in shaping the material. Then come more subtle audience considerations.

Audiences with "Attitude"

For any communication, your audience brings a specific "mindset" or predisposition toward the subject matter. In most cases, the audience will enter the viewing experience with either a positive, negative, or neutral attitude. The writer's handling of the content will vary based on the audience's initial mindset. You'd write quite differently for an audience that views the message as good news compared to one that is likely to be negative toward the communication.

Take the subject of a new product introduction aimed at an audience of manufacturer's sales representatives. At face value, this appears to be a positive communication environment. Sales people love to sell, and the challenge of a new product usually gets their juices flowing.

But consider this scenario: these sales representatives consist of a sales force brought about by the merger of two companies. Following the merger, the combined sales staff was trimmed back to a leaner, meaner group. One of the companies recently had a rash of new products "belly-up" in the marketplace. To top it off, a new vice president for sales has been brought in from the outside. Suddenly, our seemingly positive environment is fraught with negative overtones. Such information will surely influence the overall tone of the script.

The Target Audience

The target audience may not always be a homogeneous group. A company's sales force could consist of grizzled veterans alongside eager recruits. Each may respond differently to identical content. A linear media presentation cannot be all things to all people. Later, when exploring interactive media writing, we'll discuss techniques for structuring messages so differing audience or user segments can access presentations of similar content aimed at their specific needs.

In writing a target audience profile, you describe the primary audience your script will address. An analytical audience profile contains more than a two-word description, such as "sales representatives," "new employees," "security analysts," or "physicians and nurses." Those are occupational classifications, not descriptions of clearly perceived target audiences characterized by common attributes and shared motivations. Instead, strive for an audience profile that lets the client know you appreciate the nuances of its makeup.

Look at this audience profile for an internal project—a video announcing a new and massive national television advertising campaign to beef up sales for an over-the-counter multiple vitamin:

"The audience is the pharmaceutical sales force. During the past 18 months, the home office has placed a priority on *physician* details. In this video program, we will be asking the sales force to build inventories at the *retail* pharmacy level. Unless properly positioned, the sales force could perceive this as a case of conflicting priorities and lack of coordinated direction."

The writer pinpoints a characteristic of the audience that directly affects its attitude: the company's recent emphasis on physician details (pharmaceutical jargon for sales calls) rather than retail pharmacy sales. This descriptive audience profile tells the client that the writer appreciates the audience's perspective and role it plays in shaping the message.

Linear-media presentations are directed toward audiences sharing a particular interest in the subject matter. In describing the target, then, delineate their point of view toward the subject matter. Here is the audience profile for the large construction-management firm described in Chapter 3:

"Content will be skewed toward the corporate/institutional buyer of construction management services. Typically, the corporate/institutional buyer is more conservative than the entrepreneurial developer/owner. The presentation, in addition to describing Goldin/Lewis's capabilities and accomplishments, is intended to project an image that gives corporate prospects a sense of comfort with the organization."

Here the writer reports his or her research findings of the viewing audience's point of view toward the subject matter. This viewpoint will definitely be reflected in selection of key content points, motivational appeals, and narrative style and tone.

This next profile of an external, public audience is for a company that manufactures a line of high-quality home-video recording tape stock and faces a highly competitive market environment.

"This presentation will be suitable for use as a retail point-of-purchase demonstration tape for the *consumer* of blank videotape stock. As a rule, consumers of blank stock tend to

purchase primarily on price. They neither perceive nor understand that the quality of blank tape can have an effect on performance particularly in critical applications such as slow record and playback functions and during freeze frame or rapid search modes.

"This audience, however, is composed of people who have made sizable investments in home video gear and may be motivated to purchase a high-priced quality tape stock if picture quality and/or machine wear benefits can be demonstrated."

Such audience profiles are far more useful to client and writer than a terse, "The audience is the consumer of blank tape stock." A thoughtful audience profile tells the client the writer has a firm grip on the psychological makeup of the audience. To make an impact, the video will have to convincingly demonstrate benefits of a high-grade, quality blank stock. Furthermore, the writer suggests the key to motivating this audience is through appeals to their investment in videocassette hardware.

In these examples, the client is given sufficient feedback to agree with the writer's perceptions or to correct and clarify that perception. The writer may simply be parroting back what the client expressed during research interviews, but now there is a basis for consensus on paper.

Multiple Audiences

Frequently, clients expect media presentations to do double duty. Multiple audiences or audiences with vastly differing levels of knowledge or interest make a good case for an interactive media presentation. A single linear program, by contrast, cannot be all things to all viewers. So the writer should carefully consider how secondary audiences will relate to the program.

For instance, suppose our client who manufactures blank tape stock has a secondary audience in mind for the presentation: the retail floor salesperson. Here's how that secondary audience might be described:

"The retail salesperson, unfortunately, is ill-equipped to explain the differences in quality that characterize a higher-priced blank tape stock. Through this presentation, the retail salesperson will receive useful product knowledge on the interplay between home video recorder and blank stock through exposure to the presentation to consumers."

The writer has clearly positioned the primary and secondary audiences as separate and distinct groups. The secondary audience, the retail-floor salesperson, will absorb the content, viewing the program "over the shoulder" of the target audience. At no time, however, will content be presented directly to the retail salesperson. In this way, the client is forewarned there are limitations in what can be communicated to the secondary audience. You wouldn't, for example, employ a theme such as: "Remember, your profit margin is higher when you sell higher-priced tape" in a presentation to consumers!

The following audience profiles solve the problem of multiple audiences another way.

"There are two distinct audiences...

1. The Ohaus dealer representatives and inside sales personnel.
2. Prospective buyers of the GT Series precision scales.

"To develop a shooting script that appeals to the needs and interests of these two distinct audiences, we will want to talk with dealers and satisfied customers as part of our research. This will provide the insights necessary to structure the message to hit on the 'hot buttons' of target audience members.

"We also recognize a familiar problem in your desire to address two quite distinct audiences. You will not necessarily want to say something the same way to the audience of dealer representatives as to your prospects. We recommend two versions of the script using the same basic on-camera action but with narration targeted to each of the two audiences. You will get two versions of the same program, but economies of scale in production planning will minimize the additional expense."

Sometimes, scripting two versions with an eye toward using common scenes or visuals allows the client to accommodate multiple needs without the expense of two entirely separate programs. Whenever there is more than one target audience, analyze whether their points of view are sufficiently diverse to affect what content can or cannot be presented to both. Then you can identify a primary audience (the single group the content will be pitched at) and describe how the secondary audience will relate to the content. If you need distinctly different treatments of the same content to accommodate the needs of diverse audiences, you have a good case for an interactive media project.

The Viewing Environment

In the above audience profile, the writer included information about the viewing situation. The program will be seen at point-of-purchase in all the hubbub of a retail store. Playback environments and the resulting psychological effects on the audience often influence writing decisions. There's a world of difference between a message that will be seen in the structured viewing environment of a corporate conference room and one that is caught by a random, casual public

audience in a retail store.

The psychological world of viewers who are patients in a hospital is miles apart from that of a national sales meeting at a posh resort. Since the physical viewing situation has an impact on audience psychology and response, always make reference to that viewing situation and the effect it is likely to have on shaping content and creative approach.

Objectives: Statements of Expectation

Objectives express what everyone with a stake in the project expects the final product to accomplish. Presentations that satisfy stated objectives fulfill the client's expectations. No matter how loaded with special effects or innovative in style, a program that fails to deliver on objectives must be deemed a "bomb."

When the client approves a writer's list of objectives, two things occur simultaneously.

1. goals and expectations are established.
2. equally significant, the client limits the scope of the work.

In this light, objectives are as significant for what they do not state as for what they do.

Once agreed to in writing, objectives remain operative throughout the production. The writer will script to them, and the producer and production team should create the viewing experience with identical objectives in mind.

For these reasons, media writers must develop skill at expressing the intent of each communication through a precise, realistic description of what the program can achieve. Unrealistic expectations always come back to haunt the writer. Let's look at what is involved in formulating and writing objectives.

At the end of the production, you invariably return to the objectives.

At the final approval screening of a video, film, or other media presentation, I have often seen producers and writers put in this situation:

The client invites a number of cronies to sit in. Typically, these newcomers had no involvement in the creative process. At the conclusion of the screening, there's a pregnant pause. Eventually, the client says simply, "That was very good. I think that's just what we need." The ice is broken. More insightful comments surface.

Inevitably, someone ventures this opinion: "You know, I thought it was fine as far as it went. But you really didn't get into the responsibility of plant engineering to provide input to R&D engineering. How come?"

For the writer's sake, the answer to that question had best be: "We considered that point early on but determined that wasn't one of our objectives because...."

Every project must have some limitations in scope, if for no other reason than to meet budgetary and time restrictions. Objectives perform this function. Since objectives define expectations for the program, they form the foundation for the client's ultimate evaluation of the finished product.

Three Types of Objectives

An objective describes a change a media experience is intended to effect on its viewers. Change can be as internal and subtle as a heightened awareness resulting from exposure to new

information, or the change may go further, seeking to influence the audience's attitudes, beliefs, or level of motivation. Most dramatically, a program may actually attempt to change overt, observable actions—people's behavior.

These three generic objectives can be called informational, motivational, and behavioral.

If you plot the audience involvement necessary to attain these three generic types, as in Figure 4.1, there is a definite movement from a rather passive, uninvolved audience to one that must

Figure 4.1: Audience Involvement Needed to Attain Objectives

Objectives are expressions of the client's expectations for the completed program. The writer should be realistic in establishing objectives; otherwise the program will be perceived as less than successful.

Behavioral Objectives
(Active)

Audience Involvement

Motivational Objectives

Informational Objectives
(Passive)

When writing objectives, state the changes that the program intends to effect among the viewers.

become actively involved to learn a new vocabulary, set of skills, or concepts. This degree of audience involvement directly affects media selection and the mix of interactive techniques that will prove appropriate.

Informational Objectives

Programs designed to meet informational objectives ask the audience only to view the presentation to achieve awareness of a topic. The audience is not expected to *act* on information presented. The corporate television news program typifies the communication with informational objectives. Following are two examples of written informational objectives:

> "To demonstrate that Acme Industries is a key supplier of material-handling equipment, capable of delivering a wide range of products and systems to solve diverse industrial problems."

> "To show how the test kitchens are organized to support divisional development and marketing activities for new food products."

These objectives imply that information will simply be presented to the viewer. How the audience is expected to respond or act upon this new information is unspecified.

Behavioral Objectives

Programming with behavioral objectives, by contrast, occupy the opposite end of the continuum. In these instances, the target audience's post-viewing actions are specified in detail. Since behavioral changes are observable, they can be measured through pre- and post-test activities.

Changing behavior means training. That's a more complex process than simply disseminating information. In fact, the behavioral objective is synonymous with the instructional objective. Media presentations intended to teach or instruct should be described with behavioral objectives. As Robert Mager points out in *Preparing Instructional Objectives,*

in order to instruct successfully, the program designer must state the terminal behavior expected of the learner: "...an objective always states a performance, describing what the learner will be *doing* when demonstrating mastery of the objective."[1]

Here are two examples of behavioral objectives for media-based training programs:

> "Upon completion of the program, the trainee will be able to correctly apply the intervention and restraint matrix to a variety of common store security situations."

> "At the conclusion of this instructional unit, paramedics will be able to identify and classify epileptic seizures, using the International Classification System based on patient observation and analysis of brain wave recordings."

Different as the two program topics and objectives are, each contains the phrase "will be able to." By stating what the viewer or learner will be able to do after completing the program, you identify the expected terminal behavior.

Of course, the behavioral objectives above are overall course objectives. To reach the overall objective, the student must master a multitude of limited and specific sub-objectives that serve as necessary component building blocks. Here are several sub-objectives taken from a video-based training program for gas turbine operators and maintenance personnel:

> "To achieve the overall objective, content and exercises will be structured so that participants *will be able to:*
>
> 1. Identify basic turbine components: gas generator, HP compressor drive unit, LP turbine, and load.
> 2. Demonstrate an understanding of the use of control parameters to protect gas turbine parts.
> 3. Identify various control systems used to overcome compressor stall.
> 4. Select an appropriate course of action when high temperatures are present."

In all, there are 36 sub-objectives for this particular training module, each stated in behavioral terms and contributing to mastering the overall course objective.

Instructional objectives require the learner to become sufficiently involved in the content to learn the desired behavior. Instructional programming, therefore, often uses interactive-media techniques, incorporating activities that provide "hands on" learning experiences with exercises, simulations, role plays, games, quizzes, and other activities. Developing such interactivity is covered in more depth in Part II.

The ultimate experience in this vein, of course, is computer-based training (CBT) or other computer simulated experiences. In many instances, linear media is used in the classroom simply as an aid to learning—a way to disseminate content that is then integrated into behavior through classroom activities.

For now, the key point is that objectives for instructional programming must be stated in behavioral terms, describing *how* the learner will demonstrate mastery of the content.

Motivational Objectives

The motivational objective falls between the two extremes of informational and behavioral objectives. Although a definite response to subject matter is sought, the terminal behavior for motivational objectives is less specific than for instructional objectives. Take, for instance, a common corporate video communication topic: the annual report to employees. When the company has a good year, the report may be purely informational, stressing positive developments in sales, product development, operations, and markets. In a year of poor performance, however, the emphasis may shift to more motivational objectives, such as:

"To stress the need for budgetary restraint in all operations."

"To improve manufacturing productivity by reducing material waste and manufacturing defects."

"To create a greater awareness of the role of interdepartmental communication in improving customer service."

Here the audience must be persuaded to adopt an attitude that leads to more specific behaviors as conditions dictate.

Communications to sales representatives are often highly motivational. These can take the form of major large-screen presentations (even live theatre) for national sales meetings or video communications on specific products or market opportunities. In either case, getting the sales force "pumped up" and enthusiastic about the sales opportunities ahead requires a strong motivational message. Here are two examples from the pharmaceutical industry:

"To motivate the district sales organizations to make a commitment to the detailing effort required to surpass the call frequency of competitive detailing activity."

"To motivate the sales force to take the time needed to present the new medical theory that will result in market acceptance of this novel pharmacological intervention for esophageal reflux disorder."

Such media presentations are intended to influence the behavior of the viewing audience. However, unlike the instructional objective, there is no clear way of observing and measuring the change in terminal behavior. How does one measure subjective attitudes such as "greater awareness of the role of interdepartmental communication in improving customer services"? How does one know when a sales force is "motivated"?

Motivational objectives often lack definitive criteria. How *much* budgetary restraint is needed, for instance? Or *how* can production workers reduce waste and manufacturing defects? Such objectives are open to individual interpretation. This makes the motivational program more difficult to conceive and execute than either the informational or training program.

When the writer tackles a motivational program, good judgment is needed to ensure objectives are realistic. Management may expect too much from a single motivational communication. In setting objectives, the writer should clarify what the media presentation can and cannot accomplish.

A media presentation may create awareness and raise issues in exploring the role of interdepartmental communication in improving customer service, but to generate an actual effect on customer service, management may need to streamline work flow procedures, computerize order processing, or tap employee creativity through team-building activities.

An Appeal to Emotion

Motivational objectives appeal to emotions. And emotional communication is a key strength of multisensory media. The synergy between sight and sound unfolding in time can create strong emotional appeals. Study the psychology of selling, and you'll find it's commonly accepted that people buy on emotion and then justify their purchase with logic.

Consider the role emotion plays in our daily lives. Calculate the amount of discretionary income you spend on emotion. Every time you go to the movies, you "shell out" for an emotional experience. Each time you purchase audio CDs or tapes, you buy one of the purest of all emotional experiences: music. Our purchases of tickets to concerts, live theatre, and sports events all represent investments in our emotional lives.

Media writers can learn a lot from sales people. That's because we're essentially "selling" something with every script we write.

Even programs with informational or instructional objectives usually require some emotional appeal. After all, one must impart information to instruct; and one must often motivate a learner to become actively involved.

Entertainment Objectives

Because media can move people and touch their hearts as well as inform their minds, never overlook the role of entertainment in developing scripts. Writers for the movies and commercial television have entertainment as their primary goal. Entertainment may not appear often on the list of objectives for business, medical, or educational presentations, but the role of entertainment values in such programs has long been recognized by the most skilled producers, directors, and writers.

The argument is often made that viewers on the job or in the classroom come to a media experience with thousands of hours of conditioning watching commercial television and seeing Hollywood movies. The tools of entertainment and commercials have proven invaluable as learning aids in such programming as *Sesame Street*. When watching this show, it's almost impossible to say where entertainment leaves off and instruction begins.

When striving to meet motivational objectives and move an audience to think or behave in a certain fashion, the emotional appeal of a message is carried largely through the entertainment values inherent in the chosen medium. Put another way, successful programming makes interesting use of the chosen medium's strengths in dealing with the content at hand. Every medium possesses a certain "magic"; it's the writer's job to develop some sleight of hand in using the medium.

In summary, then, whatever the subject, the majority of media projects revolve around the three generic types of objectives. Moving from informational to behavioral objectives requires greater audience involvement or participation. Consequently, it's easier to measure the results of programming with behavioral objectives than with motivational and informational programming.

All objectives direct effort toward an end result. Use of the word "to" is a convenient way to ensure goal-oriented objectives. Finally, to achieve an overall program objective, several sub-objectives must be accomplished. It's not unusual for a single program to contain several informational, motivational, and behavioral objectives.

Whatever the writing assignment, take the time to state the program's objectives with clarity and precision. As Mager advises: "What we are searching for is that group of words or symbols that will communicate your intent exactly as YOU understand it."[2]

Critical Content Focusing

In his book *Adventures in the Screen Trade,* William Goldman describes a discussion with investigative reporter Bob Woodward:

> *I fiddled with the rest of the narrative...then Woodward came to my office. I asked him to list the crucial events—not the most dramatic but the essentials—that enabled the story eventually to be told.*
>
> *I think there were thirteen of them and he named them in order. I looked at what I'd written and saw that I'd included every one. So even if the screenplay stunk, at least the structure would be sound.[3]*

The quote is instructive on several counts. First, it shows the screenwriter's keen awareness of the crucial essentials involved in telling his story. Woodward and Goldman identify thirteen critical content points—elements that must be communicated to tell the story.

Second, it highlights the relationship between content and structure. Content is "what the script is about." Structure involves the sequence of events used to reveal content. The media writer must forge a strong identity with the crucial content of a communication. As Edel put it, we are "allowed the imagination of form, but not of fact."

So what facts does the writer select to focus on at the conclusion of the research phase? If your research has been thorough, you probably have more facts at your disposal than you have screen time. So what guides you in deciding which facts are crucial to the telling of your story and which are extraneous?

What Does Your Audience Need to Know?

The answer lies in examining content in light of the program's objectives and the analytical audience profile. What does your audience absolutely need to know in order for the communication or learning experience to reach the objectives? Answering that question will aid in identifying the *critical* content points—the thirteen, or ten, or maybe even three points that are absolutely crucial to telling your story.

When you can identify these critical content points with the confidence of Woodward and Goldman, you are well on your way toward crafting a content outline—the fourth writing product resulting from the assimilation phase.

That's why the content outline should be written *prior* to writing a creative concept or media treatment. The audience profile and the statement of objectives form a matrix that helps the writer identify what content needs to be communicated to the audience in order to reach the stated objectives. In reviewing research findings, begin by relating the content to the audience and objectives. Focus on those points that are absolutely essential in communicating the intended message to the audience. Information, facts, and data that help achieve an objective should be included in the content outline.

Use traditional formatting and organizational techniques to express what the program is about. If the subject matter lends itself to a chronological ordering, use that sequence. If a topical or cause-and-effect structure makes sense, then go that route. This does not mean that the content will follow in identical order in the first draft script. That decision will be made in the rehearsal phase of the script development process.

Often, the writer's perception of the communication climate has an impact on the relative emphasis given to the subject matter. For example, when research reveals morale is down, you likely face a negative communication environment. In that event, your critical content focus for a new product introduction may need to be placed on topics such as:

- Techniques to maximize time and territory management...
- The competitive viability of the product...
- The long-term potential of the product...
- Its role in returning the company to a level of profitability that supports an expanded sales force.

In this way, the outline serves as another important checkpoint between writer, client, subject matter expert and producer. With a content outline, missing points or extraneous material can be more easily identified. Shifts in emphasis on significant points can also be worked out. And it's all accomplished without the intrusion of creative concerns.

The outline excerpt in Figure 4.2 presents content points for a media program on the importance of protecting intellectual property and facility security. It is for an internal audience of employees and contractor personnel.

Figure 4.2: Excerpt: Key Content Points

Overview:

The video communication will focus on the role employees and contract suppliers should play in safeguarding intellectual products, protecting access to buildings and information, and security guidelines for visitors, resident visitors, and resident contractors.

The umbrella-like theme is that securing information and property is a matter of common-sense principles.

I. Communicate basic principles involved in protection of proprietary information.
   A. Define proprietary information.
   B. Three levels of proprietary information:
      1. proprietary
      2. confidential
      3. classified
   C. How proprietary information is protected.
   D. Employee/non-employee responsibilities for protecting proprietary information

II. Inform employees about common-sense security problems.
   A. Need for procedures to admit visitors
   B. Need to safeguard identification cards.
   C. Need to protect proprietary information, including computer software.

III. Case Study facts relating to specific security breaches in the past and the resulting legal/marketing problems created. (Specifics to be determined.)

IV. Need for procedures to take equipment in and out of buildings.
   A. Use of Personal Property Tag when bringing personal equipment to work and removing the same equipment from building.
   B. Process used to remove and return company property with a Property Removal Pass.

V. Need for common-sense computer security guidelines and the concept underlying these guidelines.
   A. For employees.
   B. For non-employees.

VI. General philosophies, summary, and conclusion.
    A. Intent of company security policy and procedures is to make *intentional theft* more difficult.
    B. Employees must follow common-sense security practices, but should not "cry wolf" at every opportunity.

Look for clues to how the writer intends to treat this material as a media presentation. If you failed to pick up on anything that characterizes this outline as specifically written for multisensory media, that's good. There is nothing that distinguishes a content outline for a videotape or multimedia presentation from an outline for print media. The function of the content outline is to focus attention solely on *what the program is going to be about.* It should not include matters of style, format, creative strategy, nor use of media techniques or effects.

Given identical audience descriptions, objectives, and research findings, three different writers should arrive at quite similar content outlines. In treating the material for the screen, however, you would expect these three writers to be totally distinctive in style, tone, and approach to the medium. One might employ humor; another, dramatization; and still a third, an elaborate stage setting or graphical interface to present identical content.

Summary

Together, the four elements of the action plan—the analytical audience profile, viewing environment, statement of objectives, and content outline—give the client a comprehensive report on your research findings. If there are problems or misconceptions, they can be ironed out before the script is generated. And with these elements formulated, the writer is now ready to shift gears and move fully into the creative process. As William Goldman put it:

In any case, before you begin, you must have everything clear in your head, and you must be comfortable with the story you're trying to tell. Once you start writing, go like hell—but don't fire till you're ready...[4]

By generating the items of the action plan, everything should be clear in your head; you should be comfortable with the story you're trying to tell.

Footnotes

1. Robert Mager, *Preparing Instructional Objectives,* 2d ed. (Belmont, CA: Pitman Learning, Inc., 1975), p. 48.
2. *Ibid.,* p. 19.
3. William Goldman, *Adventures in the Screen Trade* (New York, NY: Warner Books, Inc., 1983), pp. 235-236.
4. *Ibid.,* p. 124.

CHAPTER **5**

CONCEPT DEVELOPMENT

In the assimilation phase of the scriptwriting process, you function as an explorer, collecting raw material and sifting through it, seeking the critical content of your media presentation. Now comes the more creative phase: rehearsal.

Sounds like an odd activity for a writer—actors and musicians rehearse, writers put words on paper. But the creative process invariably involves an experimental period, a time to grope for the right voice, to play with unusual combinations, and to make serendipitous connections. It's like the painter who begins a massive work by making small, informal sketches. That's a form of rehearsal.

We rehearse the "big scenes" of our lives: how to ask for a raise or explain to the significant other how the fender got bashed. Why not also mentally rehearse the big scenes of the emerging script? Brainstorming with the program's producer, director, or art director, willing for the moment to consider any creative option, is like an actor in the early stages of creating a character, trying out lines with various interpretations.

Rehearsal is also a time to bring work done by the subconscious mind to the forefront. Often, rehearsal means setting the research results aside and turning to other activities, giving the creative child residing in your subconscious time to toy with germinating ideas. Consider, for example, Mozart's approach to writing music...

Composing in Your Mind

It was natural for Mozart to "compose" when he was traveling in a carriage or strolling after a hearty meal. Psychologist Howard Gardner, in his book *Art, Mind & Brain,* interprets the meaning of a Mozart letter describing his composing methods...

> *...and the whole, though it be long, stands almost complete and finished in my mind, so that I can survey it like a fine picture or a beautiful statue, at a glance. Nor do I hear in my imagination the parts successively, but I hear them, as it were all at once.*[1]

Gardner strives to answer the question: "How can one hear something, as it were, in the mind's ear?"

The question is worth pondering by scriptwriters. Before setting down "a chronological sequence of events" as words on a page, the scriptwriter must mentally conjure the sights and sounds that will unfold on screen. In this context, the embryonic compositional process of writing music and media scripts pose similar problems.

Gardner draws an analogy between methods used to compose music and more common activities we can all relate to: planning a dinner party or writing a letter of recommendation. There are certain mental processes you go through prior to taking physical action. The host or letter writer works from general "schemas—abstract mental representations of what a party or a letter should be like. These schemas are sufficiently general and abstract to apply to a variety of parties, a series of letters."[2]

In Mozart's day, rules for composition were clearly spelled out, with definite formulas for writing a symphony. Gardner suggests that when Mozart decided to write a symphony, many important decisions had been made in advance. Mozart's challenge was to invent promising themes for each movement, to "play" these themes in his mind against the backdrop of the compositional form he knew and then "to fashion those exciting departures and deviations that made each symphony different from the others...."[3]

As additional proof, Gardner cites a conversation involving twentieth-century American composer Walter Piston, who reported to a friend a piece he'd been working on was almost completed:

"Can I hear it then?" his friend asked.
"Oh, no," Piston retorted, "I haven't yet selected the notes."[4]

Like Piston, Gardner suggests that Mozart did not actually hear all the "notes" in a second or two. Mozart meant that crucial decisions about where sections of a piece would begin and end, where instruments would enter, when themes would recur, could all be grasped at once.

Media writers employ a similar process: they create a work's structure in the mind's eye, envisioning a beginning, middle, and end, as well as the principal media storytelling techniques, and leave detailed content to be filled in at the time of actual composition. (The focus of this process changes somewhat in a nonlinear work, but the rehearsal element is still vital.)

Before embarking on a first draft, writers make many choices: selection of formats, placement of content from beginning to end, selection of style and tone. Decisions must be made over what visual materials to use—a studio set, location footage, computer animation, special effects, chroma-key artwork, etcetera.

To ensure stylistic integrity, these decisions must be made now, in the rehearsal phase. Like

Most of Your Time Is Spent Planning

Professional writer and teacher of writing Donald Murray once agreed to become a "laboratory rat" in a writing study conducted by a colleague. Over the course of two-and-a-half months, Dr. Carol Berkenkotter studied Murray's writing methodology. Murray consented to tape record everything he did during that period and to save every note and draft. Then Dr. Berkenkotter studied the tapes and notes and interviewed Murray and observed him at work.

Murray cites the most important discovery: "...I spent three-fifths of my time, or more, collecting information and planning my writing. Most of my rewriting turned out to be, in fact, planning. On occasion, I spent 90 percent of my writing time planning."[5]

Murray sums up the payoff: "Inexperienced writers often write too soon... Much of the bad writing we read from inexperienced writers is the direct result of writing before they are ready to write."

In my introductory scriptwriting workshop, I take writers through the media writing process from assimilation to editing. About three-fifths of our time is spent in assimilation and rehearsal. I warn participants they will begin to feel "stuck forever in the rehearsal phase." That's because it is the most crucial period for the media writer.

Mozart prior to writing down a detailed musical score, the material and its treatment should be vivid in your mind. Then you proceed to drafting confident that details can be worked out.

Resist the urge to begin drafting immediately following research. Much work remains. Problems inherent in using film, television, or multimedia to reach your objectives with the target audience will be wrestled to the mat in rehearsal.

The Creative Concept

The creative concept for any script represents the underlying rationale for the entire narrative and visual experience. It's what Henry James called "the germ" for a story or novel.

Sometimes the shape, form, and style of a program literally spring fully developed into the writer's consciousness, as though the concept had been incubating throughout the entire research period. Very little rehearsal time is required.

Such creative concepts are usually a gift. Typically, strong concepts are hard to come by (for reasons we'll explore). More often, strong concepts evolve in a writer's mind through a combination of conscious effort and subconscious playfulness.

To arrive at the concept for a media program, the writer must make decisions about style, format and structure, evolving a creative strategy for the work that unifies those elements. In this chapter, we'll examine those creative elements one at a time. Then we will explore how the creative concept shapes those elements into a unified, aesthetically pleasing whole.

Stimulating a Vision with Program Formats

Despite the seemingly endless ways to treat a subject, when writing for sight-and-sound media there are only a handful of well-worn formats used over and over to convey varying content. A format is simply a generic method of presenting information in an audiovisual medium and is distinct from content, style, and structure. Content can be dealt with in any format the writer wishes, although generally some formats will be more suited to the content than others.

Visualizing your material in the following five generic formats is often a useful rehearsal technique. Some will strike you as totally inappropriate, and you can dismiss those formats for the particular content at hand. Whenever a format holds promise, focus on those content points that the format seems to suit best. It's not unusual for a presentation to contain a carefully blended mix of several program formats, each designed to carry a specific portion of the message.

The Talking Head

Imagine a speaker, put words in his or her mouth, and you have a talking head. Over the years, the "talking head" format has taken considerable abuse from media professionals; some deserved, some not.

On the negative side, the talking head makes minimal use of sight-and-sound media's strong suit: the capability to *show* while telling. As one corporate communicator put it, "Why not send me an audio tape and a photograph?"

But think of your favorite stand-up comedian in performance. That's nothing more than a talking head—but we don't find it boring visually or narratively, leading to the conclusion that the talking head format is highly "talent" dependent.

In corporate and educational media, the talking head lives on because many times, *who* delivers the content is as important as *what* is said. When the message comes from the chairman of the board, the chancellor of the university, or the physician who pioneered a new surgical technique, what is said carries the added weight of authority and credibility.

Unfortunately, executives and experts called on to deliver talking head messages rarely have the aptitude for such work nor the time and patience to prepare and rehearse.

Nevertheless, there are times when the

talking head is a necessary program element. When words you hear in rehearsal belong only in the mouth of the chairman, president, or acknowledged content expert, then the talking head is justified.

In such cases, brevity is the operative word. Seek direct input from the person going before the cameras. Talking head remarks should be written in the style of the speaker—not the writer.

As a pure format, the talking head should be used judiciously, never running more than three to 4 minutes. (Think about it—4 minutes is a long time to watch the same visual image.) Limit content to those things that only the president or an authority can say. Reserve other content points for more visual formats.

The Talking Head with Props

Give a talking head props to work with, and greater visual content results. Julia Child's cooking programs are classic examples: an enthusiastic, animated talking head demonstrates the fine points of soufflés for a viewing audience. This format is ideal for many corporate, educational, and medical subjects, particularly certain training applications. The props can literally be anything: a house, as is the case with *This Old House*; a real object, such as a computer terminal; or artwork, such as diagrams of the cardiovascular system. Set pieces and staging areas can be designed and propped to serve as functional visual elements.

Don't confine your thinking to the studio. A narrator strolling through a manufacturing plant and pointing out stages in an assembly line or touring the facility of a medical center is simply using a life-size prop to illustrate content. A training program on financial services shows a narrator in a park with two kids on a teeter-totter to illustrate the ups and downs of bond pricing.

There are, however, inherent dangers in this format. If the props used are unsuited to the aspect ratio or resolution requirements for the chosen medium, visual content will suffer. Julia Child's kitchen is laid out for optimum camera angles as well as for the chef's convenience. The set included a special mirror for looking down on the range.

Another problem may arise when a sequence of events is not structured for screen time. Consider how Julia Child chops, mixes, or bakes stages of a recipe in advance to condense the screen time. Media time differs from real time.

Visuals and Voices

With visuals and voices, the narrator is heard but not seen. A sequence of visuals fills the screen while narration comments on the action. Such visual material may be quite varied: product footage, animation, slides or photographs, artwork, charts, symbols, and other graphics—literally anything the eye can see and a camera can shoot or an artist can imagine.

The writer's goal is to structure sequences where the combined effect of picture and sound equals more than the sum of its parts. Synergistic use of pictures and sound makes the most of the informational capacity of all multisensory media. Although we call this "visuals and voices," don't overlook "visuals and music" or "visuals and sound effects." The combination of music and pictures is potent for establishing a mood or reaching an audience emotionally.

The visuals and voices format also offers tremendous flexibility for manipulating time and space. It's possible to leap from London to Manila to Los Angeles, or to make visual comparisons between Henry Ford's first assembly line and today's high-tech robotic assembly lines in 10-second sequences.

Yet for all the apparent flexibility, this is a demanding format, requiring discipline and control in scripting. Visual information must be sufficiently varied, moving from image to image and scene to scene with the pacing needed to sustain interest.

Stylistic integrity is also necessary to avoid a visual pastiche. Motion within the frame and/or changes in perspective or visual content must be frequent to keep the presentation from becoming static. Ken Burns' early PBS documentaries on the Civil War and history of baseball offer superb examples of this format.

On the other hand, although a writer may envision a flood of images, sooner or later practical production realities of shooting or gathering that footage within time and budgetary restraints must be faced.

One final point on visuals and voices. Because the narrator goes unseen, this format tends to be impersonal. Personal messages, subjects that focus on human interaction or topics where expert analysis is needed do not lend themselves to the impersonal, disembodied voice that characterizes this format.

Interviews

What distinguishes the interview from the talking head? Essentially, it is an unscripted talking head. The strength of the interview format is that it allows people to be themselves on camera. Interviews convey (for better or worse) personality as well as content. The subject's reaction to a question, the smile that crosses the face during an answer, the pause that telegraphs thought processes—all communicate as much as words themselves by placing the content in the context of character.

This program format contains two sub-categories: the on-camera and the off-camera interview. As the name implies, the on-camera interview features the interviewer as an active participant in the program, à la Barbara Walters, or Ted Koppel's *Nightline*. On-camera interviews usually give the appearance of proceeding from beginning to end.

In the off-camera format, the interviewer is unseen and generally unheard. The off-camera interview results in a less structured, more documentary style, lending itself to juxtaposing several interviews to organize content topically rather than chronologically.

The writer's role is to structure interview sequences (and questions when necessary) so that predetermined content comes out naturally and spontaneously from the subject. Note that scripting

answers is asking for trouble. The only rationale for interviews in the first place is to allow subjects to choose their own words, to be themselves. While interview topics can be discussed in advance, specific questions and answers should allow for maximum spontaneity.

Although not scripted, good interview material doesn't just happen. The interviewer must prepare probing questions and discussion points.

Dramatizations

On first perception, dramatization would appear to have much in common with the talking head and interview formats—people talking to one another. Dramatization, however, involves the assumption of character. Put two or more characters in conflict and you have the essence of all good dramatic writing.

Dramatization is most useful when subject matter focuses on the dynamics of interpersonal relationships: selling skills, employment interviewing, counseling, and other situations that depict human interaction. In this context, the dramatization can demonstrate predictable behaviors and provide role models, on topics such as how to handle customer complaints, how to conduct performance appraisals, how to overcome objections from prospective buyers.

Dramatizations can also surprise an audience expecting a more traditional treatment of the subject. In this regard, I've seen highly effective dramatizations of subjects such as antitrust law, computer accounting systems, employee benefits, and financial services. This format is a good way to build audience interest or empathy or put an entertaining twist on a subject.

The skills of bringing a character to life can also serve media writers in creating character narrations. A typical example of this technique is the use of a historical person to convey content—bringing the long-past company founder to life to describe how the business was started.

From the writer's viewpoint, two critical skills are needed to create believable dramatizations.

First, drama involves characters in conflict. This doesn't mean all dramatizations should contain the melodrama of soap opera (though I sometimes refer to this format as the "industrial soap"). For a dramatic scene, however, two or more characters must be motivated by objectives that are at cross-purposes.

Second, drama requires dialog, not narration. Playwrights and motion picture writers are known for having "good ears." Media writers who adapt this format to their own purposes must also develop an ear for dialog.

The Text Screen

Multimedia also offers writers the capability to use text on screen. Text has always been available to the video and film writer; generally it was confined to identifications of people or places, or used sparingly (a list of bullet points) to reinforce a narrator's spoken words.

The nature of how people read text displayed on computer screen make this a challenge to media writers. Chapter 13 addresses this topic in detail, citing recent research to provide useful guidelines on techniques to optimize the usefulness of text in multimedia.

Mixing Formats

An advertising friend's retort to the old adage "You can't mix apples and oranges" has always stuck in my mind. "Sure you can. It's done every day," he'd say. "It's called a fruit salad." Just like apples and oranges, these five basic formats can be mixed, matched, and combined in infinite variety to fit the content and goals of any given communication. In fact, most subjects don't fall neatly into a single, uniform format unless the program is very short, 5 minutes or less in length.

More frequently, the content of corporate, medical, or educational media programming is too complex and varied to fit categorically into a single format, and a typical production script involves mixing several formats, as shown in Figure 5.1.

A multitude of combinations is possible. When "rehearsing" formats, imagine a critical content point as it would be expressed using various formats. Then decide which format will be most effective in communicating the message, and how other content points and formats can be best integrated.

Figure 5.1: Examples of Mixed Formats

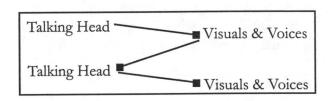

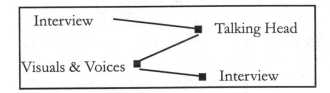

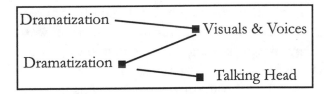

Structure

All writing has structure, and media scripts are no exception. Structure is the "chronological sequence of events" that comprise your script. In a linear presentation, it begins with an opening scene and marches resolutely through the middle and on to a concluding scene. The ultimate viewing experience unfolds in time before the viewing audience.

Critical content points often dictate the structure of a script. Your big scenes should be built around the critical content. They will become the memorable moments of your script. As William Goldman put it:

The essential opening labor a screenwriter must execute is, of course, deciding what the proper structure should be for the particular screenplay you are writing. And to do that, you have to know what is absolutely crucial in the telling of your story—what is the spine.

Whatever it is, you must protect it to the death.[6]

In linear scripts, that opening labor consists of three decisions:

1. What material to **include.**
2. What material to **exclude.**
3. The **placement** of that material from beginning to end.

The first two decisions have been made already. The content outline prepared in the assimilation phase identifies what material is included and excluded. Through that outline, you've identified what the program is about. Now you have the opportunity to explore the best placement of that material within the emerging script.

For interactive media, a nonlinear structure typically offers the audience common beginnings but offers optional paths to an end point that may or may not be identical for each user. Some nonlinear formats are never intended for each user to visit and experience all available content. Large corporate or organizational Web sites, for example, may be so content rich and varied that users explore based on their own needs and interests.

By contrast, an interactive training program may force all users through specific paths to ensure all learning objectives are met. This does not mean each user will be exposed to all media events. Optional paths may offer some learners to skip content they demonstrate mastery over. Less advanced learners may be routed to remedial content legs or have the option of learning via a variety of experiences (reading text vs. watching an animation covering identical content, for instance).

Part II addresses the relationship between content, structure, interactive navigation, and interface design at length.

Structure prepares the audience for what comes next. Sometimes you want the audience to be able to predict quite accurately what comes next; other times you want the element of surprise to work for you, letting subject matter unfold in a seemingly random way.

You can choose between two methods of structuring the content:

1. The scriptwriter can *advertise* structure as a means of gaining clarity
2. The scriptwriter's aims lead him/ her to *conceal* the structure.

Advertising the Structure

When would media writers choose to advertise structure? Generally, when writing training material. To reach behavioral objectives, most training content needs to be presented and mastered by the learner in a specific sequence. Before you can understand what happens when a centrifugal gas compressor surges, you have to understand how a centrifugal compressor is supposed to work under normal circumstances.

Often the writer finds it helpful to summarize what's been learned up to now and preview what's coming later in the program—a way of advertising the structure. This is shown in the first part of excerpt B.1 in Appendix B, an insurance sales training video excerpt on objection handling.

The track-and-field analogy provides a way of visualizing the abstract concept of handling objections. Subject matter experts use this analogy to "billboard" what will happen:

"In the next few minutes, we're going to provide you with techniques for running a sales track which has the hurdles in place...

Before getting into specific techniques for objection handling *let's define* what we mean by sales resistance and objections..."

Of course, there are many other ways to advertise the structure than simply billboarding what's coming next. Read through the second section of the sales training script in excerpt B.1 in the Appendix.

The organization of visual material as indicated in the "Video" column is designed to reinforce the distinction between insincere and genuine objections. It's achieved through the use of set pieces, graphics, titles, and a special wipe effect. Watching the program, the viewer can soon anticipate quite specifically what will happen next. When you choose to advertise the structure of your script, consider adopting these writing strategies:

1. Billboard content and tell the viewers what they're expected to get from the program.
2. Incorporate the logic of your content outline in the structure of the program.
3. Review what has gone before and set up what will come later.
4. Share the objectives or critical content points with your audience prior to in-depth development.

Concealing the Structure

Surprise is a hallmark of vivid writing. The skilled media writer can employ surprise to good advantage in programming intended to inform or motivate. There are many ways to achieve surprise, and the uniqueness of the subject matter generally suggests possibilities to the writer.

The unadvertised structure usually drops the viewer right into the action of scene one with no explanation or stage setting. (See Excerpt B.2 in Appendix B.)

Just as fiction writers surprise by manipulating time and place, scriptwriters have similar opportunities, using media capabilities for great effects. Excerpt B.3 in Appendix B, designed to motivate employees to take the time to analyze their options under a new flexible benefits plan,

moves directly into a series of dramatic vignettes, changing locations fluidly without giving the audience any preview of the specific content or structure.

The program illustrates the choices four people must make based on their personal needs and situations. But the program does not follow a predictable structure. The salesman we meet first, for example, does not reappear until the final scenes.

Programs using an unadvertised structure must still have an inner skeleton on which to hang the content. It doesn't mean the script lacks structure. Rather, you don't want the audience to be aware of the underlying framework or readily predict what happens next.

When subject matter and audience suggest concealing the structure, your script will probably not follow the logical order in your content outline. Instead, experiment with different ways of ordering the flow of events. Play with the material to create a sequence of events that keeps the audience involved in the presentation.

Style

Style is the writer's point of view toward the subject matter. Scriptwriters must consciously choose a point of view. Writers may be playful, humorous, serious, solemn, angry, analytical, theatrical—the whole range of human emotions is available to media writers. That attitude is expressed in everything the viewer will see and hear: narration, dialog, music, sound effects, on-camera talent, sets, props, graphics, transitions, and special effects.

Often, however, corporate media writers are so "buttoned-down" that they churn out script after script in what looks like "corporate Helvetica." The result invariably lacks a distinctive voice, or an attitude. Writers should consciously select a style and voice appropriate for each project, and write accordingly. The rehearsal phase is your opportunity to try out a range of styles and select the one that seems most effective, given the needs of the project.

The next two sample scripts in Appendix B are different treatments of the identical subject:

sexual harassment in the workplace. In putting forth stereotypes of sexual harassment, the writer of the script in Excerpt B.4 chose a comedic and presentational style. The music and visual transition are intended to telegraph to the audience that they are entering a fantasy world. The stylized set, exaggerated costumes, dialog, and acting style all combine to convey a comedic tone.

The lines "to camera," in which Miss Penneypinch breaks character are a theatrical device to heighten the presentational tone. Contrast this style to the different treatment in Excerpt B.5, in which sexual harassment is depicted in more subtle, realistic terms.

The dialog and action in these scenes reflect a "slice of life" style and tone. The writer strives for realism and this should be reflected in the acting, costuming and staging.

Concept Development

In his book *Writing with Power*, Peter Elbow states the dilemma all writers face: "Writing calls on two skills that are so different they usually conflict with each other: creating and criticizing."[7] Nowhere are these two polar skills more evident than during the concept-development process.

To this point, the writer has "rehearsed" the content mentally, imagining critical content in various formats, deciding whether to advertise the structure, and so on. The creative concept pulls these decisions together into a unified, aesthetically pleasing whole. Here is a definition I especially like:

> **Concept:** A storytelling theme used to provide a warm, human touch to the cold facts that constitute the content.

By humanizing the message, content becomes more memorable. A viable concept is far more than a catchy opening. Those are easy to come by. Strong, creative concepts serve the viewer well from first scene to last.

William Hoppe, a veteran corporate media producer, once used this analogy: "It's like when you go to a car wash—once your car is hooked up, it's out of your control. But it's pulled effortleslly through each stage of the process." A good concept functions the same way.

Also, strong creative concepts are invariably deceptively simple; almost obvious once expressed. They take only a line or two to describe:

> "We'll use a doll house and then chroma-key hands wearing white gloves and a suggestive piece of clothing, to visualize key points about preventing burglary."[8]

> "Since this is an audiocassette training program on a new antiseizure drug, let's structure the presentation in the style of "All Things Considered," including mock interviews with neurons and feature stories on how the brain functions."[9]

> "Let's get five characters from different Materials Management departments stuck on an elevator, forcing them to interact (reinforcing the theme we're all in this together') and letting them become multiple narrators."[10]

> "We can shoot the presentation from subjective camera point of view to heighten audience awareness of the importance of vision and threat of glaucoma."[11]

You're after an interesting, compelling way to communicate the content, using the strengths of the chosen medium. It usually takes lots of brainstorming. Sometimes the writer is able to brainstorm with the producer or art director. Other times, the writer must brainstorm solo.

To generate as many interesting, whacky, off-the-wall, playful, and potentially useful ideas as possible, banish the critical "judge" who resides within, giving your creative child a safe haven for playfulness.

Only after you feel you've exhausted the creative possibilities should you enter a more analytical mode. First, review the doodles, notes, sketches, and scraps of paper you probably generated. Look for relationships, contrasts, or connections. Circle and join ideas that have the most promise.

One of two things will happen. First, you may strike upon a creative concept so compelling that it dominates your thinking on how to write the script. The concept comes to you "full-blown"; you envision the various parts of the program fitting together like movements of a symphony. The experience is Mozartean.

Or, your movement toward a concept will be more evolutionary. You may take various approaches, combining or refining them into that single idea that shapes style, format, content, and structure into a unified, aesthetically pleasing whole—an approach to the story that provides a warm, human touch to the cold facts that constitute content.

This is where Elbow's dichotomy between creating and criticizing is most apparent. However you generated the concept, you've been in the creative mode—giving free rein to your playful side. Now don the judge's robes, and put your concept "on trial" to identify weaknesses. A useful tool for making such judgments is the "Concept Evaluation Matrix" (Figure 5.2).

Concept Evaluation Matrix

This is nothing more than a series of questions you should ask in order to evaluate the validity of your concept. The answers will reveal if your approach merits full-blown development, some modification, or sends you "back to the drawing board." There are seven criteria you must apply to the concept:

1. Content Origination: Does the concept spring from careful consideration of the subject matter or is it arbitrarily imposed upon the subject? The decision to write a script encouraging eye checkups for glaucoma from a subjective camera point of view arises from consideration of the content.

The notion of doing a "Star Trek" takeoff to communicate key features of a 401k investment plan is arbitrary and indulgent. Originality involves finding the "hook" inherent in your material, not coming up with an idea and then forcing the material to fit.

Figure 5.2: Concept Evaluation Matrix

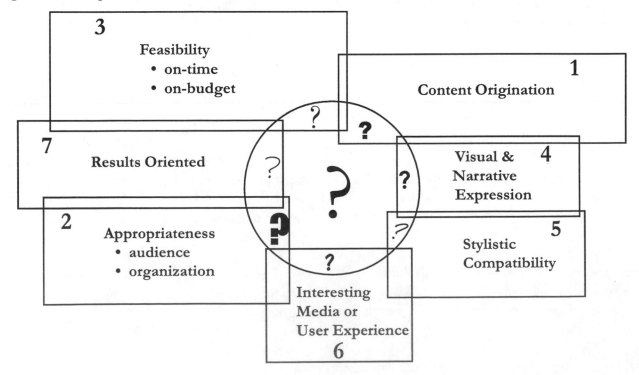

To return to Rachel Carson: "...the discipline of the writer is to learn to be still and listen to what his subject has to say to him."

2. Appropriateness: Your concept must be appropriate for both the organization and the audience. The sleek, handsome set made from polished Plexiglas may be quite appropriate for the high-tech electronics company but totally off-key for the Wall Street international investment bank. The approach you take to reach an audience of sales people will differ from your appeal to unemployed blue-collar job seekers.

3. Feasibility: If a good concept cannot be properly executed within the "givens" of the assignment—time, money, and talent—you must either refine the concept accordingly or explore other options.

4. Visual and Narrative Expression: Your concept should allow for a synergistic use of the chosen medium's capabilities. Inexperienced media writers often begin by scripting the audio side of a video script first, totally ignoring the visual potential. Good media writing links words with images.

5. Stylistic Compatibility: All the elements of your concept (mix of formats, structure, style, use of talent, etc.) must be organically integrated, meaning if you use comedy in one section, and a more straight narrative style in other sections, you need to seamlessly integrate the two. Do all your "main themes" work together?

6. Interesting Media or User Experience: What will the user's experience be like? Your concept should be intrinsically interesting. Whether working in film, video, multimedia, or audiocassette, you have at your disposal tools that have been used imaginatively to plumb the depths of almost any subject known to man. If you can't think of an interesting way to use the medium for your material, you're either in the wrong business, or you haven't worked at it hard enough.

7. Results Oriented: Go back to your objectives and ask honestly whether your concept will achieve results that match the client's expectations.

Remember, to generate intriguing concepts you must be in a receptive, creative state of mind. To test the validity of your concepts, examine them critically, according to the criteria of the matrix.

Award-winning writer Donna Matrazzo adds one more question you must answer: "Can I write this well?" The most challenging concepts often stretch a writer to the outer limits of his or her capabilities. If you're up for the challenge, go for it. But if you honestly think a concept is beyond your ability to carry off, it's only prudent to go on to another idea. In a year or two, you may feel that you're ready for a similar challenge.

Writing the Treatment

At the end of the rehearsal phase, you're ready to generate the next writing product: the treatment.

The treatment expresses the writer's emerging vision of the viewing experience in simple narrative prose form. To write a treatment, you simply transcribe the sights and sounds imagined during rehearsal. The treatment describes the eventual viewing experience from beginning to end, indicating format, hinting at style, and revealing structure.

Inexperienced writers often forego treatments, unless client or producer demands it, leap-frogging directly to a first-draft shooting script. A descriptive treatment, however, is a valuable tool with many benefits at this stage of the writing process.

A well-crafted treatment serves the following functions:

- helps overcome script "illiteracy" on the part of your client, content experts, and other nonmedia people involved in the project
- identifies issues relating to production requirements
- helps develop a production budget

Finally, the scriptwriter uses the treatment as a road map during the drafting phase to produce a first-draft script.

Guidelines for Writing Treatments

Bear in mind that the treatment is a narrative description of the program you see and hear in your mind's eye and ear. Keep the prose simple, and follow these guidelines:

1. Develop the treatment according to the chronological sequence of events you imagine unfolding on the screen.
2. Describe the location and principal on-screen participant for each major scene.
3. Describe "sights" and "sounds" that will appear in the script.
4. Indicate major transitions.
5. Describe important sets, graphics, animations, or special effects.
6. Don't overwrite. The treatment is a general description of how the program will unfold. Leave flexibility for the drafting phase.

Like composer Walter Piston, who reported that a piece he'd been working on was almost finished but that he "hadn't yet selected the notes," the media writer will not hear every word of narration nor see each visual in the program. Whereas a script contains detailed instructions on how to produce the program, the treatment is a tool for communicating and discussing the creative concept you are proposing as a solution to the training or communications problems of the project.

To illustrate these guidelines, two annotated excerpts from treatments prepared for linear informational programs are included in Appendix B. The excerpts depict a variety of formats, and visual and narrative styles. Numbers in parentheses in the text correspond to the comments that follow

each excerpt and point out how the writer follows the basic guidelines for writing treatments. You should be able to visualize a viewing experience from each treatment.

The Complete Action Plan

Combine the writing products generated in the assimilation and rehearsal phases of the process, and you have the elements for presenting a complete project proposal to clients or management. These documents not only illuminate the need for the project and demonstrate the validity of the writer's recommendations, but they also function as guidelines for budgeting and scheduling the production.

The complete action plan—including objectives, audience profile, content outline, and media treatment—marks the end of the research and conceptual phase of a project. Once the client and producer/director approve the action plan, the writer turns to execution and the detailed work of constructing a comprehensive shooting script.

Although there are additional considerations when developing digital interactive projects, these initial tasks will still be performed. Some, such as analyzing the audience, establishing objectives, and conceptualizations will be more critical and require more sophisticated use of these skills.

The value of such preliminary work cannot be overemphasized. Although some things evolve, change, or grow on the road to a final shooting script, the essentials of form and style are established through the treatment. Those with the most at stake in the project have agreed to pursue a specific course of action.

If a decision-maker or writer has reservations or doubts about the direction the project is taking, now is the time to retreat and regroup. If that means returning to the drawing board and developing an entirely new approach, so be it. Generally, however, sound research, analysis, and conceptual work to this point will result in an approach that is greeted enthusiastically.

A creative concept that is on target will result

in a good production, even in the face of some calculated budgetary, production, and time limitations. By contrast, no amount of cosmetic production value can compensate for a bankrupt creative concept. Spend $100,000 or more producing a fifty-cent concept, and you still end up with a fifty-cent concept! And as for the old saying "we'll fix it in postproduction"—that's like trying to clean up an oil spill.

Footnotes

1. Howard Gardner. *Art, Mind and Brain* (New York, NY: Basic Books, Inc., 1982), p. 358.
2. Ibid., *p. 362.*
3. Ibid., *p. 363.*
4. Ibid., *p. 360.*
5. Donald Murray. *A Writer Teaches Writing,* 2d. ed. (Boston, MA: Houghton Mifflin Company, 1985), p. 17.
6. William Goldman. *Adventures in the Screen Trade* (New York, NY: Warner Books, Inc., 1983), p. 196.
7. Peter Elbow. *Writing with Power* (New York, NY: Oxford University Press, Inc., 1981), p. 7.
8. A concept of scriptwriter Ed Schultz for a Citicorp project.
9. A concept of scriptwriter William Van Nostran for an Ortho Pharmaeceutical project.
10. A concept of scriptwriter William Van Nostran for producer/director Kim Cloutman and the SNET Corporate TV Center.
11. A concept of writer/director Jack Pignatello for a Crum & Forster project.

CHAPTER 6

THE IMAGINATIVE EYE

"To draw is to put down your thoughts visually."

Fritz Scholder,
Native American painter[1]

Where are we in the creative process? The writer has collected the information needed to identify and address the communication/training challenges. Several writing products have been generated, including content outline and treatment. By writing the treatment, the writer chose a specific creative strategy to capitalize on the strengths of the medium then described the general chronological sequence of events that will unfold on screen.

Now comes a turning point in the process—that period when the complete shooting script is fleshed out in painstaking detail for the first time. The result: a full second-by-second description of the viewing experience. Is it any wonder the initial result, the first draft, is often rough and unpolished?

Sight & Sound Symbol Systems

What makes the work of drafting a media script a challenge is the coordination of sight-and-sound symbol systems. Media writers need to be "audiovisual thinkers." To get maximum "bang for the bucks" from sight-and-sound media, scriptwriters must leverage the potential synergy between two different, distinctive symbol systems.

Painters or sculptors focus solely on visual modes of thinking, rehearsing, and creating. Novelists and essayists rely primarily on the effect of words on paper. But like a switch-hitter in baseball, media writers must be adept at thinking visually, verbally, and aurally in a simultaneous, synchronous mode.

Most ballplayers are comfortable swinging

Words and Pictures

In *Philosophy in a New Key*, aesthetician Susanne Langer describes the difference between what she calls a "discursive symbol" (such as language) and a "presentational symbol" (such as a painting). Words communicate through "a linear, discrete, successive order; they are strung one after another like beads on a rosary." In this sense, all language has a "form which requires us to string out our ideas even though their objects rest one within the other; as pieces of clothing that are actually worn one over the other have to be strung side by side on the clothesline." Langer calls this property of verbal symbolism *discursiveness.*

The laws that govern visual communication are totally different from the laws of syntax governing language. The most radical difference is that *visual forms are not discursive.* They communicate their meaning *simultaneously* (rather than successively, like language), so the relations determining a visual structure are grasped in a single "act of vision." In this way, visual symbols are *presentational* rather than discursive. (This distinction may partially explain why inexperienced scriptwriters, especially those with print backgrounds, overwrite narration and underwrite the visuals. By training, writers are more comfortable with discursive symbols.)

Narration, unfolding in linear form, takes more *time* to comprehend than a picture, which can be grasped almost instantaneously. A portrait conveys incredible detail, for instance, because we do not have to stop to construe verbal meanings. Says Langer, "That is why we use a photograph rather than a description on a passport..."[2] This is simply a variation on the theme that a picture is worth a thousand words. It is also why effective visualization in an audiovisual presentation generally reduces the need for explanatory verbalization.

Print writers use discursive symbols to express their ideas and emotions. Photographers and graphic artists use presentational symbols to express their visions and emotions. The media writer uses *both* discursive and presentational symbols *simultaneously to* express ideas, visions, and emotions.

from only one side of the plate. Switch-hitters, by contrast, are ambidextrous. Media writers need to develop the facility to work with so-called right- and left-brain symbol systems, switching gears and moving smoothly from one mode to the other. Insight into these contrasting symbol systems is found in the works of philosopher and aesthetician Susanne Langer (see sidebar).

My initial writing jobs were in print-oriented public relations departments, writing news releases and feature stories. Although I had done graduate work in TV and film, the daily print-oriented writing strengthened my verbal muscles while the visual ones atrophied.

Later, when I began working in corporate television, I had to concentrate on exercising my visualization muscles. It took a lot of work. It took several years until I felt some sense of balance between my verbal and visual skills—like the switch-hitter whose left/right batting averages are about equal.

Visual and Verbal Frames of Mind

All of us have been taught, with varying degrees of skill and success, to use language. (And as with any skill, in putting what has been learned into practice, we may develop bad habits along with the good.) Childhood socialization and formal education places heavy emphasis on developing and refining verbal thought and expression. After the primary grades, development of visual modes of thinking and expression is left largely to chance. What distinguishes the two? Allan Paivio writes:

> *While language is a socially constructed and conventionalized mode of expression, no corresponding single visual language exists... This is one of the classical behaviorist arguments— imagery is subjective and inferential, and words are objective and manageable.[3]*

This viewpoint contradicts popular wisdom. A picture is supposed to be "worth a thousand words," implying that pictures communicate with greater precision or clarity than words. In truth, however, pictures and words can function as either highly precise or highly ambiguous symbols.

In college freshman communications courses, students learn that "meanings are in people, not in words." The same can be said of visual images. "Meanings are in people, not in visuals." What is obvious and clear to one viewer may be loaded with ambiguity to another. (What does the burning candle flame symbolize in the motion picture *Blue Velvet?* Who knows the significance of the woman's apartment building being on Lincoln Street? Why is the robin at the end of the movie a mechanical bird?) What is provocative to one audience is offensive to another. A comforting message to one group patronizes the next.

Scriptwriters face other creative paradoxes. Painters, sculptors, and potters create visual works that are tangible expressions of their own—direct by-products of their craft. They paint, draw, shape clay on a revolving wheel. A potter can set a bowl on the table and say to those around: "This is what I made today."

Scriptwriters also communicate through visual imagery, but most trust collaborative craftspeople—directors, set designers, graphic artists, computer animators—to realize their images on screen.

Another paradox. Even though working toward a visual mode of expression, the scriptwriter communicates function, style, and pacing of visual material via words on paper. And as Vera John-Steiner points out, there is a dichotomy between language and imagery:

> *Language is a highly conventionalized form of expression, but images—the constituent forms of visual thought—are hard to standardize or to define. There is no dictionary of images, or thesaurus of photographs and paintings...[4]*

Ironically, then, scriptwriters must use a highly conventionalized form of expression (words) to describe forms of visual thought (images on a screen) intrinsically difficult to standardize or define. However, our clients expect us as professional communicators to deliver content to the target audience with absolute clarity every time out of the chute. The client expects every member of the target audience to walk away from a viewing with identical messages.

Indeed, management often cites consistency and uniformity of the communication as prime benefits of media presentations. Every member of an organization, all across the country, sees and hears the same message. How can there possibly be room for individual interpretation? How could communication breakdown happen?

Quite easily. And more frequently than professional communicators would like to admit.

In writing workshops, I use a series of slides displaying minimal graphic symbols like those in Figure 6.1 and ask participants to jot down what the image means to them. Since these symbols are taken directly from the *Symbol Sourcebook,[5]* each has a precise "conventional" meaning. Yet few participants are familiar with the coded meaning of each symbol, so, when asked to generate a meaning or association on the spot, their spontaneous responses vary widely.

The teaching point is that each visual elicited a powerful instantaneous response from each individual—and the meanings are valid from each person's frame of reference. It's what they see; what they "get" from the visual. But those responses are never uniform. *"Meanings are in people, not in visuals."*

The Media Writer's Code

Screenwriter Paul Schrader summarizes the significance of this to writers of sight-and-sound media when he says:

> *I am not a writer. I am a screenwriter, which is half a filmmaker. I can't be a writer because words are not my code; words and sentences and punctuation. My code is far more elaborate. It has to deal with images. Montage. Cinematography. Editing. Sound. Music.*[6]

Figure 6.1: Selected Symbols

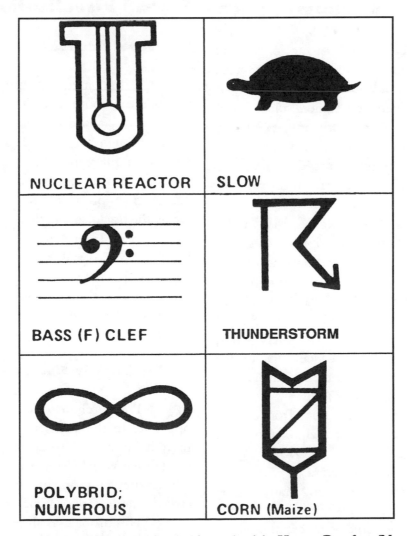

Source: Adapted from the *Symbol Sourcebook,* by Henery Dreyfuss (New York: McGraw-Hill, 1972).

Schrader captures the essence of media writing. Like screenwriting, it is not putting words on paper. He views scriptwriting as constructing a viewing experience from a "chronological sequence of events."

The "code" Schrader and all screenwriters employ to describe visual images and events is the code of media production terminology. In this chapter, we'll focus on practical aspects of using standard media production terminology when drafting the "chronological sequence of events" that describes the intended viewing experience

Time and Space: The Audiovisual Continuum

Within the confines of a motion picture screen, TV set, or computer display, a linear media program consists of a continuous evolution of spatial relationships between camera and subject, coordinated with a sequence of audio events. To describe those spatial relationships and their synchronization with audio events, the writer uses the language of film, television, and, more recently, multimedia production.

The visual "language" of media communications is rife with descriptions of spatial relationships. Most describe spatial relations between camera and subject, such as the classic progression from "Long Shot" (LS) to "Medium Shot" (MS) to "Close-Up" (CU) to "Extreme Close-up" (ECU).

Camera movements such as PAN, TILT, DOLLY, TRUCK and ZOOM (see Glossary for definitions) describe movements of the camera over, across, or in and out on the subject.

Terms to describe transitions from shot to shot or scene to scene imply spatial juxtapositions between two images: "CUT", "DISSOLVE", "WIPE", "PAGE TURN", etcetera.

In multimedia production, many of the terms have similar meanings. In addition, this medium employs codes unique to creating visual images for computer interactivity. "ROLLOVER TEXT", for example, refers to text or graphics that are displayed only when a mouse "rolls over" the area of a specific hot zone.

Write Down What You Visualize

All writing is problem-solving, and the problem of which pictures and images should accompany what words is the essence of linear media writing. So let's look first at typical pitfalls in writing the visual portion of a shooting script, then we will explore techniques to improve and clarify descriptions of what viewers should see.

Typical Visualization Problems

Verbal Dominance

Often, media scripts are visually weak because the communication is driven by verbal expression. Visual expression is considered only as an afterthought, or not at all. This is not to say that all programming must be highly visual. When the purpose of the communication is to reveal the chairman's or president's thinking on a critical issue facing the organization, there may be little need for visualization. Too often, however, wall-to-wall text is scripted for a narrator while only the most cursory consideration is given to what will be on the screen throughout the recitation. Strong visualization never results when the left side of the page is treated as an afterthought.

The Kitchen Sink Syndrome

The kitchen sink syndrome is just the opposite. In the writer's zeal to visualize, every narrative point has an accompanying illustration. While each visual element may be appropriate for that particular moment, there is no underlying stylistic framework or visual theme.

This problem is always compounded when the client wishes to integrate a variety of existing visuals, or assets, into the program. The writer may be faced with old film footage, videotape from a

Figure 6.2: Using a Visual Analogy

Methaphors, analogies, and similies are useful ways of making abstract subject matter more concrete. This sales training program likens handling objections to track-and-field events. Runners who train with hurdles (buyer objections) take those hurdles without breaking stride. Likewise, the salesperson who prepares and practices overcoming sales resistance and objections raised by the prospect will also take them in stride.

The analogy is carried out visually in the studio set design, which incorporates hurdles as a way of illustrating specific types of objections.

Photo courtesy of the Prudential and Kinder Bros. & Associates.

previous presentation, slides from the photo library, and artwork used in a promotional print piece. Different people, of course, will have produced each element at different times, for unique purposes, with no thought of the project at hand.

Inexperienced writers may embrace this material and begin plugging it all into the visual side of the page. Unless this is done with extreme sensitivity and skill, however, the result will be a hodgepodge of visuals lacking clarity and unity. Visual style and point-of-view will disintegrate.

Inappropriate Visualization

Sometimes visual material may not be suitable for the medium you are writing for. Charts or graphs that may work as projected slides, for instance, might contain far too much information and detail for resolution on a television screen.

Another form of inappropriate visualization is more stylistic. Earlier, directors were characterized by their fondness of the verb "to see." Another word directors like is *look*—used as a noun. The look and feel of a program describes its visual style: a "documentary look," for instance, or a "high-tech look." Every media presentation is characterized by its own individual look, which should also be a reflection of the medium itself. (The look chosen for a video presentation should be appropriate to the resolution and color rendering characteristics of the video screen. Graphics for a computer presentation may need to be treated somewhat differently given that medium's resolution and color palette characteristics.) Writers should feel confident the look they call for in production is appropriate for the specific content, audience, and objectives of a project.

Abstract computer-generated graphics are not likely to be appropriate for a presentation that focuses on the history and heritage of a time-honored organization or institution. Whimsy and humor are not likely to win the hearts and minds of an audience of individuals who have just been diagnosed with a life-threatening disease such as cancer or AIDS. This doesn't mean we never want

to shock the audience or be provocative, which lends a certain ambiguity to such choices. Writers must develop a refined sense of visual literacy and taste.

In a studio set, for example, the distinction between wood-paneled backdrops with leather chairs versus Plexiglas panels with contemporary furniture makes a definite statement about the style and culture of an organization. Both may be handsome, but they imply something different simply by the selection of materials.

Likewise, the typeface selected for theme titles in a large-screen sales meeting media module should fit the organization's image and purposes of the meeting. The typeface selected for an audience of tire dealers will likely be different than the one chosen for an audience of neurologists. In describing locations, studio sets, graphics, photography, film footage, animation, special effects, or any visual element, the writer should strive for a look that is compatible with the overall tone, purpose, and stylistic integrity of the presentation. Avoid visual incongruity.

Guidelines for Effective Visualization

Determine the Function of Visual Material

Visuals serve many purposes in media presentations. On the most literal level, you may be using the television camera to show how a task is performed, for example, in a training program on unloading liquid hydrogen. In that instance, you will be quite literal in describing graphic elements.

To explain the inner workings of an internal combustion engine, a program might use computer animation, a sequence of still diagrams, or a cutaway scale model. Such visuals serve a specific tutorial function, leading the viewer to focus on principles of motion, not the artwork itself. In such cases, the function is straightforward illustration.

Given other subject matter, however, visuals serve to create interest, or stimulate the imagination, calling attention to the style of the visual material.

Figure 6.3: Use of Setting and Backdrop

The writer's description and handling of settings and backdrops should be as well conceived as narrative copy. The oversized typewriter functions as a display area for writing samples in a business correspondence course. Courtesy Crum & Forster Corp.

Cartoon style artwork conveys a whimsical air. Abstract computer animation, by contrast, has high-tech connotations.

Similarly, sets or other backdrops can range across the spectrum in terms of function. But they're also staging devices meant to be impressive and attention-getting.

In a humorous training program designed to serve as a discussion starter on the importance of strategic planning in business, offbeat painted backdrops and set pieces convey the slightly surrealistic tone of the piece. Symbols, abstractions, even "magical" computer-generated animation video effects offer still other methods of making striking visual statements.

Documentary style footage, on the other hand, may be the most functional when seeking to establish credibility. Media often serve as windows on the world, giving your audience a glimpse of unfamiliar realities. To illustrate the world of a youthful prison inmate making a new start through a special parole program, for instance, documentary footage serves the writer's purposes.

Sometimes you may choose 3D animation because it is necessary from a functional standpoint. For other subjects, 3D rendering may be used as a means of creating interesting high-impact visuals.

By carefully considering the function your visuals should perform, you will arrive at valid decisions about the *form* visual material should take. Form should evolve naturally from function. Answer the question: "What do I want visuals to *do* for the viewing audience in this program?"

Make Stylistic Decisions Early

Problems like verbal dominance or inappropriate visuals generally result from inattention to the visual style of the program in the concept stage. The writer can avoid many visualization problems by thinking through the visual style of the program before doing any narrative writing. In fact, if you follow the process described in Chapter 5, you are forced to deal with what the viewer will be seeing, as well as hearing, long before you script narrative copy.

For preliminary visualization, you don't need to have every single graphic, camera angle, or special effect clearly in mind. Rather, focus on the potential for visualization in the overall context of the program. What look or style will serve your communication goals?

If you envision a studio set, what elements should the set contain? What function do they perform? How are they integrated with the narrator or other on-screen participants?

If you're combining a variety of visual assets, how will they be integrated to result in a unified, aesthetically pleasing whole? If you see action unfolding in multiple locations or sets, what is the rationale for using each location? How are they linked together?

Don't forget the relationship between visuals and voices. Is your talent on- or off-camera? If on camera, what environment will talent appear in? If you're suggesting totally off-camera narration, do you have sufficient visual material to engage the viewer's eye?

Often, there's no simple answer to these questions. Your decisions will be influenced by content, budget considerations, production resources, logistics, client needs—and the audience. By giving early consideration to the style of your visuals, you ensure that individual shots, graphics, and titles fit into the overall visual framework.

Identify the Big Building Blocks

When toddlers construct with building blocks, they learn to select big ones first, put those in place, then add smaller ones as the structure grows more complex. Scripting is somewhat the same. Once you have the component building blocks in mind, it's simple to write "ZOOM in for ECU on Block C. CUT to TWO SHOT of Blocks K and F..." If you've thoroughly identified the functions of your visuals, this step is simply an extension of that process.

If, for instance, you've pictured a set with multilevel staging areas as the functional method of visualizing a program on writing business letters, you next need to clarify precisely how many staging areas are needed. What is the specific purpose and function of each? How often will each be used? How will transitions from one area to the next be accomplished? The writer should answer these questions before drafting the shooting script.

Suppose you've determined that an animation sequence is a functional way to illustrate the action of a new drug. Now you need to identify how many different content points will use animation. How many animated scenes does that require? How will these scenes fit together?

If you will be visualizing principles of medical malpractice law with a sequence of short dramatic vignettes, you must determine how many vignettes the content requires, what settings are needed (emergency room, doctor's office, courtroom, etcetera), and what action takes place in each locale.

At this point, it's helpful to construct lists of such elements or, if you're one of the fortunate writers who can also draw, sketch them out. You're still not down to writing shot-by-shot descriptions or creating a comprehensive storyboard. But like the toddler, play with the big blocks first, arranging them until they fit together well.

If you plan to illustrate a historical narrative with still photos and period artwork, you must determine that there is sufficient source material available to sustain the piece visually. Granted, you may not know yet the sequence of these visuals or the specific camera moves you'll script. But if you anticipate a five-minute narrative and can locate only six relevant photos or pieces of art, you're still in search of a visual solution. If the multilevel staging area set you envisioned will cost $30,000 to construct for a project budgeted at $38,000 total, you need to rethink the set and its elements. Again, the starting point for this visualization should have been reflected in your treatment.

Camera and Staging

When you've arrived at a clear perception of the function and style of visual material and have the big building blocks in place, you can get down to the detailed construction of the shooting script. Many beginning writers are uncertain as to what to include and how detailed a description is needed when writing shooting-script visuals. Screenplay writers simply indicate locations and time of day or night in their scripts—detailed camera directions are considered amateurish.

In media writing, however, where the subject matter is highly specialized and the purpose of programming goes beyond entertainment, it is imperative for writers to specify shots, camera angles, and transitions. This doesn't mean directors will follow your descriptions slavishly or that production logistics won't alter the writer's suggested visualization. But since almost every corporate, medical, or educational program requires a one-of-a-kind format and visualization, it's up to the writer to include sufficient detail for the script to function as legitimate instructions on how to make the program—a blueprint for the production team.

Set the Stage

By all means, describe the overall function, style and look you wish to establish. Usually, this visual description occurs on the first page or two of a script. In the excerpt in Figure 6.4, for instance, the writer devotes nearly an entire page to describing the style, function and component elements of a studio environment.

The writer has a specific style clearly in mind

Figure 6.4: Excerpt Describing Video

VIDEO

FADE UP ON:

CU—Camera pans across studio backdrop, which consists of flats painted with freestyle rendering of an office setting and perhaps an AT&T truck parked by telephone pole. This artwork is executed in a sketchy, minimal, freestyle form. It is not intended to be realistic.

The art is done in monochromatic shades: gray and black or tan and dark-brown, for instance.

These flats are cut out and arranged in front of a plain studio cyclorama; (see Glossary). The appearance is like a life-size children's pop-up art book.

The same style is used to represent two classroom flip charts. Throughout the program, the Narrators refer to these charts as SUPERS appear in handwritten style to highlight key points. These flip charts also serve as display areas for transitions to and from case study vignettes.

For the opening, the main title…

Sexual Harassment: Fact or Fiction?

appears over shots of these backdrops. Then…

Cut to TWO SHOT on male and female Narrators. They sit on simple stools in foreground area.

Source: From "Sexual Harassment: Fact or Fiction?," written by William Van Nostran, directed by James G. Libby, produced by William J. Benham for AT&T Corporate Television. Used by permission.

and shapes that vision through text such as: "...executed in a sketchy, minimal, freestyle form...not intended to be realistic...monochromatic shades..." Additionally, the writer explains how certain building blocks will be used throughout the presentation: "...the Narrators refer to these charts as SUPERS appear in handwritten style to highlight key points. These flipcharts also serve as display areas for getting in and out of vignettes."

Initial descriptions of visual content are extremely important in conveying the images in the writer's mind to the client and the director. These descriptions help those all-important script readers to visualize the viewing experience as you intend.

Describe Action

The writer is the first member of the production team to stage action. Although the writer's imagined actions are modified and refined as the production takes on its own life, initial indications of on-screen activity are essential. Figure 6.5, for instance, shows the opening shots for an employee orientation to the Maxwell House Coffee Company history.

The writer uses television production terminology to describe the activity. "P.O.V." (an abbreviation for point of view) indicates that the camera should assume the vantage point of a shopper entering the store. "TRUCK" tells the director the camera should physically move down supermarket aisles. The writer also describes actions the on-camera narrator will perform and calls for close-up shots of brands as insert material. Directions are specific enough that the script readers have an understanding of what shots are needed to construct the scene; at the same time, the directions provide sufficient latitude for adjusting to shooting environment logistics of the supermarket location. Later, this same script (Figure 6.6) calls for an actor to portray Joel Cheek, originator of the Maxwell House blend. He recalls how he went from wholesale grocery representative, working his territory on horseback in 1873, to found the Cheek-Neal Coffee Company, which first marketed

Figure 6.5: Excerpt Describing Video

> **VIDEO**
>
> **FADE UP ON:**
>
> MONTAGE of shots in supermarket environment. (Could be shot P.O.V. of shopper entering store.) We pass by checkout counter and ZOOM to can of Maxwell House being rung up.
> Action moves into supermarket aisles as we TRUCK down coffee aisle.
>
> [SUPER opening titles.]
>
> Establish Maxwell House Sales Rep putting up display.
>
> Feature "The Best Coffee Company" slogan.
>
> DIFFERENT ANGLE as Narrator enters scene and addresses camera.
>
> NARRATOR strolls down aisle, referring to shelf facings.
>
> Insert CLOSE-UPS on cans and jars.

Source: From "The Best Coffee Company," written by William Van Nostran, directed by Robert Shewchuk and James G. Libby, produced by William Hoppe, General Foods Corp. Used by permission.

Maxwell House. The left side of the television script contains these descriptions.

Much of this is stage business for the actor to perform. More detailed camera directions are not necessary since camera placement is the director's prerogative, dictated by physical environment and practical blocking of stage business.

Script the Camera Directions

A functional shooting script provides camera directions to the extent that they are necessary. This does not mean each and every shot will be described in the shooting script. Camera directions should correlate to the specificity required by the subject matter.

A training tape for anesthesiologists on how to administer an injection anesthetic, for instance, would call for many more specific camera directions than a dramatic vignette of an employment interview. In the case of the anesthesiology training tape, the writer will identify specific close-ups on action relating to the induction and maintenance of the anesthetic during surgery.

> CU as nitrous oxide is
> administered.
>
> CU as oxygen is
> administered…
>
> …and airway protection
> provided.
>
> ECU as muscle
> relaxant injection is
> administered.
>
> Insert ECU on hand
> adjusting rate of
> microdrip anesthetic.

All such specific action would be detailed in the shooting script and linked to the narrator's off-camera explanations.

When drafting a dramatic vignette, however, specific camera directions may be quite minimal unless there is a key bit of action or reaction that is important for the viewing audience to see at a given moment. For example:

> CU on job applicant;
> her face registers
> confusion in response
> to the interviewer's question.

Usually, however, the director's blocking and staging of dramatic scenes determine camera angles and cuts. As a general rule, if you want the viewing audience to see a specific image on the screen at a precise moment in the script, then describe the shot accordingly.

Figure 6.6: Excerpt Describing Stage Business

VIDEO

Action begins as actor portrays Joel Cheek.

Cheek moves about in office with turn-of-the-century memorabilia. He uses props and photo album to illustrate his story.

He goes to map on wall. ZOOM to CU on map: follow route of Cumberland River.
MS on Cheek as he moves to saddlebags slung over chair. INSERT CLOSE-UPS as he pulls coffee bean samples from the bag.

Moves to copper kettle and empties samples into kettle.

INSERT CLOSE-UPS of beans, as appropriate.

MS as Cheek moves to photo album. Begins to leaf through. ZOOM CU on photos or art of Maxwell House Hotel.

Source: From "The Best Coffee Company," written by William Van Nostran, directed by Robert Shewchuk and James G. Libby, produced by William Hoppe, General Foods Corp. Used by permission.

Indicate Titles and Supers

When you want the viewing audience to see text or other graphic or visual effects, write it in the visual descriptions column. The superimposition of text over a scene should always be indicated by the word "SUPER." A sales training program in which track hurdles are used to symbolize the prospect's objections would be written as follows:

> MS on two sales
> trainees by two
> hurdles.
>
> SUPER:
> (Above each hurdle)
>
> ***Genuine Objection***
> ***Insincere Objection***

Indicate the appearance of arrows, to draw the viewer's attention to a portion of the image, or other graphic superimpositions, in a similar manner.

CU on map.

SUPER:
(Concentric circles to indicate possible customer service driving routes.)

When describing superimpositions, the parentheses indicate that you are describing a visual effect as opposed to text that appears on the screen. Program titles, directions to pause or stop the program, identification of a speaker's name and job title are typically indicated as SUPERS.

Describe Visual Transitions

Just as a series of individual shots creates a scene, a total program consists of a series of interrelated scenes. Obviously, scene changes occur whenever action moves from one location to another. Additionally, major shifts in subject matter, introduction of new faces or voices, or passage of time may also call for a scene change.

Sometimes, scenes are delineated by a significant change in program format—say, moving from an interview segment to a section containing visuals and voices. Introducing a new style, mood, tone, or tempo may even cue scene changes.

The bridges linking one scene to the next are also written using media production language. The following terms describe the transitions employed most frequently in linear visual media.

Fade Up/Fade to Black

All television and film programs begin and end in "black." The very first image fades up from a black screen, and the final image returns to black. In addition, a momentary fade to black (sometimes referred to as "touching black") then fading up the next scene can also be used as a transitional device

to bridge program segments. Generally, this transitional effect is too interruptive to serve as a frequent transition between one scene and another. However, training programs designed for group discussion or workbook often employ eight to ten seconds of "black" to allow for the mechanics of stopping and restarting playback equipment.

Cut

A cut is nothing more than an instantaneous change between two shots or images. The final frame of Scene A is followed by the first frame of Scene B. (The term *cut* originates from motion picture editing, where one piece of film is literally cut and butt-spliced to the preceding shot. Later, in the heyday of live television, the cut, or "take," from one camera to another became a standard transition.)

Although a writer may use a cut to go from one scene to the next, it doesn't mean every cut is a transitional device. The simple cut from one camera angle to another, from one image to the next, is the normal method of going from shot to shot. In drafting the shooting script, a cut between one shot and the next is always implied unless the writer indicates otherwise.

Dissolve

Because cuts appear with great frequency, they usually do not signal a shift in locale, time, or content as vividly as the writer might like. In a dissolve, the tail end of Scene A fades out while the first frames of Scene B simultaneously fade in. The two images overlap for a period of time. It's a fluid transition and since the effect itself requires screen time to occur, it telegraphs to the viewer that a change is taking place.

Wipe

The wipe is sometimes described as a hard-edged dissolve. To the eye, it looks as though Scene A is being wiped off the screen by the appearance of Scene B. A hard line separates the new scene from the previous scene. The midpoint of a wipe is like a split screen with half of Scene A on one side and half of Scene B on the other. (Like most visual effects, a verbal description sounds more complex than it really is.)

A wipe between scenes can move from screen left to screen right, or vice versa. A vertical wipe moves up or down the screen; a diagonal wipe starts out in one of the four corners of the frame. A series of wipes between relatively short but closely related scenes can be an effective, upbeat way of going from one to the next.

Stylistically, the wipe calls attention to itself more than the dissolve. Always be certain the transitional effect is appropriate to the style and tone of the program.

Special Effect Transitions

When a writer feels the need for a more pronounced transitional device, a variety of special effect transitions may be written into the script. Here's where a good grasp of the chosen medium's capabilities, editing equipment, and techniques helps express visual continuity on the printed page in practical production terminology.

In television, effects are generated electronically in the editing suite; in film, through optical printing techniques; and in multimedia, through computer software.

In video, digital effects generators offer videotape editors unusual flexibility in manipulating the size and perspective of a single image. Using these digital effects, transitions such as simulated page turns, flip-flopping pictures, infinity zooms, and other types of optical magic can be created with a few simple key strokes. Software programs such as Microsoft PowerPoint™ make many of these same digital effects available on a laptop computer. The relative ease with which these striking effects can be created makes video post-production ideal for many situations, even material shot on film is often transferred to tape and "posted" as video.

Custom Transitional Devices

Sometimes the writer will even customize a unique transitional device as part of the overall visualization. A custom-tailored transitional effect should, however, be genuinely motivated by content. In the case of the American Express script (Figure 6.7) part of the intended message was to dramatize the worldwide application of the new computerized Travel Information Processing System (TRIPS). In that instance, the writer magically transported the narrator to American Express travel offices around the globe through a specially devised three-dimensional cube, which appeared initially as the American Express logo. (Figure 6.8) shows how the transitional effect was described in the shooting script.

Such a unique and technically complex transition was justified in this instance because of the importance of the communication, overall production values, and substantial budget. Effect for the sake of effect, however, is invariably self-defeating. Ninety percent of the time, you will be well-served by cuts, dissolves, and simple fades. Special effects and digital effects transitions should be the exception, not the rule. Otherwise, they become unspecial effects.

Describe Special Effects

When the writer feels an electronic video effect is critical to telling the story, the effect should be vividly described in the left-hand column. Terms such as *chroma-key, squeeze zooms, halls of mirrors,* and *tumbling pictures* are well known to video directors. If you have something more unusual in mind, write out your vision as precisely as possible so the production team can execute the effects precisely. Here's an example:

> Computer generated graphic simulating aperture of a camera lens. Matte title graphic, "Focus on Research" in center.

Figure 7.7: Excerpt Describing Transition

VIDEO	AUDIO
MS on Narrator by computer terminal.	**NARRATOR**: ...TO SEE THE RESULTS OF THAT PLANNING AND DESIGNING, LET'S LOOK AT TRIPS IN ACTION AND SEE ALL THE THINGS IT CAN DO FOR THE CUSTOMER—AND FOR US! OUR FIRST STOP IS OUR PARK AVENUE OFFICE IN NEW YORK CITY.
On his final word, the picture FREEZES and the camera PULLS BACK to reveal frozen image on one face of blue American Express cube. The cube begins to rotate... ...it continues to turn until the new face, containing a frozen image of Narrator outside Park Avenue office is full-front and the preceding scene is gone. Camera moves in, losing the box, as the scene comes alive.	**MUSIC**: (Transitional "tag" theme comes up to accompany scene change.)
MS on Narrator. Follow as he enters office.	**NARRATOR:** WHEN AMERICAN EXPRESS ENTERED THE TRAVEL BUSINESS BACK IN 1915, PROVIDING TRAVEL SERVICES AND MAKING TRAVEL ARRANGEMENTS WAS RELATIVELY SIMPLE...

Source: From "Trips: Your Selling and Servicing Partner," written by Allen Neil, directed by James G. Libby, produced by Video Marketing Group for American Express Travel Services. Used by permission.

Simple animation to simulate closing and opening shutter. Scene of new R and D construction is now matted into the shutter area.

No matter how precise we try to be, visual effects are difficult to describe with words since they have the characteristics of presentational symbols. Make a point of discussing the function of an effect with the director and technicians who are required to execute the effect. (I have often been surprised at a first screening of a program for which I wrote the script but had no hand in the production process. Sometimes the surprises are pleasant; other times, not. In such instances, I have regretted not being more emphatic in describing ideas for sets, staging, style of artwork, etc.)

Computer-Generated Images & Animation

In most areas of slide and video production, the computer has taken the place of the artist's table, photographer's copy stand, animator's cell art, and even live action shoots. Computers generate the vast majority of business, scientific, and industrial 35mm slides used in presentations today. In addition, the computer often serves as the display device or is wired to a projector to accommodate large audience presentations.

Computer-generated art is ideal for the typical business slide: bar charts, graphs, trend lines, etcetera. Text is easily integrated with artwork or graphic symbols. The software ranges from user-friendly programs such as Microsoft PowerPoint™

Figure 6.8: Using a Custom Transitional Device

For a project on the American Express TRIPS system, the writer suggested a custom transitional device: a cube that reveals upcoming scenes as it rotates. Courtesy American Express Travel Services Division.

and Lotus Freelance™ and Persausion™ for Macintosh to packages that require considerable artistic and computer training to operate.

Many sales representatives are capable of creating extensive mobile sales presentations on laptop computers. Computer-generated presentations are easily updated or changed, since the original artwork is stored on hard drive or disk. When it's time for an update, only the changed data needs to be re-entered into the computer.

Computer-generated art is not limited to the business data slide, however. In the hands of a skilled multimedia artist, such programs can be used to generate imaginative graphics, three-dimensional objects, and sophisticated animation. The more sophisticated artwork usually requires more computer time to create—and that can quickly add to a production budget.

Computer Animation

Likewise, computer-generated animation has also become routine in both television and multimedia production. While such effects play "starring roles" in many Hollywood blockbusters, the cost of computer-generated special effects for film is often prohibitive for most industrial work.

The output of the computer can be recorded directly to videotape, providing opportunities for a wide range of graphics and animated effects from rudimentary pop-on style animation to highly sophisticated three-dimensional creations limited only by the computer animator's imagination, time, and budget. (Network news, sports, program openings and local TV station IDs, and the venerable *Monday Night Football* opening are replete with examples of the most glitzy computer animation.)

Whether developing a simple slide show, video presentation, or multimedia program, writers should be familiar with the potential, as well as the limitations, of computer-generated graphics systems. This field changes so rapidly, that a description of all two- and three-dimensional software would soon be obsolete.

Implications for Media Writers

As with any type of visual or special effect, computer-generated graphics and animation should be used because they play a functional role in the communication, not for the sake of glitz. Media writers need not become experts on these systems to script imaginative graphics or animation effects. But it is imperative to define the graphics/animation needs of the project and match these to the capabilities and resources available to the production team. Medical and engineering programming often cry out for computer-generated animation—but frame-by-frame pop-ons, arrows, and titles may suffice instead of full-fledged animation.

Interestingly, 3-D animation, in particular, uses media production terminology found directly from film and television. A 3-D animator readily understands what terms like ZOOM, TRUCK and PAN mean as well as terms describing shots such as medium shot or close-up.

Whatever the application, the writer should meet with the computer-graphics artist and explore the capabilities of a specific system prior to writing such programming. Detailed storyboarding is usually a required step in developing computer graphic or animation sequences.

By consulting and collaborating with the director and multimedia artist, the writer can develop scripts that are imaginative yet appropriate for the application and feasible given the production logistics and budget.

Summary: Keep It Functional

Visual descriptions in a shooting script communicate the sequence of visual events that will comprise the viewing experience. The writer must think visually, conjuring up appropriate, purposeful imagery in the mind's eye. Communicating visual ideas with words on paper is complicated by the contrasting nature of presentational and discursive symbol systems.

You need to supply sufficient instructions so that client and crew understand how the content will be visualized. You must also use the language of media production as a shorthand to communicate how visuals should be executed. Descriptions of screen action, camera shots and video effects represent a practical, pragmatic kind of writing.

Keep video instructions functional and realistic. If you have a clear perception of visual style and content before writing detailed shot descriptions, you should find the writing flowing logically from image to image. As you gain experience anticipating and solving visualization problems before they develop, you'll find first-draft shooting scripts will have an inherent cohesiveness and unity that stamp them as the work of a professional scriptwriter.

Footnotes

1. Vera John-Steiner, *Notebooks of the Mind* (New York, NY: Harper & Row, Publishers, 1985), p. 38.
2. Ibid., *p. 28.*
3. Ibid., *p. 83.*
4. Ibid., *pp. 82-86.*
5. Ibid., *p. 83.*
6. Henry Dreyfuss, *Symbol Sourcebook* (New York, NY: McGraw-Hill Book Company, 1972), *pp. 39, 56, 80, 123, 157, 212.*
7. John Joseph Brady, *The Craft of the Screenwriter* (New York, NY: Simon & Schuster, Publishers, 1981).
8. Vera John-Steiner, pp. 23-24.

CHAPTER 7

THE IMAGINATIVE EAR

> "Sentences are not different enough to hold the attention unless they are dramatic. No ingenuity of varying structure will do. All that can save them is *the speaking tone of voice somehow entangled in the words* and fastened to the page for the *ear of the imagination.* That is all that can save poetry from sing-song, all that can save prose from itself." [Italics mine][1]
>
> **Robert Frost**

A "speaking tone of voice" written for the "ear of the imagination" is all that can save narration from the listless, bland corporate style. Read annual reports. They seem to be created in sterile rooms, much like computer chips. The prose contains no surprises. The anonymous writer (more likely, committee of writers) hides from view. Neutered, the resulting text lies on the page like T.S. Elliot's evening sky: "A patient etherised upon a table."

Donald Murray, the writing coach mentioned earlier in this book, describes "voice" in the context of newspaper writing:

"Voice, the way the story *sounds,* is the distinctive element...that gives the illusion of individual writer *speaking* to individual reader. [Italics mine.] It is the element of the story that carries its emotional force. The story may be detached, angry, humorous, caring, sarcastic, ironic, sad, amused. The whole range of human emotions is available to the writer using voice."[2]

Frost and Murray attribute the aural qualities of language as the key to unlocking secrets of style. When writing narration for media, the way the story *sounds* is paramount. Your audience reads nothing on paper. Their viewing experience consists solely of sights and sounds unfolding in time. Usually, viewers hear your words one time only at a predetermined pace. Media writers must become proficient at sculpting vivid narrative copy that communicates ideas with verbal and *aural* clarity.

Writing for the Human Voice

Narration is the workhorse of corporate and educational media programming. In writing for the ear, one fact is paramount: a living, breathing human voice brings words on paper to life. Good scriptwriters develop skill creating vivid narrative copy that communicates ideas with verbal *and* aural clarity. Writing for the ear is really not so difficult. Often, it's just a matter of common sense—don't write sentences so long and complex that they cannot be spoken in a single breath.

Generally, narrative copy falls into one of four general categories:

- On-Camera Narration

- Off-Camera Narration

- Executive Message/Subject Matter Expert Commentary

- Character Narration

Narration written for a professional spokesperson is either delivered on-camera (talking head/talking head with props format) or off-camera to be synchronized with visuals (visuals-and-voice format). The two may also be mixed, juxtaposing blocks of on- and off-camera narration.

The medium also influences selection of a narrative technique. On-camera narrators appear in both films and videotapes. But television's live presence creates greater intimacy and immediacy between audience and on-camera personalities.

Many documentary films, by contrast, consist solely of visual-and-voice off-camera narration. (Interviews are also more frequently seen on television than on film, again, owing to the "live" look of videotape and the medium's reliance upon close-ups.)

Mixed-media presentations, often staged for live national sales meetings, are invariably high on motivational copy. They may incorporate a live host or hostess—sometimes even a cast of actors, singers, and dancers—integrated with corporate speakers and media presentations.

Professional or Nonprofessional Talent

Typically, professional narrators are the ideal choice to deliver off-camera copy. Nonprofessionals, especially content experts and organization leaders, are usually included to lend credibility or authority. Generally, such nonprofessional on-camera appearances should be brief and to the point.

When detailed content points must be delivered precisely, or when copy is motivational in tone, professional narrators are the best choice. Despite being outsiders in presentations designed to communicate inside information, professional voices have the distinct advantage of being able to read narration conversationally. (Hence, they appear to the ear as an insider.) When the voice is "disembodied," expression comes solely from vocal inflection, timing, and pacing. This requires someone with performing and interpretive ability and experience.

Writing informational copy for the on- or off-camera professional, the writer must settle into an appropriate narrative "voice." Donald Murray describes the range of styles or "voices" available to writers:

> *Journalism once attempted to achieve a single voice as if an institution were speaking. Today, journalism not only allows increasingly diverse voices, it encourages them so that the reader hears writers speaking. It is our responsibility as writers to develop a range of voices with which we feel comfortable, and then to try them out by drafting leads to see which one will work best on a story. If we discover the voice then we usually have the lead.*[3]

Corporations and organizations often speak as if an institution were speaking. Media communications, however, require humanity, drama and interest. Interest, as Frost observed, results from dramatic sentences. A distinctive narrative voice is an ideal way to achieve such drama.

Try this experiment. Think of a talking head or visuals-and-voice presentation that you know well. Perhaps it's the script you just completed. Maybe it's a TV commercial you've heard so often that you know it from memory. Perhaps it's a message from the chairman of the board that you edited.

Whatever narrative thread you select, make a "mental loop" of the audio track about a minute in length. Keep playing the words and content of that loop over and over in your head. (In workshops, I have participants close their eyes and go into a trance-like state until the narrative copy becomes a mantra.) Then, as this narrative copy plays on and on, start changing the narrator. First, make your narrator Barbara Walters, then, change to Bill Cosby. Next, make your narrator Woody Allen, or John Madden, or Oprah Winfrey. And finally, make the narrator Kermit the Frog.

Do this exercise with a group of people and you'll notice grins and giggles at different voice/content combinations. For many choices the incongruity between narrative voice and content is sufficient to create laughter. More significantly, however, when you ask how many people began to *change the copy* with change of narrator, at least half the people usually raise their hands. Such is the power of voice—it will dictate the words, sentences, and pace of the narration.

The secret to writing distinctive, yet appropriate narrative voices results from discovering a suitable voice in your inner ear, then locking into it as you draft narration or dialog.

I once wrote a training program for frozen-foods-broker sales representatives. These men and women go into local supermarkets and compete for freezer space, shelf positioning, and merchandising programs for frozen food products made by big companies like Kraft or Stouffer's. It's a shirt sleeve job, in and out of supermarkets all day.

In drafting narrative copy, I sought to establish a real down-to-earth voice. Lots of short, simple sentences but very action-oriented. When I began writing, I had to strive consciously to achieve the desired tone. But once I "locked into it," the inner ear took over; the voice became second nature.

In media presentations, communication takes place on many levels. Establishing emotional rapport with viewers is often overlooked in the mechanics of nailing down content. Striking the ideal narrative tone is a surefire way to connect with your audience emotionally.

Executive Messages and Subject-Matter-Expert Commentary

The third type of narrative writing also calls for a personal style and voice, not the writer's, but the *speaker's*. The in-house spokesperson should be used when *who* delivers the message carries as much weight as the specific content. When the recognized expert on centrifugal gas compressors speaks, other engineers listen. When the president of the company talks, employees take content to heart.

In drafting on-camera comments for such speakers, the media writer's search for voice begins with the executive or subject-matter expert. The speaker's attitude toward the content and his or her management style, speech patterns, and rhythms all influence the writer's task. As in more traditional speech writing, the writer "ghosts" for the busy executive or expert. Sufficient personal knowledge and insight into the speaker's character lead naturally to a voice compatible with that individual's own style. Later in the chapter, you'll find specific suggestions for doing this.

With these narrative types in mind, let's discuss techniques for achieving clarity in a conversational writing style—no matter what the voice.

OBSERVE THE ELEMENTS OF STYLE

Strunk and White's *The Elements of Style* is a classic on writing with brevity, clarity, vigor, and authority. Although written with print writers in mind, this model of brevity certainly applies to scripting narration. My advice: commit *The Elements of Style* to memory. (More practically, read Strunk and White every six months to imbed its wisdom in your mind.)

Three of Professor Strunk's stylistic rules have particular relevance for writers of narration:

1. Use the active voice.

"The active voice is usually more direct and vigorous than the passive."[4]

Direct, vigorous writing has greater impact on the ear than vague, indefinite passive constructions. The active voice gives writers of narration a better shot at aural clarity.

2. Put statements in positive form.

"Make definite assertions. If your every sentence admits a doubt, your writing will lack authority."[5]

Media presentations play to captive audiences expecting to receive useful information or learn new skills. The more positive and forceful your narration, the more likely the viewing audience will feel it is receiving a worthwhile, meaningful communication.

Writing that lacks authority is not worth the expense of mounting a media production. It also places the narrator—your flesh and blood transmitter—in the awkward position of sounding indecisive. As Murray says, "Good writing is always based on a firm foundation of authority—there is a significant relationship between the word 'author' and 'authority'."[6]

3. Omit needless words.

"Vigorous writing is concise. A sentence should contain no unnecessary words... This requires not that the writer make all his sentences short, or that he avoid all detail and treat his subjects only in outline, but that every word tell."[7]

When writing narration, words translate into screen time, which, in turn, translates into money. Working in media that gobble up time and money, the writer owes it to audience and producer to be economical in every sense. Become ruthless. "Omit needless words."

Observe these three principles, and you've taken a big step toward ensuring that your own narration can be spoken easily and will be clear to the listening audience.

Keep It Conversational

Narrators in voice-over sessions are often asked, "Make it a little more friendly." The admonition should be applied first to the writer. A narrator can't take convoluted, formal text and make it sound like a chat over the back fence simply by reading with a big smile. The following principles characterize a conversational style.

Conversational Writing Is Informal and Personal

Unlike a speech, which addresses a group using rhetorical and declamatory conventions, good media narration is written as a conversation directed to an audience of one. So write the way people speak. That doesn't mean narration must be riddled with slang or take on the random structure of a spontaneous conversation. But it should convey informality and have a personal tone, as though the narrator is speaking to an individual.

As an example, here are two versions of the same information. The copy in version A contains legal jargon, which often crops up in corporate projects. While this may be marginally acceptable in print, it becomes totally sterile and impersonal when read aloud. (Go ahead—try to read that copy aloud and sound friendly and personal.) Version B, by contrast, is written as one person might express that thought in conversation with another person.

Narration copy A

> To qualify for an allowance, all advertising must be prepared in accordance with the terms and conditions of the current Cooperative Advertising Allowance Agreement...

Narration copy B

> To receive your allowance, make sure ads conform to requirements spelled out in the current co-op Ad Agreement...

Several factors make version B more appropriate for a narrator to read conversationally. First, it uses personal pronouns, "you" and "your," acknowledging that the comment is directed to individuals. Words such as "advertising" and "cooperative," are shortened to a conversational form, "ad" and "co-op." The legal jargon such as "in accordance with" or "terms and conditions" are simplified through a less formal vocabulary: "conform to requirements." Notice, too, the conversational version "omits needless words."

Develop an ear for the simplicity that characterizes spoken conversation. Contractions and simplified syntax, for instance, lend informality to narrative copy.

Instead of...	Write
we will	we'll
cannot	can't
automobile	auto or car
due to the fact that	because

Write With Pictures in Mind

Words without pictures are simply a speech. Don't write narrative copy without knowing what the accompanying visuals consist of. The most obvious reason for this is to avoid picture/text redundancy—describing through narration what is perfectly obvious visually. Narrative copy should enhance the visual portion of the presentation, adding perspective and interpretive viewpoints.

Use the Language of the Audience

On the surface, this suggestion seems to contradict earlier advice to use the simplified, straightforward word form. In reality, however, it recognizes that audiences of insiders often have their own trade or professional shorthand. The writer's initial research should include developing a working knowledge of that professional or industry lingo. For instance, in the insurance industry, otherwise common words such as "risk," "exposures" or "surplus" have unique connotations. In the pharmaceutical/medical community, words and phrases like "efficacy," "indications," "over-the-counter," "well-tolerated" and "mode of action" all carry specific meanings.

However, when the communication is directed to an outside audience—the general public, opinion leaders, or other industry outsiders—then special terminology should be avoided or explained. The conversational standard, then, is determined not by the writer or the client, but by the audience.

Avoid Hyperbole and Hype

Bold claims and superlatives belong to the advertising copywriter. When your audience consists of employees, stockholders, students, faculty, physicians, lawyers, nurses, or other specialists, straight talk and logic make for the most credible message. If you want a narrator to sound sincere, knowledgeable, and convincing then write narration that is sincere, knowledgeable, and convincing.

To tout a product or generate enthusiasm for a new policy or program, substantiate positive sentences and claims by offering proof that a product or program is the "best on the market." Sales representatives need real features and benefits and hard data to make a good sales presentation. They also need to be prepared for marketplace realities.

Selling sizzle in place of the steak usually leaves the audience hungry for more. Honesty of purpose always shines through the glitter of media presentations and touches the audience directly.

Don't Overwrite

The audio column is not just for words. It also includes music and sound effects. When writing for the ear, keep in mind that, at certain strategic points, it's most effective to allow the narrator to step aside for a musical or sound effect interlude. Some of the best accompaniment to a visual is nothing more than silence.

Test Your Copy

The acid test for narration is foolproof: read it aloud. Better still, sit down with the producer or director to read your first draft aloud, making notes about what needs improvement. This is the quickest, surest way to detect and fix narrative problems. If you, the writer, can't read the copy comfortably, something's wrong. For instance, read this copy aloud right now.

> OUR NEW "SNEEZE" COMMERCIAL WILL BURST INTO THE HOMES OF MIL- LIONS OF AMERICANS STARTING THE WEEK OF NOVEMBER SECOND AND WILL IMPACT ON THE COLD AND FLU TARGET AUDIENCE THROUGH A MIX OF PRIME TIME, LATE NIGHT AND DAYTIME EXPO- SURE AT THE ONSET OF THE COLD AND FLU SEASON.

A third of the way through one is gasping for breath. It also makes two references to a specific time frame: "November second" and the "cold and flu season." Here's one possible rewrite.

> OUR NEW "SNEEZE" COMMERCIAL WILL BURST INTO THE HOMES OF MIL- LIONS OF AMERICANS THE WEEK OF NO- VEMBER SECOND. AT THE ONSET OF THE COLD AND FLU SEASON, THE COMMERCIAL WILL REACH THE TARGET AUDIENCE THROUGH A MIX OF PRIME TIME, LATE NIGHT AND DAYTIME EXPOSURE.

Now, see if that isn't easier to read conversationally. Also, the connection between "November second" and the "cold and flu" season is clarified—yet we've omitted the duplication of the phrase.

Writing for the Nonprofessional Reader

Certainly, the same stylistic principles that guide writing narration apply when writing for the executive or content expert. In fact, it's even more important to write for the speaking voice. Trained professionals can adapt to an unusually long sentence or successfully navigate a tongue-twisting phrase. But the majority of nonprofessionals are at a distinct disadvantage reading aloud.

When scripting for an executive, then, the writer must gain insight into the individual's personality and style to adopt a fitting tone. Are you writing for an executive who's strong and forceful, a captain of industry, or one who comes across as one of the boys, folksy and down-to-earth? Is the executive one who takes a rational, reasoned approach to the business or is she or he a motivational leader who appeals to the emotions?

Staff writers usually possess an advantage over the freelancer in such cases, having more opportunity for direct access. Yet even in-house writers are often isolated from busy executives. Both staff and freelance writers should try to review an executive's past speeches and video appearances to get a feel for rhetorical style. It's also important to meet with the executive, if only for 15 minutes, to hear firsthand what the executive hopes to accomplish.

If you're scripting for a content expert, your role is to help that person express his or her knowledge through the chosen medium. In addition to gaining insights into personality, consider what visual support will help convey content. Will the person work best with physical props, or will cutaway graphics prove more functional?

Two or More Narrator Voices

Sometimes, you may opt for two or more narrators. The technique is often used in lengthy scripts containing blocks of narrative copy. Alternating two voices, especially a male/female combination, helps delineate transitions and changes in subject matter.

If, however, a writer produces a single lengthy narration, then simply assigns every other paragraph to each of the two narrators, an opportunity to have dual voices play functional roles or contrasting characterizations is missed. A more imaginative solution is to identify a specific role and voice for each narrator, then script narration accordingly.

For instance, the frozen-foods broker's training program I referred to involves a male and a female narrator. They play different roles in the delivery of the content. The male narrator serves as a studio-based anchorman, while the female narrator appears on location, delivering reports from the frozen-food aisle of a local supermarket. The male narrator's tone is more matter-of-fact than the female narrator, who is down-to-earth and warmer and more personal in tone.

Music and Sound

The right side of a dual column video script is labeled "AUDIO." For most informational and educational programs, narration and dialog usually dominate the AUDIO column. As a result, scriptwriters often fail to leverage the power of music and sound effects to establish mood, stir the audience, fulfill motivational objectives, and raise the spirit.

In *Philosophy in a New Key,* Susanne Langer traces musical aesthetics from a historical perspective, then offers this insight into music's appeal:

Another kind of reaction to music, however, is more striking and seems more significant: that is the emotional response it is commonly supposed to evoke. The belief that music arouses emotions goes back even to the Greek philosophers. It led Plato to demand, for his ideal state, a strict censorship of modes and tunes, lest his citizens be tempted by weak or voluptuous airs to indulge in demoralizing emotions. [8]

Music can provide an injection of emotional appeal to your audience. Consider how important emotion is in nearly every human communication or enterprise. While doing a series of sales training scripts one summer, I was confronted with the assertion that "people buy on emotion, then justify their purchase with logic." I kept resisting that notion, putting more credence in rational behavior.

Then, the course designer made this observation: "Think how much of your disposable income you spend to purchase 'emotional experiences.' When you buy tickets on the 50 yard line or behind the dugout, you're buying the emotional experience of being part of the crowd, yelling and screaming for your team. Or consider the money you spend on books, theatre and concert tickets, artwork, compact discs, the movies—the list goes on and on."

In almost every project and assignment, scriptwriters are overtly or covertly playing on audience emotions, trying to sell the benefits of new products, the importance of learning procedures for operating centrifugal gas compressors, or the need for following bank procedures in the event of an armed robbery.

Hospitals use video the day before surgery to reassure anxious patients. Corporations sell stockholders and security analysts on the company's accomplishments and performance through image pieces.

Music offers a direct path to an audience's heart and soul. Why, then, is music used inappropriately or totally ignored in so many corporate media productions?

For starters, scriptwriters often fail to envision and assign a specific communication function for music.

Many years ago, my wife and I accompanied our daughter to her college freshman orientation weekend. Among the evening activities was an illustrated lecture on "Dying and Death in Alfred Hitchcock's Films." The professor was provocative and witty (in a macabre manner), introducing themes about Hitchcock's depiction of on-screen murder.

While showing scenes, he made comments to the darkened audience: "Look at his use of quick cuts here. . .see? The villain's screen left; the hero, screen right...." At one point, he intoned, "Listen to his use of music here...."

During the postmortem (pun intended), a parent raised the issue: "Why did you make so much fuss over music? I was taught the best movie music was in the background. You're not supposed to be aware of it."

"Why not?" crackled the graying Prof. "You make a conscious effort to notice editing. You're aware of composition, lighting, action within the frame, special effects—and the more sophisticated the viewer, the greater the appreciation of such cinematic elements. Why not pay attention to the music? How is it playing against the picture? What's its storytelling function?"

I realized then why I've always disliked most stock library music. The pieces are meant to serve as "background" music. That's why I'm burned out on insipid, synthesized music played by unskilled, uncaring anonymous musicians. So let's bring music to the foreground and see how it can improve our media communications.

Foreground music says, "Pay attention! I have a role to play in this communication. I've been carefully placed in this script by the writer to serve a purpose."

Okay. So music should be functional. What roles can music play in media scripts?

- Establish mood
- Cue a transition
- Underscore a point
- Support the pictures
- Play "against" the pictures
- Provide a rhythmic bed for editing
- Communicate an emotion
- Offer a change of pace
- Surprise the audience

Notice what is not on this list: "open the program," "close the program," "provide background music." The misuse of music is often most evident in programs that begin with music, end with music, and have music running under the entire narrative track.

Certain content or viewing situations do call for "wall-to-wall" music. Programs used in booths at convention trade shows may need a sustained music track to gain attention. Most audiovisual communications, however, require more purposeful, intelligent uses of music.

It starts with a writer identifying the function of music and making it an integral element of the viewing/listening experience, as Excerpt B.8 in Appendix B shows.

Music and sound effects can play highly specific, functional roles in telling a story. To use music functionally, writers need a range of musical listening experiences to draw upon: classical, pop, rock, folk, hillbilly, jazz, avant garde, show tunes, blues, film scores, etcetera. The writer may not be a musician, but the complete scriptwriter will be conversant with music in many forms to envision imaginative uses of music within the structure and content of a script.

Today, the rapidly changing technological developments in creating and recording music make media producers less dependent on prerecorded library music. Although bewildering, such things as composing by computer, synthesizer, and digital sound manipulation have brought the practicality and cost of original scores within the range of many media producers. Even library music, in the hands of a skilled audio engineer, can produce intriguing results through editing, mixing, and electronic manipulation. But it all starts with a writer whose "imaginative ear" hears *where* music would be effective and explains *how* in the script.

Scripting Audio Programs

When I bought my first word processor many years ago, the equipment came with a stack of manuals and a package of audiocassette tapes to "talk you through" each lesson. That's one example of an "audio only" application. Here are others:

- Some video-based classroom training programs make extensive use of audiocassette segments to convey specific, detailed, and nonvisual content.
- Sales managers, recognizing their sales force spends hours every day strapped into an automobile, commission informational and motivational audiocassette messages to reinforce previous training, sales-meeting themes and home-office direction.
- Ironically, because digitized audio requires much less bandwidth to stream than video, sound bites and other audio content is easily integrated into Web sites, voice mail, and other digital media presentations.
- And there's a whole industry built around the appetite for books on tape.

Even though I'd written several "audio only" scripts, it wasn't until I was invited to conduct a workshop for writers forming a team to turn out an extensive series of training-oriented audiocassettes on high-tech information that I began to consider the genuine potential of the medium.

Pebbles of Meaning

Fortuitously, I was researching American Indian myths for a personal writing project. Digging into this oral-based culture offered insight into verbal storytelling qualities. I discovered the oral traditions and experiences of American Indians are quite different from those of our written culture.

Every culture responds to language differently. For us, a word consists of highly abstract symbols (the alphabet) such as those you read now. These symbols occupy *visual* space on pages. Because of Western civilization's deeply ingrained literacy, words are largely (but not exclusively) visual entities.

For a nonliterate culture, however, the word is experienced *solely* as an oral/aural entity. There is no visual alphabet to distract from the experience of sound in space and time. No words, sentences, or punctuation on paper. The nonliterate is more comfortable with the sense of language as a flow of sound (just like narration) because that is how the ear perceives language. With the image of written language cues, explains one Native American, we have "no difficulty imagining what the aural poet means if he says that words are pebbles of meaning, but that very image of written language makes us see as a metaphor what he may mean as a literal statement..."[9]

Which brings us full circle to Frost! Writing for the ear requires the "speaking tone of voice," that sense of language as a *flow of sound*. To craft good audio scripts, develop your appreciation for the full, rich potential of the aural medium at your disposal—not only speech, music, and sound effects but also the *visual* potential. What struck me reading American Indian literature was its vivid, imaginative visual imagery.

Like our grandparents sitting around the first radios, Indians around the campfire under an evening sky were free to let their imagination take whatever flights of fancy the night's storyteller could invent. And so Native American tales are full of images of animals who take on human form or humans who become birds or insects as an integral part of the plot.

An Audiovisual Medium?

Radio writers used to refer to their medium as "theater of the imagination" and wrote vividly in all manner of genre—soap operas, westerns, cops and robbers, science fiction, comedy. They challenged their audiences to use their imagination and "see" literally anything possible to envision in the mind. (In this sense, television takes something away from a viewer's imaginative participation.) Today, most such aural writing is limited to radio commercials or found in Garrison Keilor's theatrical radio sketches, such as the adventures of his detective Guy Noire.

As Robert Hilliard says in his book on writing for TV and radio, radio allows writers "complete freedom of time and place. There is no limitation on the setting or on movement in time or in space. The writer can create unlimited forms of physical action and can bypass in the twinkling of a musical bridge minutes or centuries of time."

Hilliard cites Orson Welles's radio treatment of H.G. Wells's *War of the Worlds*. He refers to a similar but unsuccessful televised version of the story. "Limiting the action to what one can present visually restricts the imaginative potentials of word and sound,"[10] concludes Hilliard.

So in a sense, radio and audiocassettes are visual media. The audience plays an active role envisioning what the writer suggests the listener *see*.

Another potential for expression in audio-only media is the nonlinear counterpoint and overlaying achieved by mixing several auditory sources: music, sound effects, dialog, narration, or interview comments interwoven to create a collage of sound. It is what the late eccentric Canadian pianist Glenn Gould called his polyphonic radio documentaries: contrapuntal radio.

"...We tried to have situations arise cogently from within the framework of the program in which two, or three, or four voices could be overlapped, talking essentially about the same thing... treating those voices as characters—as all the material... was gained through interviews. It was documentary material treated as drama."[11]

The audiocassette scriptwriter works in a similar imaginative realm. Anything is possible: talking electronic typewriters, a sales representative in heaven or hell, a radio call-in show about the fine points of zero-based budgeting—give your mind free rein. Not long ago, I wrote an audiocassette primer on epilepsy for pharmaceutical sales

representatives in the style of NPRs "All Things Considered." A radio reporter interviewed a fictional medical illustrator working on anatomical diagrams of the brain. A mock travel writer took us on a journey from one neuron to another to illustrate the flow of an electrical charge across a synapse.

For your own inspiration, turn to the spoken arts section of the library record collection. Check out old Mel Brooks/Carl Reiner 2000 year-old-man routine. Listen to Bob and Ray's fictitious interviews. Go even more theatrical with the Fireside Theatre creations. Get hold of old Stan Freberg radio spots. Check out early Woody Allen monologues. And read some American Indian myths. They will set your aural imagination on fire with the visual possibilities of a "sightless" medium.

The script excerpts in Appendix B illustrate imaginative approaches to informational or instructional subject matter delivered through the audiocassette medium.

Salespeople spend lots of time in their cars. Audiocassette programs are an efficient way to reach them with informational or sales training material. Excerpt B.9, from a General Foods sales training audiocassette series, uses takeoffs on familiar radio broadcast formats as a way of developing a fast-paced style that gets the message across entertainingly.

In this introductory module, the audience is introduced to the concept through a mock traffic report and call-in show. Within minutes, other callers give the flip side of the coin—the customer's viewpoint . Shortly, a Dr. Ruth parody introduces the sales therapist for the series.

The overview and format parodies continue with a soap opera spoof, "As the World Sells." Notice the use of sound effects to create visual imagery in the listener's mind.

A sports event offers yet another familiar radio format and an opportunity to allow the imaginative listener to participate in an active way.

Next, review an audiocassette script aimed at salespeople, in this case, pharmaceutical sales representatives. Excerpt B.10 involves a prescription product to treat irregular heartbeats known as arrhythmia. Although the writer takes a more traditional narrative approach, note the use of music and sound effects as a means of illustrating and reinforcing key copy points. A mix of voices, additional music cues, and an audio interview are used to convey content while generating a sense of pace and vivid listening experience.

While radically different in style and tone, these two sales-training excerpts illustrate the potential for creating interesting, informative, and involving listening experiences when writing for the human ear.

Summary

When writing for the ear, it is easy to underestimate what the combination of narration, dialogue, music, and sound effects can achieve as well as the technical craft needed to fully capitalize on such potential.

The key lies in realizing that viewers never see words on paper—they hear words unfold in time as "pebbles of meaning." Achieving aural clarity with dramatic sentences a narrator can easily articulate results from the "speaking tone of voice" writers are encouraged to use by developing an "imaginative ear."

Footnotes

1. From liner notes to "Robert Frost Reads His Poetry" (New York, Caedmon).
2. Donald Murray, *Writing for Your Readers: Notes on the writer's craft from the Boston Globe* (Boston, MA: Globe Pequot, 1983).
3. *Ibid.*
4. William Strunk, Jr. and E. B. White, *The Elements of Style,* 3rd Ed. (New York, NY: Macmillan Publishing Co., Inc., 1979), p. 18.
5. *Ibid.,* pp. 19-20.
6. Murray, *Writing for Your Readers.*
7. Strunk and White, *The Elements of Style,* p. 23.
8. Langer, *Philosophy in a New Key,* p. 211.
9. Brian Swann, ed. *Smoothing the Ground, Essays on Native American Oral Literature* (Berkeley, CA: University of California Press, 1983).
10. Robert L. Hilliard, *Writing for Television and Radio,* 3rd. Ed. (New York, NY: Hasting House, Publishers, 1976), p. 13.
11. "Glenn Gould: Concert Dropout, a Conversation with John McClure" (New York, NY: a Columbia Records Masterworks recording, stereo BS 15).

CHAPTER 8

MAKING THE MOST OF FEEDBACK

It's an old story I heard, supposedly about Mel Brooks. It's a rewrite session during the so-called golden age of television. A large group from Sid Ceasar's *Your Show of Shows* is gathered around a table to provide feedback on Brooks's latest sketch. One by one, they offer analysis of what was wrong with every aspect of the sketch. "O.K., O.K.," said Brooks. "But where were all you guys when the pages were *blank?*"

"Re-vision: to see again." There are many ways to see our first draft scripts "again." One is through the eyes of others—client, content expert, producer, director, boss, writing buddy, wife, or husband. That's called "feedback."

Another way of seeing first draft scripts "again" is through the eyes of the writer. Only the writer relates to the shooting script as both creator and critic. It is "whole-brain thinking" epitomized. A response from both the artist and the judge.

Yet overall, revision is the phase in the scriptwriting process when we are at our most critical. As von Oech would put it, this is the time to don the "judge's wig" with all its authoritarian associations.

Reactions to scripts come in many guises— and sometimes disguises. What does the perturbed chairman of the board mean when he says, "It misses the mark. It just misses the mark!" What does the content expert mean when she says, "You don't seem to be focusing on the real core of our problem." What does the hurried client mean when he says, "I don't know, it's just not what I had in mind somehow."

At this turning point, the scriptwriter must sometimes play the dual roles of salesperson and psychotherapist, gently questioning and probing to clarify what the buyer or patient really means. Is the script in need of major surgery? Or are the problems largely a matter of style and voice? Did the writer's creative boldness push the producer further out on the "creativity/risk" limb than he/she is comfortable with?

Or, the most alarming scenario of all to the

writer, has something in the overall nature of the project changed? Perhaps the target audience has been expanded; or maybe some new, unforeseen and unspoken objectives have crept into the parameters defining a project's scope and boundaries.

Whatever the nature or significance of feedback, the scriptwriter must now work to understand each script "reader's" perception, then determine how to accommodate that perspective in a second draft script.

Unfortunately, some writers attach negative meanings to words such as *revision, re-write* and the like. Perhaps it's a carry-over from high school English teachers and torturous college term papers. But strong, vivid narrative media writing does not spring full-blown in one draft. Often directors are literally forced to rip the pages from a scriptwriter intent on polishing and reworking up until, and even past, the final hour. (I think that's why many directors don't like writers hanging around on shoots.) As one director, Jim Libby, aptly puts it, "Scripts are never finished; they're simply abandoned." Prior to abandonment, however, there should be a period of studied, analytical, and skillful rewriting incorporating relevant feedback and reactions from all involved—including the writer.

Scriptwriters walking into the meeting following circulation of a first-draft script have cause for trepidation. The handful of select "script readers" have read and reread. Now they gather (like vultures?) around a table to offer feedback. Each responds from his or her own, usually highly focused perspective. (Content experts focus on content, clients on objectives, producers on dollars, directors on logistics, etcetera.). Depending on the size of the group, it's easy to feel lonely or a tad defensive: "Just where were all you folks when the pages were blank?"

Feedback in the Writing Process

Feedback plays an integral role in each phase of the scriptwriting process. We write content outlines and treatments for the express purpose of soliciting feedback before spending the time and energy a first-draft script demands. In evaluating such feedback, the scriptwriter needs to consider three related factors:

- When does it occur in the writing process?
- Who is the feedback coming from?
- What is the substance of the feedback?

When does it occur in the writing process

With experience, you come to expect certain types of critical reaction at different stages of a project. Discussions about the creative concept should be flushed out and resolved at the treatment stage. "If it's not working at the treatment and outline stage," says scriptwriter Donna Matrazzo, "then it won't work as part of the script."

When both content outline and creative approach are approved at the conclusion of the rehearsal phase, revisions to the first draft script most often focus on: additions, deletions, or editing.

If the scriptwriter begins to hear feedback relating to the premise of the entire creative treatment on a first draft, serious problems are afoot. These concerns should have surfaced long ago and been addressed head-on before writing a firstdraft shooting script.

Hearing such feedback at this stage of the project indicates one of several possible problems:

1. The treatment did not fully indicate to the client, content expert, or producer the full ramifications of the creative direction and its implications.
2. Or, some new element relating to objectives, content, style, budget or use of the program has been injected into the project without the writer's knowledge. In other words, the parameters or "givens" of the project

are being changed.

3. Or, it is also possible that the writer strayed significantly from the original content/treatment rationale in executing a first draft.

Who does the feedback come from?

Feedback relating to content most often comes from subject matter experts. Writers should realize that significant content revisions can, and often do, occur at the first-draft stage. Although the content outline performs a function similar to that of the treatment by communicating what the program is about prior to a first draft, considerable detail is added to the content outline in a first draft—especially for technical or complex subjects with training objectives.

Often, when expanding content in the first draft, technical errors, omissions, and ambiguities surface. Conscientious content experts are sticklers for getting it down right. Depending on the topic and situation, clients may also have a significant amount of input relating to content. I've even participated in script sessions where differences between content experts and clients arise. This is always a great spectator sport.

Who the feedback comes from is important in a larger context. Various industries, businesses, educational, and medical subjects have languages of their own. Often the writer may have a good grasp of the subject but fails to use the precise words or "jargon" the intended audience will relate to. (I experienced this problem in a project for the United States Golf Association. I wrote, for instance, "from tee to putting green." It was changed to "from tee to green." Obviously, I don't spend enough time on the "links.")

Each industry has a unique vocabulary. In time, that vocabulary becomes second nature to the scriptwriter. But when you're new to a specific field, your first draft often requires some reworking to capture those nuances.

At a first draft reading, feedback from producers and directors is likely to fall into two areas: style, and budgetary or logistical issues. For the most part, major questions of style would certainly surface in the treatment. But while the treatment conveys the conceptual "germ" and creative schema, the first draft reflects a precise working out of this approach—scene by scene and shot by shot.

Perhaps a disturbing inconsistency in style or voice crept into narration. Maybe the balance between formats appears differently in the first-draft script than it did in the abbreviated style of a treatment.

Their comments tend to be quite specific on style, narrative voice, visualization, the function of each scene, format, pacing and length, use of graphics, music, and sound effects—those elements that comprise the "production terminology" of a media script. Comments on presentational or stylistic aspects of the first draft from clients and Subject Matter Experts (SMEs), on the other hand, can sometimes be taken with a grain of salt.

So at a first-draft meeting, writers not only need to listen to the substantive message of the feedback, but also consider who is offering each comment. This helps assess the nature and interrelationship of various responses to the script from the differing perspectives of each script reader.

What is the substance of the feedback?

Initially, the scriptwriter must discern the nature of everyone's response. The most terrifying feedback comes in the form of information that clearly indicates the project parameters have changed. Somehow, the givens are different now than at prior meetings on content and objectives.

Another equally frightening form of feedback occurs when the content expert says, "I don't think you really understand what we're trying to teach about how a centrifugal gas compressor works." If you get a sinking feeling in the pit of your stomach, the SME's probably right. Often, such comments result from clients hoping to expand on the uses of the media program:

"We'd not only like to show the videotape to our dealer sales reps—we want a shorter, edited version aimed at consumers for dealer reps to play at point-of-purchase."

Or...

"This script isn't meaty enough. We not only want to use it to *introduce* the product—we wanna build some training sessions around it."

Or the producer explains...

"The budget has changed, and we're gonna have to come up with a less expensive approach."

Such feedback indicates the media writer may have to rethink the project—take one step forward and two back by returning to the concept development stage. If a client wants to change the audience or objectives, it's up to writer and producer to explain the consequences on scripting and production. When told they cannot meet all their needs without developing two distinct versions of the media presentation, resulting in additional production costs, clients may reconsider and return to a more limited approach.

If not, then the writer must assess how the new parameters affect the existing first draft. The impact usually cannot be fully determined right on the spot. Reaching two distinct audiences may require more research with the content expert. It might mean shaping two versions of the script using a common concept and format, and common production elements. That's a conceptual matter requiring problem identification, analysis, and solution. It's more than a rewrite; we're talking a "rethink," and that calls for "time out" to regroup. (Changes in the original specifications usually impact the total production schedule. It's not "kosher" to expect the writer and production team to stick to initial commitments without some give-and-take in

the schedule. If that's not possible, the writer, at least, is facing overtime. Clients should pay for such overtime.)

Sometimes feedback coming from different sources has multiple effects on the script. Often only the writer is fully aware of the significance of such changes. For instance, I once used dramatization and a concealed structure for a program on employee benefit changes. For reasons having to do with the company's policies and commitment to equal opportunity employment, the actions and motivations of two characters (a black female clerical employee and a white female professional employee) were reversed. On the surface that doesn't seem like much of a rewrite—simply switching names and a few lines of dialog should easily respond to the client's concern. In this instance, though, I had to do major surgery on the highly fluid and flexible concealed structural spine to accommodate the change. Sometimes, only the writer fully appreciates the scope and consequences of the feedback. And only the writer can go off to sift through it all and fix problems.

In short, whenever the writer hears feedback that indicates a major problem with the concept, content, or structure—the revision process is likely to go beyond the adding, deleting, or editing normally associated with revision.

Handling Objections

For a time, all my projects were on the same subject: sales training. I'd never had much respect for selling and salespeople. (Most consumers don't. We're usually distrustful and wary of salespeople, sometimes even adversarial, especially when buying an intangible product like insurance.) Not only was I writing a lot of training material, but I was writing material related to selling insurance!

So, of course, I learned about the sales process. And sales training courses place considerable emphasis on objection handling. Once I dug into the content and spent time discussing selling skills with subject matter experts, I began to realize that handling objection is exactly what writers do during script conferences. So the skills used to handle objections can be readily adapted to make the script conference more productive and less traumatic for writers. For instance, one of the first objection-handling rules is to anticipate the objection.

Anticipate the Objection

I met to discuss feedback on the United States Golf Association script mentioned earlier in this book. The objective was to illustrate the causes and cures of slow play, golf's most serious "disease." Two pros, Fuzzy Zoeller and Amy Alcott, were to be the spokespeople. The treatment proposed a solution for the major scripting problem: how to demonstrate the wrong-way causes of slow play. Figure 8.1 shows a portion of that treatment.[2]

Figure 8.1: Treatment in relation to anticipating objections

CREATIVE STRATEGY

The Challenge

There is an inherent challenge in communicating this content via film or television. On the one hand, these media are ideally suited to capturing and demonstrating both the causes and cures of slow play. The challenge, however, lies in developing a stylistic approach to ensure on-screen demos of slow play don't result in a viewing experience that is also slow and protracted.

A Solution

The following treatment addresses this problem head-on with a creative concept designed to "speed up" the action and viewer interest of slow-play scenes while illustrating negative behaviors.

The solution involves what we call the "home movie" effect:

Television Treatment

Home movies—even home videos, for that matter—have a characteristic, amateur look (hand held shooting, overuse of zooms, scratchy prints, etc.) which often makes the action mildly humorous. At the same time, home movies appear slightly speeded up when transferred to video. Our concept is to shoot "wrong way" scenes in the style of a home movie or videotape.

Basically, here's how the program would unfold…

The producer/director and I were both comfortable with the "home movie" device for illustrating slow play. But prior to the client meeting, we tried to anticipate potential objections, confusions, or questions. Other than total rejection, we could come up with only one objection: the treatment focused on describing the "home movie" technique for illustrating wrong-way examples. On reading the complete treatment, however, one might assume the majority of screen time and emphasis went to the "home movie" segments, leaving our professional golfers a minimal role.

The treatment appropriately explained what was most difficult to envision—how the home movie technique would be executed and integrated into the body of the program. Scripting the "right way" commentary of the pros required little explanation. However, should the client raise the objection that the "stars" might be overshadowed by the wrong-way hackers, we had a response in our hip pocket. No "think on your feet" adlibbing would be necessary.

So, begin by considering the script or treatment, the players and politics involved, and then anticipate areas most likely to raise questions or concerns.

Hear the Objection Out

Next, salespeople are tutored to "hear the

objection out. Keep your mouth shut. Let the buyer get the full concern on the table." Usually, the "buyer" (client, producer, or SME) feels better simply for having voiced his/her objection. And the salesperson (writer) has not short-circuited the process by jumping in and answering an objection too quickly. After all, without hearing the objection out, we may miss vital information—the key to unlocking "the sale."

Clarify the Objection

Now it's the writer's turn to speak, but it's still too early to answer the objection head on. Instead, use the salesperson's technique of analyzing and clarifying the objection. You do this by asking a question or two in return to make certain you understand: "Let me make certain I follow. Are you saying you're not comfortable with the home movie technique itself—or are you concerned about upstaging the pros?"

It's the salesperson's technique of making the buyer answer an "either/or" question. The real objective may lie beneath the surface. Also, listening to a client's feedback (or anyone's feedback on your writing) requires "third ear" listening skills. Often what's not spoken, but implied or buried in rhetoric, carries the heart of the issue.

Remember, people buy on emotion, then justify their purchase with logic. The same applies to scripts and clients. Their most important reactions are emotional and affective. Often they're trying to like the script, but they need help. Sometimes, all that's needed is for the writer and producer to bolster the client's confidence by saying they know what they're doing, and the resulting program will work with the target audience.

Answer or Defer the Objection

Once the objection has been clarified and you feel you understand the client's genuine point of view, the writer must decide, "Do I want to answer this objection?" And if so, "Do I want to

answer it now?"

Not every objection requires an answer. Some (known to sales types as "minor point objections") are simply too picayune to bother with. Others point to additional problems the client or content experts need to get off their chest. So allow them to "hold court." Give them the floor. Listen carefully. Listen for what they do and don't say.

Are you hearing objections you expected to hear and have ready answers for? Are you hearing minor points that can be fixed through rewrites? Is the client/content expert having trouble with the concept? Or, do they find the treatment or script lacks effectiveness and impact?

Classifying Objections

Answers to these questions determine your response. New salespeople are taught to classify objections according to type. The most dismaying is the hopeless objection:

"I just don't like this script at all."

"I was dubious of this as a treatment. Now I'm convinced humor is the wrong approach for our audience."

"I think we should go back to my idea for opening the program with comments from the Division VP."

Such statements are big, bold oral rejection slips. Just as salespeople are cautioned not to take rejection personally, writers need to steel themselves against such criticism. If you've done your best work, adopt a Zen-like attitude.

So they didn't like your script. The sun still rises in the east tomorrow morning. Or try this mental self-talk: "If the client can't see the merits of my work, that's his/her problem, not mine. I'll complete the assignment as best as I can and move on to more appreciative clients who respect me and see the merit of my contribution."

But what to do after the mental pep talk?

David Lyman, founder and director of the Maine Photographic Workshops, says that sometimes "creativity is knowing when to let go. . . to recognize you're in a no-win situation and that it's a waste of creative energies to swim upstream any further."

So you have to write it the way the client dictates. They wear you down. When you know the resulting program will be a dull, lifeless, ineffective use of the medium, with little audience appeal, it's like rubbing salt in the wound. But take the most businesslike, professional approach possible under the circumstances. That's what you're paid for.

There will be other clients, other opportunities for scripting the award-winning program. And even recalcitrant clients can wise up in a hurry when the jury of audience opinion votes. To sum up, the various types of objections and the appropriate responses are listed below:

1. Hopeless objection: requires no defense. It's time to retrench.
2. Minor objection: usually needs little discussion. When facing only minor objections, you're home free.
3. Genuine objection: the client raises relevant shortcomings in the first draft. This is the most important objection to overcome or address through revision. You must overcome this sales resistance or agree to make changes to resolve the issue.

Handling Genuine Objections

When you hear the client pose a genuine objection, you may have one of several initial responses:

- Total disagreement
- Total agreement
- Uncertainty—you're not totally sure whether to agree or disagree
- Confusion

When you disagree with the client's point, your instinct will be to do battle for your work:

CLIENT: "I don't know. Seems to me like the 'home movie' stuff is upstaging the pros who are supposed to be the stars."

WRITER: "I'm glad you brought that up. In the treatment, the 'home movie' action does seem to predominate. But that's primarily because the technique is difficult to visualize, and we wanted to flesh it out for you. Believe me, in the first-draft script, the home movie action will be about 25 percent of the screen time; the pros will be in the spotlight for three-quarters of the time."

Often, when you answer an objection head-on and do so convincingly and professionally, the client will acquiesce. After all, they've said earlier they like the concept; they're simply voicing concerns. If you allay their fears, they will trust your judgment. (However, if the first draft script of our slow-play golf program comes in with 50 percent of the screen time devoted to the "wrong way" home movie content and 50 percent on Fuzzy and Amy, the client has a legitimate beef at the script session.)

Next, suppose you agree with the client's feedback? Does this happen often? Yes. Sometimes, especially at the treatment or first draft stage, a section of the script may bother you as writer, but you don't know quite how to put it right. If the client points to the same concern, you both know the problem needs fixing. Talk openly and honestly to the client, seeking their thoughts and ideas. Try to avoid being defensive or having guilt feelings that your writing falls short.

Writing is not a discipline with right and wrong answers to problems. Rather, there is a range of solutions, some better than others, to most writing problems. Sometimes it helps to share with the client why you find the section difficult to write. Verbalizing and discussing the difficulty may help solve the problem itself.

Sometimes, though, feedback on your work

may come in shades of gray. This occurs when the client's comments relate to a topic you had not considered before. Or perhaps your client expresses a viewpoint in an insightful way, forcing you to see the script or writing problem in a different light. An idea has merit, but it also may mean changing tone or structure or some other aspect of the draft. Will the new approach pay off or simply lead you down a sidetrack?

Responding to this type of feedback, you're not necessarily prepared to don the warrior's helmet and rush in to defend what's presently on paper. Neither do you want to dismiss the comments as irrelevant. Generally, a positive yet noncommittal response is most appropriate: "Gee, that's an interesting idea. I never thought about it that way. Let me mull that one over for a while." It's short, honest, and leaves all doors open.

There really are a number of ways in which to respond to feedback on your work at any stage of the writing process. Understanding and rapport with the client, producer, director, and subject matter experts (as well as plain old tact) create a climate in which you can accept feedback in positive, constructive ways.

For more insight into adapting objection-handling skills to the writing process, delve into some sales training books. Bookstores and libraries sag under the weight of all these self-help books. And most are surprisingly consistent in analyzing the sales process.

The Most Important Reader

Earlier, we introduced the scriptwriter as one of the handful of select individuals to actually function as a reader of shooting scripts and participate in review sessions. Yet novice writers are not always aware of their role in the review process.

Granted, we participate as readers during the physical drafting of the script, moving from what Lucy McCormick Calkins calls "passion hot" (when we're writing freely and easily) to "critic cold" (when we allow the "judge" to peer over our shoulder and critique the emerging text). And we often read first

draft scripts aloud when presenting them to clients and content experts, commenting on relationships between visual and narrative copy.

But I'm talking about something different. The idea can be found in the roots of the word revision ("to see again"). Calkins and other writing teachers describe the writer's function in revision as one of distancing yourself from the drafting process so that you can read and respond to the script from several perspectives. Time provides the necessary distancing. Set your emerging manuscript aside for a period. Return to it later with fresh eyes and renewed enthusiasm.

Put yourself in the shoes of your target audience. Then read your draft. How do you like it? How do you feel about it? Something I've learned over the years is that your writing is never as brilliant, insightful, and inspired as you think it is during feverish inspiration.

Neither is it ever as dreadful and ineffective as you fear when the writing was difficult and painstaking or when you felt totally uninspired. With a little distancing (sometimes as brief as a day or two for short scripts; weeks or even months for longer works), you find yourself responding more normally to the work.

So how do you like it? Anything you want to change? After a first draft, you invariably find things to improve. Maybe it's simply a matter of word-smithing, or perhaps you see how a simple structural change might make the program more effective. Do you feel the script is too long? (I always have that problem.) How about the balance between two chosen formats? Happy with how that worked out?

You can ask yourself innumerable questions about your emerging text. Figure 8.2 is a list of "revision strategies" I adapted for Audio/Visual writers from Lucy McCormick Calkins' book.

Obviously, you'll probably never undertake all these strategies on a single project. Use it as a checklist to decide what you wish to focus on as a reader of your own script. As you read and re-read with fresh eyes, you'll find yourself responding alternately as "artist, judge, even warrior and explorer" on occasion.

So drive around the "race track shifting from gear to gear," as Roger von Oech would say, depending on the nature of the project and your response to what you've written. You'll find things you want to change. Oddly enough, one of the most frustrating, unusual experiences of my scriptwriting career resulted from a client who liked my first draft so much that he wanted to proceed directly into production—no revision necessary.

I told him there were things I really wanted to change, but he was content. He didn't feel a rewrite necessary! Believe me, this doesn't happen often.

EDITING

If you return to the media writing process

Figure 8.2: Twelve Revision Strategies

1. Change a section from one format to another.
2. Rework a confused section—the ending, the opening, a key point, an important transition, etc.
3. Reconsider tone or voice. Try on a different voice. See if it improves the script.
4. Make a long script shorter.
5. Take a short script, and expand it into a more detailed version.
6. Try different openings.
7. Predict the viewers' questions, then revise in order to be sure they are answered, ideally in the order in which they are asked.
8. Read the script aloud—listening to how it sounds. Revise accordingly.
9. Reread the draft, evaluating what works and what doesn't. After identifying what works, write another draft or portion of a draft, building on that strength. Decide whether to delete, repair, or ignore what does not work.
10. Put the draft aside and return to it another day.
11. Talk with someone about the subject. Then rewrite the draft without looking back at the previous versions.
12. Read the script looking at only one aspect, such as:

    • Narrative style and voice
    • Visualization
    • Structure and pacing
    • Formats
    • Transitions
    • Music and sound effects
    • Visual effects

Source: Adapted from Lucy McCormick Calkins, *The Art of Teaching Writing.* Portsmouth, NH: Heinemann Educational Books, Inc., 1986

diagram (p. 24), you'll see we're approaching the final destination: an approved shooting script. After revising the first draft script, the client, content experts and production team all get another crack at reviewing your work.

If you did a thorough, detailed job, you should now be home free. Major objections to content, style, voice, visualization, or other first draft issues will have been addressed in your revisions. At that time, you added, deleted, or changed a portion or all of the script. Now, the content expert and client should be down to nit-picks. If the project has been on track to this point, the production team may even begin the early stages of the production process, from preproduction planning to execution.

As a reader of your work, you, too, will have played a role in shaping the substance, focus, and style of the second draft shooting script. You should be comfortable with the story you've told and how you used the strengths of the chosen medium to convey that story. You are also entering the nit-picking mode.

You may or may not have another roundtable meeting with all the principal players. If your first draft was well-received, the team is probably confident that any major changes have been incorporated, and they may opt to read the second draft and submit comments through notes or a phone call.

If you have the luxury of time, now is your final crack at responding to the soon-to-be-abandoned script. Maybe you take it on an airplane flight for an objective reading. Maybe you sit with the director and read the copy aloud one final time. Now is the time to ask these simple questions:

- Did the first revision remain true to the concept, structure, style and tone of your original intent?
- Do any changes made by client, SME, producer, or director stand out like a sore thumb? Perhaps it's only a word or two, but those words matter. A quality shared by all creative individuals is persistence

coupled with a drive for perfection. Writers may be sloppy in other parts of their lives, but they must be brutally honest, self-critical, and meticulous in the editorial process.

- Is everything in the visual portion of the script appropriately described?
- Does the voice remain constant throughout? The longer the work, the more difficult this becomes. The more narrators, speakers or characters, the more difficult it is to be consistent.
- Do you still like the script? If not, can you say it is a craftsman-like solution to the writing problems, given the compromises you were forced to make?

This last question is tough. After living with a project day and night for weeks or even months, it's only natural for a certain weariness to set in. In the corporate and organizational media world, you rarely reach the end of a project without having to make some compromises along the way.

You often feel ready and willing to "abandon" this child, turn it over to the production crew, and let them wrestle with all its shortcomings. Resist.

Give yourself one last unhurried, careful rereading of the material. Experience has shown that just as the client, SME, and production team want to make subtle last-minute changes, the writer will also see small things that can be fixed when moving from the second (or third or fourth) substantive revision to finished production script.

You may want to pull out the thesaurus to search for a more precise meaning for just one word. Perhaps you discover a section of narration that can be made more conversational simply by using more contractions. Maybe you have an inspired idea for a transition. As long as such "tweaks" remain within the practical realities of the production budget and timeline, go for it.

Once these detailed revisions are made—you can lean back, kick your feet up, and say, "By God, we did it! Made ourselves a media script! Created something that simply didn't exist before." It's a good feeling.

Footnotes

1. Peter Elbow, Writing With Power, *Techniques for Mastering the Writing Process* (New York, NY: Oxford University Press, 1981), *p. 7.*
2. From a proposal by William Van Nostran for a United States Golf Association project.

INTERACTIVITY

Like so many things about so-called "new media," interactivity has roots in technologies and principles that are anything but new. Today's CD-ROM, CD-i, DVD formats and World Wide Web are fourth and fifth generation attempts to marry the computer with media technologies.

Computers as teaching machines, or electronic tutors, date back to the 1960s. Computer programs were written so the learner's responses or choices triggered the computer's next move. In this way, computer-assisted instruction (CAI) and its media rich offspring is similar to playing chess against a computer. Instruction is nonlinear and individualized, allowing a learner to repeat material that proves difficult or skip information already mastered. Each move of the chessmen the user makes is countered by a computer move.

But in the 1960's, computers were limited to alphanumeric display. So the other half of the earliest interactive media systems, the laser videodisk, offered a tool for bringing media richness to the learning experience.

Originally conceived as a consumer item, the early interactive videodisk was similar to today's digital laser disks, except much larger—the size of a twelve-inch, LP phonograph record. When first introduced in 1980, the videodisk failed to capture broad consumer acceptance for one simple reason. In this original form, it was a "read-only" playback device, unable to match the "time shift" capabilities

of competing videocassette recorders (VCRs) which could tape programs off-air for playback at a later date. Combined with the camcorder, the VCR also served as an upgrade for the home movie market, allowing instantaneous playback of the family picnic or high school play.

When it first appeared, however, corporate and military trainers seized upon the optical videodisk for one major feature: random access. Anyone who's experienced the difference between searching for a song on audiocassette tape versus accessing a song on a laser CD player appreciates the power of immediate random access. In videodisk form, it provides nearly unlimited branching capabilities.

But random access without "intelligence" would be of little significance. The most revolutionary feature of early interactive videodisk technology was direct computer interface. By linking the random access capabilities of the disk with a computer and customized software, you gained all the benefits of computer-assisted instruction combined with the media rich potential of full motion video, sound and graphics.

User Control

With such technology, however, users must have some means of "talking back" to the TV screen. In the late 1970's, early 80's, a host of ingenious devices were employed—keyboards, specially designed keypads, touch-screen light pens, touch-screen technology (still widely used for kiosk installations), joy sticks, as well as a hand-held device named after a small, nimble, furry rodent.

A Technology for Teaching

From the outset, astute trainers recognized the potential synergy resulting from the combined power of a teaching machine (the computer) with a more personal, highly visual, and very familiar "instructor" (television). Branching required for teaching could now become quite complex, because a single response may lead to a variety of follow-up interactions to confirm the learner understands or to correct mistaken answers.

Still more sophisticated applications involve simulations. A case study scenario is established, and the learner tries out various solutions with more or less success.

Design components may include a combination of linear segments to present new information, followed by interactive techniques to test the learner's comprehension or to apply new concepts to a given situation.

Learners work through the material individually in nonlinear fashion and at their own pace, based on their specific needs. The computer can be programmed so those learners cannot proceed to new material until successfully demonstrating mastery of prerequisite content. This is achieved by "competency gates"—tests, quizzes, on-screen visual identifications, simulations, or any interaction to demonstrate the learner is prepared to receive new instructional content.

Monitoring and Measuring

By capitalizing on a computer's memory, learners and their "human" instructors can capture the results of the learning experience for analysis and recording proficiency. Program designers and trainers can analyze comprehensive data on the performance of individual students as well as on a group of participants.

In this respect, interactive training lends itself to highly measurable, quantifiable subjects. Little wonder the U.S. Army, faced with the need of training large numbers of people with varying backgrounds, educational levels, and learning abilities, was an early adopter of both computer-based instruction and the interactive video disk.

Knowledge Storage and Retrieval

In addition to instructional and communication uses of interactive media, an equally powerful use of the technology has emerged more recently in the area of storing and accessing knowledge. Although an individual computer may have limited memory capacity, networked computers possess seemingly unlimited memory. Networked computers can become a tool for sharing data, information, and knowledge.

The Internet is the most ubiquitous example of a broad knowledge repository. Through a combination of computer memory, the ability of computers to "talk" to one another, and software that automates data searches (search engines) and hypertext, technology is playing an increasing role in making information and knowledge more accessible.

"Technology's most valuable role in knowledge management," observe Thomas Davenport and Laurance Prusak in their book, *Working Knowledge*, "is extending the reach and enhancing the speed of knowledge transfer."[1]

Davenport and Prusak define knowledge as "broader, deeper, and richer" than either data or information. (Information possesses more value or usefulness than pure data because it has context—it is "data that makes a difference.") [2]

Corporations and organizations are making greater, ever more sophisticated use of information and knowledge data bases through intra- and extranet applications as ways to improve internal communication, training, customer service, project management, and research.

Writing for the Internet requires an understanding of interactivity, but it also involves an appreciation of how many large organizations, such as corporations, structure information for Internet access and the influence such structures have on the introduction and flow of information through the site over time. In addition, Internet writers must be mindful of how the on-line reading habits of people differ from their off-line approach to reading. Hypertext links confer the power to jump immediately to related information—even different sites. While such features offer site designers useful tools, they also make special demands upon content developers and writers.

PART II: CONTENT

Part II focuses on the writer's role in developing and creating successful interactive projects. It offers proven tools and techniques for combining content with interactivity. Unlike Part I, which is process-oriented and requires a step-by-step linear reading, Part II focuses more on discrete topics. All these interactive techniques, however, require the same disciplined approach to the writing process. If anything, in fact, writing for interactivity requires a discipline and persistence exceeding that of many linear scriptwriting assignments.

Production Script Revisited

The Introduction to Part I concluded with a media shooting script definition. As we begin Part II, let's revisit that definition, modifying it to accommodate interactive multimedia writing.

A multimedia script is the written description of events depicting the relationship between sights, sounds, graphics, animation, and text using a mix of media while providing users control over which events they experience, in what sequence, and for how long. Users may also make choices or input information that will automatically prompt specific events.

Footnotes

1. Davenport, Thomas H., and Prusak, Laurence, *Working Knowledge, How Organizations Manage What They Know*, (Boston, MA: Harvard Business School Press, 1998). p. 125
2. Ibid., pp. 3-4.

CHAPTER **9**

THINKING INTERACTIVELY

Suppose the following five activities were meant to be done in a strict linear sequence:

1. Drink juice
2. Eat bagel
3. Drink coffee
4. Read newspaper
5. Wash dishes

To arrive at activity number two, eating a bagel, activity one must be completed in its entirety. Nor can coffee be enjoyed until the bagel is completely finished. Only after the last sip of coffee can one turn attention to the day's newspaper, and so on. To almost everyone, this would seem a rigid, arbitrary way in which to proceed through breakfast.

I myself begin by drinking juice *while* eating the bagel *and* perusing the newspaper. (Since I take a morning vitamin, I'd interject a sixth activity not even on the list at this time.) Notice, too, that I wouldn't do the three activities completely simultaneously. If someone were carefully observing, however, there would be a specific sequence of events: a sip of juice, a bite of bagel, read the paper. Another two bites of bagel *while* reading the paper. A sip of juice.

I'd generally pour coffee *after* finishing juice and bagel, but I'd continue reading the newspaper for a time—and, only reluctantly, clean up by taking care of the dishes. This more random nonlinear

approach to breakfast is analogous to the difference between thinking in a linear or interactive mode when presenting information.

Until the advent of the computer, nearly all media experiences were linear with a finite beginning, middle, and end. Even once computers made random access possible, early computer-based training ("teaching machines" dating back to the 1960s) often resembled more linear models (electronic workbooks with multiple-choice questions) than a true nonlinear experience. Text-heavy by necessity, early computer-based training used the multiple-choice question as the key form of interaction between learner and subject matter.

Those who have contributed most to developing interactive media syntax did so by discovering tools and techniques for breaking new ground. They learned nonlinear thought processes, applying them through tools such as branching, creating a multisensory experience built around user input, and adopting various ways of structuring and organizing content.

Branching

Branching is another nonlinear thinking characteristic. For example, to determine your need for further information, select the answer that best fits your situation:

1. I have written interactive CD-ROM training programs and am intimately familiar with the concept of tactile viewer involvement and the potential of various branching possibilities.
2. I have written Web sites and get the idea of branching. Tell me more about this concept of tactile viewer involvement.
3. Don't tell me how the watch is made when all I want to know is the time. Can't you just summarize what's different about writing for interactive media?
4. Hey, I'm new to this. How is branching any different from a multiple-choice question technique?

If this book were an interactive CD-ROM, your selection would lead you to a specific content segment designed to respond to your personal level of interactive-media interests and knowledge. This interactive design element is well known to those working on the Internet—where users seek information relevant to them while ignoring other content and "drill" to the level of detail they seek by selecting the most direct path to a specific topic.

Instructional designers use branching techniques when creating interactive case studies that have multiple outcomes, or when two answers to the same question continue down different content paths. A correct answer leads to new content. An incorrect answer leads to additional material explaining the topic in greater detail.

A Multisensory Experience

With ever-greater frequency, interactive programs are true multisensory experiences. PC-based multimedia programs (such as CD-ROMs) offer visual "treats" for the eyes in the form of colorful graphics, photography, animation, film, and video footage. Music, sound effects, narration, and dialogue stimulate the ear and offer another avenue for communicating content.

Writing well for the eye and ear as described earlier in this book is a skill that can be directly translated to the interactive digital-media world. The ability to combine, blend, and integrate these elements in the service of communicating content represents the core challenge of interactive-media writing. It is not enough to use such tools simply because they are available to the media writer—the challenge is to use them effectively and appropriately in the service of communication and training goals.

Which leads to an often-overlooked aspect of true interactivity: storytelling. It has been said that with linear media someone "tells you a story." With interactive media, however, "you tell yourself a story." The "give and take" interplay between the participant and the medium should emulate the illusion of personal dialogue between two individuals.

This illusion of dialogue results from the combination of nonlinear possibilities with sensory input on the participant's end, leading to appropriate digital-media output. The goal is to simulate a dialogue between user and computer.

In her book on computer-based training, Gloria Gery further distinguishes interactivity by who initiates the give and take. An interaction is "either a course-initiated or learner-initiated stimulus-and-response cycle with the added dimension of having either the learner or course evaluate the response and then take another action that requires some response."[1]

Passive to Participatory Continuum

The more frequent the opportunity for sensory input, the more immediate and appropriate the response to that input, the greater the sense of dialogue. Stimulus-and-response activities are, by nature, interactive experiences. You can plot all human activities along a continuum that describes the level of interactivity. (See Figure 9.1)

It's interesting to note that play and games are all highly interactive and involving—some

Figure 9.1: Passive versus interactive media experience

Passive to Participatory Continuum

All media experiences inhabit a continuum of interactivity. On the passive side of the scale are activities such as reading a book or watching a movie. Taking part in an evening of improv comedy, by contrast, can be somewhere in the middle (if you're in the audience), or highly interactive (if you're a performer). Almost any experience can be placed along this continuum. Use it to analyze your own daily activities and experiences. Ask: "What could be done to make a passive experience more interactive?"

Passive	**Interactive**
Reading	Having a conversation
Attending a lecture	Attending a discussion group
Listening to a symphony	Playing in an orchestra

physically, some mentally, and sometimes, both together.

Sensory Input

To interact with a computer requires mechanisms for providing input for the user. What are ways to provide sensory input? Keyboard and mouse are currently the most common. Touch screens and joysticks are other methods for users to provide sensory input. As voice-recognition technology matures, interactive training is sure to be enhanced by the ability to use spoken language as input. Sales trainers can create ever more realistic simulations of buyer-seller dialogues. Foreign language training will be vastly improved, as your computer will correct your pronunciation or suggest a more colloquial expression.

The Time Issue

Time, which tends to be fixed in many linear experiences, is highly relative, by contrast, in interactive media experiences. Watching a 30 minute video takes 30 minutes, as does listening to a 30 minute audiocassette or CD. The time required to read a book depends on how quickly and thoroughly the reader can comprehend the material. There is

also an enjoyment factor. One may linger over an Emily Dickinson poem, savoring the interplay of imagery, wordplay, meter, and rhyme far more so than when reading a business memo.

With multimedia learning, by contrast, time is relative to the expected outcomes and depth of the subject matter. A CD-ROM with 60 minutes of video could take as little as 90 minutes or as much as two days of involvement. Conversely, developing 30 minutes of activity might require only a few minutes of video with extensive exercises or 20 minutes of video and audio with only a few text-based exercises and activities.

Like Einstein's theory of relativity, there is elasticity to time in the interactive media experience. If you are a frequent Web surfer, you've probably experienced the trance-like state that allows you to skip from site to site and topic to topic without realizing that an hour or more has passed.

For some reason, we have a much stronger sense of time as passive viewers. Some of this is because of ingrained linear formulas—we sense when a 30 minute sitcom is about over because we are so familiar with the storyline arcs. Even coming out of a darkened movie theater, we can usually tell rather accurately about how long we've been in the world of the film characters before seeing a clock or noticing that it has gotten dark outside.

Interactive Media Organizational Tools

Those who design and create content for interactive experiences need working knowledge of topics that are of minor or no relevance when writing a linear media experience. These disciplines include:

Navigation—how is content organized to capitalize on the interactive experience? What categories of topics will information be grouped under? What, in fact, are the various ways in which information may be organized?

The organizational structure that may suffice for a linear presentation may not be the best or most appropriate if we want to convey the same information in a nonlinear structure. The first step in exploring information and transforming it is to play with its organization.

How will users return to higher levels, main menus, and home pages? What other branching options will be available to users? Will there be multiple ways to arrive at the identical content? Can certain content be selectively ignored or bypassed?

Navigation is often expressed through tools such as flow charts and diagrams, Web-site maps, and other pictorial/graphic aids that illustrate the underlying skeletal structure of content. Figure 11.5 shows a sample of navigational flow charts.

Interface Design—creation of text and graphic elements (often taking the form of icons) that allow users to move logically and easily through the content.

Interface design and navigation are easily confused. Think of navigation as the skeletal structure for organizing content.

Interface design is the craft of giving users fast, ready access to the content chunks. Of course, the degree of access desired is a variable determined by the nature of the target audience and the goals of the project.

Sometimes the intent of the project leads designers to want to give all users fast, simple access to any content element. For example, a corporate Web site designed for the general public to learn about products, services, corporate earnings, and other news. In such cases, the interface must be designed to make any and all content accessible. Other times, when access to Internet information may be restricted to a specific audience, or when instructional designers of a training program want learners to progress through a series of screens and video clips in a specific order, the interface will be more restrictive. In this instance, we give random access to a linear information "chunk," then expect the user to progress through content in a relatively linear sequence.

Figure 9.2 illustrates an interface tool designed to facilitate user movement through the structure. Both navigation and interface design will be fully explored through example in later chapters.

User-friendliness—We hear a lot about intuitive, user-friendly interfaces but not so much about what makes them user-friendly. It's a bit like the old saw about what makes great art: "I can't tell you what it is, but I know it when I see it."

Knowing it when we see it isn't helpful when you're in the midst of creating an interface. Later in this section on interactivity, we'll examine human interface principles such as use of metaphors, consistency, feedback and forgiveness,[1] and through use of techniques such as icons, roll-overs, pull-down menus, and the like.

Bombardment—Use of the multimedia delivery capabilities of interactive digital media is another method for engaging the audience to maintain interest. This is also an instructionally sound principle, since individuals exhibit various learning styles. Some respond to text on screen, others to visualization. Still others to dramatic

Fig. 9.2: Using a highway metaphor as a graphical interface.

Source: "The Road to Cure, Collection Tools and Techniques," produced by VuCom newMedia for Chrysler Financial Company LLC. Used by permission.

storytelling or demonstration by a role model. While some prefer to learn by doing. When a training program can be designed to include a media-rich environment, it is more likely to contain the variety that stimulates continued interest.

Bombardment, a multisensory technique in which a single screen or event employs several simultaneous yet distinct expressions of the same message, helps reach all audience members via their preferred learning modality. Such reinforcement also improves retention.

Summary

With this introduction to the world of interactive multimedia, the following chapters address the media writer's role in the process, highlighting organizational, conceptual, and writing skills that differ from those used when developing scripts for linear media experiences.

Based on my own experience working in both worlds, the skills are adaptive and additive. Craftsmanship as a linear media writer forms a solid foundation for successful writing in nonlinear formats. There are, however, new challenges. The remaining chapters should offer tools for coping successfully with these challenges and for creating interactive programming worthy of the name.

Footnote

1. Gloria Gery, *Making CBT Happen* (Tolland, MA: Gery Performance Press, 1987), p. 14.

CHAPTER 10

INTERACTIVE OBJECTIVES & CONTENT DEVELOPMENT

When a project involves interactivity, your assimilation phase writing products are likely to be somewhat different from those you create for a linear media presentation of content. The audience profile and viewing environment description is likely to be identical. You might, however, need to address the level of computer literacy of your audience as well as of the user environment (a sales presentation versus trade show or museum kiosk).

If you're developing a training program for home health aides, who often come from a low socioeconomic status, their computer literacy and keyboard skills may be marginal. Address that fact and the impact it may have on the program design. By contrast, if your program is targeted to engineers, you can expect an existing degree of computer literacy.

In addition to viewing environment, you may also need to describe the technical specifications for a program. Is it being mailed to users' homes, where a wide range of computers with differing specs, capabilities and available memory can affect playback. Or is the program intended to play off the hard drive of a single dedicated computer system in a museum?

Whenever programs are designed to play on a wide variety of computers, it is important to describe minimum system requirements. The client must understand issues raised by playback on differing computers and how that impacts

performance of features such as sight-and-sound synchronization, video playback (quarter screen versus full screen, etc.) and speed of animations or other bit-heavy events.

For the most part, however, the audience profile and viewing environment description you draft for a linear presentation will not differ significantly from that for interactive media. The major differences will surface in stating objectives and developing the content outline.

Is Interactivity Necessary and Purposeful?

One of the first questions that should be addressed with a client in the research phase of an interactive project is *why* the program should be interactive in the first place. Here are some legitimate reasons for interactivity:

- To give the user the opportunity of creating customized sales presentations by quickly accessing content that is relevant to a specific prospect.
- To give the user instantaneous access to a specific subject by employing the computer's random access capabilities. Museum kiosk installations often employ this feature.

- When a high degree of interactivity is required to meet instructional objectives or to simulate a "real world" situation or human behavior, such as the unfolding process of a sales call.
- To attract and hold a user's attention. For example, a computer game used in a trade show environment.

Not all communications topics fall into such categories. In fact, for many communications, a linear presentation of information is not only appropriate, but also preferable. In the rush to enter the World Wide Web, many companies constructed first-generation Web sites that were nothing but mere extensions of their brochures and print materials. This is neither a reason to be on the Web nor an intelligent use of that medium's unique interactive characteristics.

Other companies have created so-called interactive computer-based training programs that do not go beyond mere electronic page-turn versions of printed training manuals.

So prior to establishing specific content-related objectives, consider what will be gained by making this subject an interactive experience in the first place. As Edwin Schlossberg writes in his book, *Interactive Excellence*, "Most interactive designs are misnamed. They are not based on involving the audience in a compositional or collaborative experience. Instead, they are built on the capabilities of the device or computer to put some simplified story in motion... Inviting people to see an illustration simply makes them passive observers, even if they have to push a button to see it. Asking someone to join in a game, on the other hand, requires him or her to be involved in the experience. Interaction is the beginning of a relationship between the person participating, other people in the environment, and/or the person who composed the experience."[1]

Instructional Objectives

Clearly, one of the most compelling reasons

for interactivity between user and subject matter is to marry the capabilities of computer-based training with the sight-and-sound stimuli of multimedia. Yet here, too, not all subjects will translate equally well into Computer Based Training (CBT) formats, nor is multimedia always the most effective way to meet instructional goals. In this era of distance-learning hype, it is vital to remember there are still many virtues to stand-up classroom instruction. Nor can one study the novels of Jane Austen without first *reading* them in a traditional linear manner.

The following material elaborates on the role of interactivity in achieving instructional objectives and provides initial guidance on determining when interactivity, content, and learning goals are in sync. The intent is to further clarify not only the characteristics of well-designed multimedia instruction, but also the boundaries and limitations of *all* CBT instruction.

Figure 10.1: Five Stages of Learning

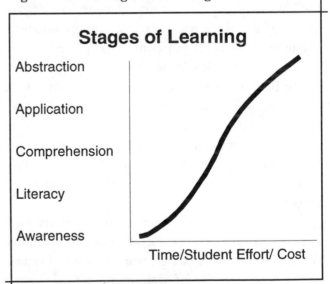

Dr. Michael Ezzo, a psychologist with extensive experience using computers for teaching adult learners, brought the learning model shown in Figure 10.1 to his work at VuCom newMedia Learning. The model depicts five stages of learning—beginning with "awareness" and "literacy" and ascending to "abstraction." Each learning stage is defined and described on the next page:

1. Awareness—The learner gains appreciation of *why* information is important to him or her. By becoming aware of why it is important to learn the subject, he/she can then become sensitive to the scope of issues, boundaries related to the issues, learning expectations, and objectives, and gain sufficient familiarity with the material to be able to reference topics when triggered by related events.

Example: New Employee Orientation

For most new-employee orientations, content focuses on introducing the company or organization, its mission and values, the new employee's role in the organization, and what further training or integrating experiences will be provided in the days and weeks to come.

2. Literacy—Training to this level means the learner is not only familiar with the topic, but also can begin to formulate questions appropriate to continued learning. You can begin to use the vocabulary of a given field of learning: the court system, for instance, or the steps involved in performing a certain procedure. You may not know how to perform the steps (whether an intellectual process or set of motor skills, such as swinging a golf club) but you know the terminology associated with the subject matter.

Example: New Employee Orientation

Many components of new employee orientation must achieve this level of learning. If you are going to work for a retail merchandise chain, your orientation might include: store department names and functions, special terminology (associates = employees; customers = guests) and other important policies or procedures.

3. Comprehension—Building an understanding of underlying priciples and concepts. A concept is made up of groups of words. Training to this level requires more human effort as the chances of misinterpretation increase. Based on the potential consequences that might result from misinterpretation, a component of this training should involve some face-to-face interaction, to verify that the learner is capable of using the concept appropriately.

Example: Discrimination or Sexual Harassment Training

Discrimination and a corporation's expectations of employee behavior in the workplace are complex concepts. Computers can be used to make someone *literate* about the topic and comprehend basic topics such as what constitutes sexual harassment. However, a company or organization would probably want some additional level of face-to-face assessment to be assured each individual knows the range of circumstances that could constitute discrimination and possesses skills necessary to properly conduct new hire interviews or employee coaching and counseling sessions.

4. Application—At this level, the learner is able to combine concepts and/or execute skills (a skill requires using a sequence of motor movements or intellectual actions) with proficiency. Reaching a level of understanding means the individual knows how to apply or do something (such as preparing a checkout counter register for the first customer).

Example: Supermarket shelf management

When an individual is asked to follow a rule or regulation the explicit goal is that they become fluent about the issue, they recognize when it is appropriate to act and can follow the steps involved as outlined. How to recognize under- or overstocking in a specific store department and what actions to take to solve the problem is one example of combining concepts and executing a skill.

5. Abstraction—This final stage of learning involves a level of mastery of material, practice using relevant skills, and the capability to create beyond the presented scope or boundaries of the material. Through integration and synthesis, the learner becomes facile applying content to new and/or abstract situations.

Typically corporations do not train groups of people to a level of abstraction. This is reserved for individual efforts in more formal learning settings—an MBA program, for instance.

The graphic in Figure 10.1 also illustrates the strong correlation between the amount of student time, effort, and corresponding development cost needed to reach each succeeding stage of learning. As the figure illustrates, reaching subsequently higher stages of learning requires ever-increasing levels of student time, effort, involvement and participation.

- When building awareness, the emphasis is on *disseminating* information.
- To achieve literacy, the learner must begin interacting with content in ways that foster use of terminology and demonstrate understanding of key concepts.
- To move the learner from awareness through literacy to comprehension and applicationtion requires more involved and creative use of the available interactive multimedia features by combining the computer with various sight and sound media.

This includes engaging participants in on-line case studies or problems drawn from real-life experience, or using the computer as a research tool to access and analyze data, and then developing a course of action.

Consider, too, that for many topics, moving beyond the literacy level requires instructional experiences that stretch the limits of computer-based training. Sales or negotiating skills are prime examples. The elements of a sales or negotiating skills model can be easily taught to the literacy level. Role models of the appropriate use of such skills can be presented with video segments. Students can even begin to practice using these skills in simulated interactive sales situations.

The best practice of such skills, however, is actual role-playing in a classroom environment, followed by a critique from a master instructor and then a period of being observed using new skills in actual field situations with individual coaching to reinforce appropriate use of new skills. Clearly, even a highly sophisticated computer simulation including voice responses cannot achieve a comparable level of learning experience, observation and personalized coaching. Exploring a second explanation of training levels explains why…

Kirkpatrick's Levels of Training

In his book, *Evaluating Training Programs, the Four Levels*, Donald Kirkpatrick offers a model for assessing training programs. It consists of these four levels:

Level 1: Reaction—Measures how those participating in the program react to it. Kirkpatrick likens this level to "customer satisfaction." Often measured in the form of the postcourse evaluation feedback questionnaire, Kirkpatrick points out this is more than "happiness sheets… If training is going to be effective, it is important that trainees react favorably to it. Otherwise, they will not be motivated to learn."

Level 2: Learning—Defined as the extent to which participants change attitudes, improve knowledge, and/or increase skill as a result of the training experiences.

Level 3: Behavior—The extent to which change in behavior has occurred because the participant attended the training program.

Level 4: Results—The final results that occurred because participants attended the program. Examples of results include:

- increased productivity
- improved quality

- increased sales
- decreases in number and/or severity of accidents
- reduced turnover

As Kirkpatrick points out, such results are often the ultimate rationale for most training programs in the first place.[2] In addition, Kirkpatrick makes a special point of stating conditions influencing Level 3 results. For change to occur, he writes, four conditions are necessary:

1. The person must have a **desire** to change.
2. The person must **know** what to do and how to do it.
3. The person must **work in the right climate.**
4. The person must be **rewarded** for changing.[3]

Training programs can have a direct effect upon the first two conditions. The second two, however, are dependent upon factors that are not within the trainer's direct control. They involve issues of supervision, management, working conditions, and workplace environment. Much training has limited impact at the behavioral level because the learner returns from a training program to a work environment that is unchanged. Colleagues and supervisors may not even share the same levels of literacy or conceptual insight that the trainee has learned. As a result, new skills cannot be reinforced and are soon overwhelmed by the inertia of "doing things the way they've always been done."

With this as background, it's vital to consider the limitations of CBT in achieving instructional objectives with certain types of subject matter. One can teach the principles of how to draw blood, or give a patient an injection, but would any of us want to have a needle stuck in us by someone who had no more experience in the process than a computer-based training program? Most motor skills require a level of practice and performance in order to achieve a level of competency.

Likewise, a CBT program on how to stock shelves in a mass-merchandise chain store can bring an individual to a level of literacy, even competency, in how to read store layouts (planograms) and rotate stock, thereby condensing the time it will take a supervisor to bring the studies to the application level in the physical store environment.

Far more can be expected of a computer-based training program designed to teach credit analysts how to interpret credit applications and credit bureau reports and apply consistent principles in determining creditworthiness. It is an activity performed largely on a computer. The principles involved are intellectual and judgmental: "When this condition exists, do or consider this…"

Case-study scenarios can be created and presented via information and data on the computer screen.

The line between instructional design and scriptwriting duties is not always clear. Typically, an instuctional designer performs up-front analysis with someone who is able to bring the adult learner to the desired learning level. The media writer then receives the assignment to carry out scripting based on predefined instructional goals and strategies.

Other times, media writers are expected to serve the role of instructional designer. Some are prepared to do so, others are not. It's important to know your own strengths and weaknesses and be prepared to recommend an analysis of content, goals, audience, and delivery methods by an instructional designer when that is in the client's best interest.

Stating CBT Objectives

Most instructional designers will specify what learning level you intend to achieve. If, in your mind, you are aiming for literacy with subject matter, and the client expects participants to achieve compehension, performance expectations are clearly not in synch.

Put computer-based training in the context of the total supervisory environment. Describe skills that will require practice in a classroom setting or on the job.

Indicate what material must be memorized and what material is for reference purposes on the job.

A recent project of mine involved training for court clerks within the Michigan judicial system on how to direct the public to the proper court based on their circumstances. The computer-based training focused on an explanation of how all Michigan courts are organized and taught key principles of jurisdiction and venue for major court functions—criminal, civil, family matters, etcetera. The program also included a printed job aid, offering a summary of these principles as well as a listing of court locations and telephone numbers for reference on the job.

An on-line computer help system is another common form of job aid. Often, then, CBT instructional objectives are framed within the context of an existing aid or one that will be created. CBT then teaches to the job aid so participants will know when and how to use the reference as a performance aid in the work environment.

In addition to your description of audience, objectives, and content, interactive proposals, sometimes known as high-level design documents, consist of additional elements addressing aspects of interface design and navigation. The next chapter focuses on aspects of digital interactive media that the writer will need to understand in order to create a high level design document.

Footnotes

1. Schlossberg, Edwin. *Interactive Excellence*. New York: The Ballentine Publishing Group, 1998, pp. 80-81.
2. Kirkpatrick, Donald L., *Evaluating Training Programs, The Four Levels*. San Francisco: Berrett-Koehler Publishers, 1994, pp. 21-26.
3. Ibid., 23.

CHAPTER 11

WORKING INTERACTIVELY

In developing interactive media, writers must not only grapple with the communication of content through a mixture of sight and sound, they must also become adept with the elements of digital media that allow the user to navigate and interact with the screen. Typically, this includes three interrelated disciplines:

1. **Navigation principles**—How content is structured and organized for user-friendly access
2. **Flow-charting techniques**—Creation of a visual map representing the navigational structure of specific content
3. **Interface design**—Providing user tools (icons, buttons, hyperlinks, etc.) to access content and events

A Navigational Case Study

To appreciate the subtle complexity of navigation in an interactive communication and the value of a flow chart to interactive media production, look at the simplified flow chart shown in Figure 11.1.

A main menu offers three options—each takes the user to three subtopics, allowing access to additional events. These "events" provide more detailed information or interactive experiences pertaining to the subtopic. An event may consist of text only, text and graphics, animation, or a media event such as playing a video or audio clip.

Assume each screen or event offers the user three navigational choices:

- **Forward**—takes the user to the next event in the subtopic
- **Reverse**—returns the user to the previous event
- **Return to Main Menu**—allows the user to immediately access the main menu for exploring one of the other two sub-topics.

As a user, suppose you are working down "Subtopic One" in relatively linear fashion. Event "One-B" of this leg, however, offers an additional option: a hyperlink (text or graphic), that when clicked, takes you not to the next frame within "Sub-Topic One"—but directly to "Sub-Topic Three-D"—an event deep within the third leg.

You opt to access that frame. You spend time there, exploring the content. Then, you activate the "reverse" button. Where should that send you?

It could send you back up the "Subtopic Three" branch or leg. Suddenly, as a user, you would be adrift at sea. You will have lost your navigational bearings with your interactive compass awry.

Figure 11.1: Hypothetical program flow

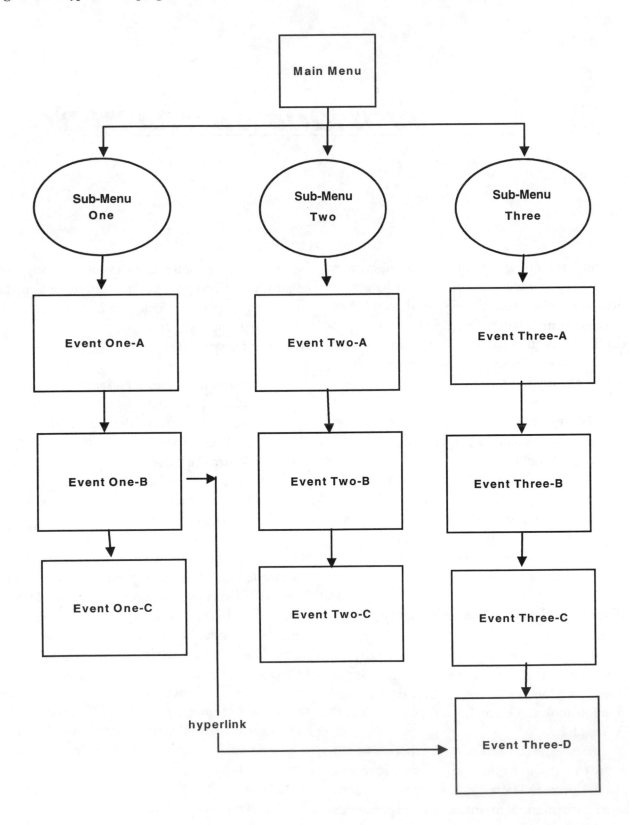

From the user's perspective, it is more logical and intuitive if activating the "reverse" button returns you to the screen within the leg that brought you there. Now the backward/forward navigational paradigm is intact.

Of course, some users will not activate the "Event one-B" hyperlink. So when they eventually arrive at "Subtopic Three-D" and activate the "reverse" button, they will rightfully expect to return to the previous frame within the "Subtopic Three" branch (Three-C). Therefore, the program must be authored so the "reverse" button functions *differently* based on how the leg-three event is accessed.

As this example demonstrates, advancing from one screen or event to the next is usually the easy part. It's going *back* that often creates a dilemma.

Unfortunately, such decisions are often not confronted until the programmer is in the throes of creating the code and must make the decision him or herself or must call an ad hoc production meeting to get direction. A comprehensive, detailed flow chart, however, will provide all such navigational information.

Expressing Structure With a Flow chart

A flow chart is a visualization of an interactive program's navigational structure. It expresses two significant elements of an interactive program simultaneously:

1. How content is "chunked" into individual topics.
2. The arrangement of those "chunks" and relationship between them.

Flow charts are essential to developing an interactive media script, representing an additional writer's product to create at the conclusion of the rehearsal phase.

Just as a shooting script serves as a blueprint for the production crew showing "how to create this viewing experience" for a linear media project, flow charts serve a similar function in an interactive production. They are schematics depicting how navigational structure and interactivity are organized.

Like content outlines and creative treatments, navigational structure must evolve from a clear understanding of how content, audience and objectives interrelate.

Ways to Organize Content

Whether your content is information or data (in the digital domain, some argue that all content is data), it represents the product of your research and assimilation. Suppose you are developing a tutorial on world theatre. The history of world theatre involves a massive amount of information, facts, photographs and drawings, interviews, stories, anecdotes, literary materials, and media assets. The way in which you organize this material to create an interactive experience on the user's behalf is what transforms information and data into useful, meaningful knowledge.

By placing raw data into a context that reveals relationships and patterns, you make it accessible to the user. In today's business lexicon: organization *adds value* to information and data.

That context will vary based upon the target audience and the objective your client seeks to achieve with the interactive experience. The skills involved in describing the target audience and identifying goals and objectives are equally essential when looking at ways of adding value to information through interactive access. (Another way to think of navigation: it is the way in which users will access specific information.)

Nathan Shedroff, an interactive design consultant, describes seven ways of organizing things:

- Alphabetically
- Numerically
- by Location
- by Time
- across a Continuum
- into Categories

• Randomly (not organizing them, or using chance as the organizational principle)

Almost every card game consists of taking cards that have been shuffled to create randomness and then bringing some organizational form to them, generally by a combination of categories (clubs, spades, hearts, diamonds, kings, queens, jacks) and numbers (the four of clubs, etcetera).

Maps organize places by geographic location. But most maps also have an alphabetical index that correlates to a mathematical/numerical coordinate to aid in identifying specific locations (a city or town) quickly.

Card games and indexed maps are examples of multiple forms of organizing information. Just as a linear video program may use a mix of formats (talking head to dramatization to visuals & voice, etcetera) you may also employ multiple organizational principles to chunk information and design a navigational structure for accessing various topics.

For example, if you are creating an interactive tool that allows the user to find a store near his or her home, you might begin with a map of states (organization by location), which accesses an alphabetical list of cities offering the option to see a store's location on a local street map.

Multiple organizational methods help users find things more quickly. They may also help people see relationships between concepts with greater insight. Turning a list of categories into a continuum, for example…

Data   Information   Knowledge

To create a flow chart, take your content outline, and look at ways to "chunk" the information into organizational patterns. Then begin to play with these chunks like building blocks and create flow charts to express how various topics can be grouped and accessed. One of your first considerations is the relationship between breadth and depth.

Breadth vs. Depth

The typical multimedia flow chart is two-dimensional—the horizontal axis expresses "breadth" while the vertical axis expresses "depth." The flow chart in Figure 11.2 is an example of treating a subject in great breadth but almost no depth.

It offers the user a top-level introduction to World Theatre. In terms of a college curriculum,

Figure 11.2: **Flow chart depicts covering a subject broadly, but with little depth.**

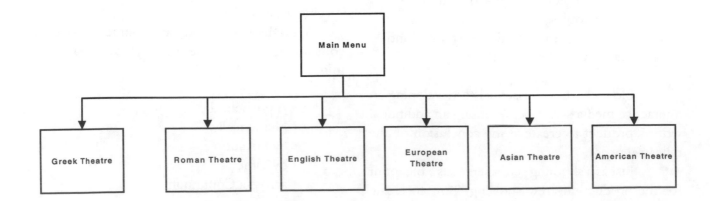

this emphasis on breadth corresponds to the typical "survey" course.

Figure 11.3 is an example of treating a single portion of the material presented in greater depth. This is simply one way information about American theatre could be "chunked" to provide user access to various topics in greater detail than is possible with a "top level" survey approach.

We might further segment this information to provide more specific access to topics as shown in Figure 11.4.

This structure offers breadth with depth by combining a chronological and categorical "chunking" of information. There is symmetry and consistency to the visual flow. While this orderly parallel construction may suit some topics, for the subject at hand, and probably the vast majority of content, it is beginning to seem arbitrary and forced.

Early American theatre, for instance, is not distinguished for playwrights, producers and directors, nor stage and costume designers. Colonial American efforts at the theatre were not so formally organized, nor was it considered a business or art form. Its interest lies more in the social uses of theatre and adaptation of European traditions in the New World context.

Somewhat later, emerging American forms, such as minstrel shows and even the itinerant medicine show would be more relevant to address in an interactive knowledge repository.

A more useful structure for a tutorial on American theatre, therefore, would not rely on such parallel symmetry as an organizing principle.

Figure 11.5 illustrates a less rigid, more organic approach. The top level retains a chronological segmentation to provide *broad* access to the subject matter, while allowing content to dictate the subtopics contained in the *deep* analysis of each period.

Naming & Numbering Conventions

A well-prepared flowchart is an essential production tool for interactive media. Topics should be named with the user in mind. Strive for the greatest clarity with the fewest possible words.

A corresponding numbering system aids immensely in identifying, cataloging and storing various media assets during production and programming. Figure 11.5 illustrates using both shapes and numerical designations as organizational tools during writing, production and most especially, programming. Any text, photos or media clips on *The Gershwins and Other Musical Masters* can be designated as belonging in file #340, for example.

This numbering convention is even more important if you look at the legs coming off the numbers 400 and 500 sub-menus. Many menu choices are identical: "Actresses," for example. When organizing copy and assets for production, only the numerical designation distinguishes those that belong in *The Post-War Period* from those belonging to *The Modern American Theatre*.

Interface Design Basics

Metaphors take advantage of our existing knowledge of the world around us and, as such, can be quite useful in designing an intuitive interface. The choice of a "desktop" (a two-dimensional space on which objects are placed) as a metaphor for navigating through a personal computer is an early, enduring example. Icons for file folders and trashcans make the metaphor vivid and functional.

The interface combines a clear, finite set of objects with a clear, finite set of actions to perform on those objects. (You may "open" or "close" a folder. You may drop and drag it to "copy" its contents to another folder, etc.)

Interface design is the creation of text and graphic elements, often taking the form of icons, permitting users to move logically and easily through the content. Users perform actions by choosing from alternatives presented on the screen.

Several principles govern interface design. A main menu interface should provide ready access to all the "level one" subtopics, for instance. Based on subject matter and audience, the overall interface may take the form of an environment—a kitchen

Figure 11.3 is an example of treating a single portion of the same material presented in greater depth.

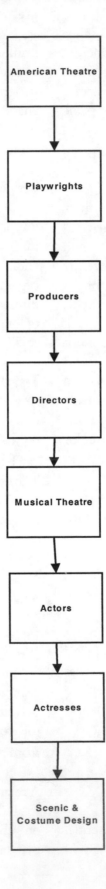

Figure 11.4 This flow chart illustrates a combination of breadth and depth, yet it also suffers from an attempt at too rigid an organization.

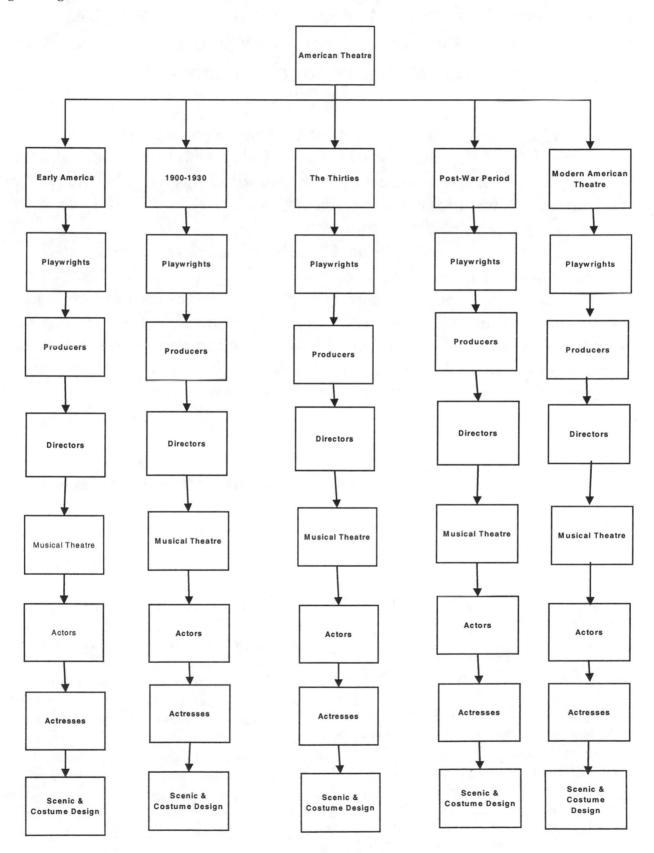

Just as a creative concept should be motivated by the content, a user-interface metaphor should also spring from analysis of content, audience, and objectives.

A recent VuCom newMedia project involved a large client in banking and financial services. The client was in a period of growth through acquisition and came to us for help in creating computer-based training for the teams involved in analyzing and converting the newly acquired bank to existing corporate standards and procedures.

As a group, we brainstormed and presented three concepts for an interface design. One used the metaphor of building bridges. The client settled on this one not only because it offered visual opportunities for the training as well as the interface, but also because it offered a subtext reinforcing the overarching theme: the metaphor of bridge building applies to the process of two separate organizations becoming one. The bridge is what joins them. But until the bridge is built, they remain two isolated entities.

for a program on cooking or foods; a carnival or playground map as an interface environment when children are the target audience.

Or the environment may take on a more metaphorical nature—using an archeological dig in the desert as a metaphor for telephone collection work. Here is a writer's description of such a fanciful metaphorical interface:

"Just as an archeological dig involves a painstaking, disciplined search for pieces of a puzzle, so, too, does the collection agent's probing of each individual creditor's circumstances. Much like an archeologist, the collection agent knows in advance what he/she seeks. He/she is trained in skills that facilitate the search—it is not just random excavation; but also probing, purposeful digging. A fragment of information mentioned casually over the phone by a creditor can shine light on a path that will lead directly to buried treasure."

Icons and other Interface Tools

Once you settle on the overall interface, you can focus on the specific functions required and how to translate them into a user-friendly graphical interface. This is where icons, symbols, pull-down menus, and rollovers come into play. Screen design is also the province of the computer graphic artist. However, content developers and writers have significant input and often will collaborate, review, and critique the art director's work. So it's important to appreciate the role played by icons, pull-down menus, and other tools used to bring functionality to the interface.

An icon, in this context, is when a single image represents a potential user interaction. The most functional, intuitive icons bear a pictorial relationship to the action the user can perform—the icon resembles the action it depicts. A pair of scissors to stand for the action of "cutting" a portion of text, for instance, and a clipboard to communicate the action of "pasting" that same text.

When creating icons, strive for graphic images that clearly represent the concept and action they depict. Insight into the characteristics of your target audience gleaned during research and assimilation can help guide you in creating metaphors and icons that are both appropriate to the content and to the audience's experience and expectations.

Symbols are images used to represent concepts, ideas and philosophies. The meaning of a symbol, however, is not implied in its visual content. In the case of symbols, meanings are in people, not the symbol. There is nothing inherently peaceful in the "peace" symbol.

You can certainly use existing symbols, or create new ones, to aid in a user-friendly navigation. But be sure the target audience will attach the appropriate meaning to the symbol. Physicians will likely respond to medical or biological symbols; engineers, to engineering symbols.

As a rule, the pictorial nature of an icon makes it more user-friendly since its meaning is largely intuitive. Of course, not all topics or functions lend themselves to metaphors, analogies, and use of graphic icons or symbols.

This is when you may want to consider more text-based interface tools such as pull-down menus, dialog boxes, or "rollover" features.

Pull-down menu: A menu that is hidden from view until activated by the user. Once revealed, the menu presents the user a list of text-based choices or commands. Pull-down menus are appropriate when users face many possible choices—a list of the 52 states, for example. (A graphic map of the United States. with point-and-click functionality, however, offers a faster method of accessing the same information.)

Rollover: A rollover often describes the function of icons that may not be self-explanatory. Placing the cursor over the icon activates a dialog box to provide a verbal description of that specific function.

Writer's Product: The High-Level Design Document

Just as the writer creates several products at the conclusion of the assimilation phase, many interactive projects involve creation of a high level design document prior to initiating detailed scripting. Typically this document includes items such as those listed (items in bold identify those that are unique to interactive projects):

- Instructional objectives

- Analytical audience profile

- Content outline

- **Flow chart to communicate structure and navigation**

- **Interface design**

- **Types of interactive experiences (multiple-choice questions, "drop & drag" activities, etc.)**

- **Media mix (use of video and/or audio clips, animation, etc.)**

- **"Look & feel" samples of main menu and other screen graphics, animations, additional menus, and other key screens, as appropriate**

- Media treatments and/or storyboards to indicate narrative style

Figure 11.5: This flow chart offers a more organic treatment of the subject. The topics going down each leg are germaine to sub-menu. Notice, too, the numbering system, and the use of ovals to designate a menu screen.

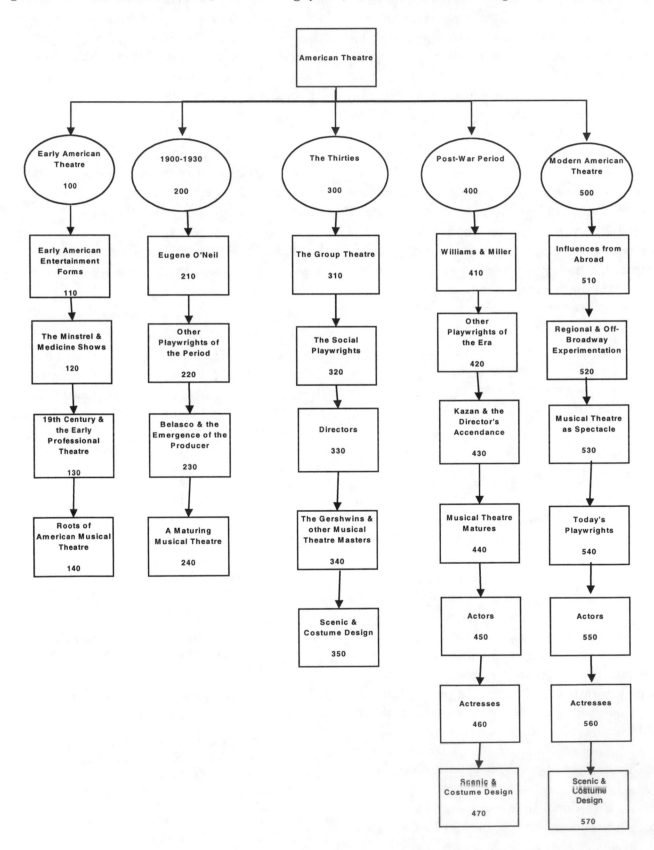

- **Technical specifications/requirements**

- **Testing tools and methods (use of pre-test, post-test testing integrated into instructional content)**

- **Simulations or interactive games**

- **Tracking mechanisms (software programs that facilitat management's ability to track a learner's progress and test results)**

- **Production plan and schedule**

Some, such as "look & feel" samples of the main menu are efforts requiring an artist and art direction. Technical specifications and requirements often involve input from a programmer or technical director. The producer may specify a certain authoring package in order to meet the client's testing and tracking needs. Interactive projects, therefore, are often highly collaborative, even at this early stage in the development process.

Once the client approves the high level design document, the writer or writing team may be at work for weeks or months developing scripts. Since those responsible for the graphical interface, screen production, and programming have all offered input up front, however, the technical, screen design and programming issues will be resolved in advance of writing actual scripts and screen text.

Sample excerpts from a high level design document are contained in the Appendix (Sample A.7). The program, designed by Digital Techniques, Inc., was developed for an interactive kiosk placed in the United States Golf Association's museum.

This award-winning interactive exhibit (designed at the time for interactive video disk) brings the museum to life by involving the visitor in a "hands-on" way. Visitors can not only peruse endlessly through golf's golden moments but they also have the opportunity to design their own golf course, match wits with a partner in a golf quiz, or compare the swings of pros throughout history (see how Arnold Palmer and Tiger Woods match up, for instance).

The design document contains a balanced mix of treatment style narrative prose, screen samples, and a simplified flow chart.

SUMMARY

Navigation involves analyzing content in relation to user needs. What is the optimal combination of breadth versus depth for the navigational model? What is the most logical method of organizing content for the user—by categories, as a continuum, by location, or chunking content in a variety of ways?

Flow charts are used to visualize how content is organized and how the user will access it. Interface design involves creating the icons and graphical screen design that helps make user access friendly, intuitive, and consistent. Combining principles of sound organization with useful navigation and helpful user interface is what comprises the discipline of information architecture.

CHAPTER 12

THE WORLD WIDE WEB OR "SKATING LIKE A WATERBUG"

"On February 18, 1997, IntelliQuest Information Group, Incorporated, released the results of its latest survey, estimating some 47 million adults (age 16 and above) in the United States in the fourth quarter of 1996 had been on the World Wide Web."[1]

That same week, IntelliQuest's CEO, Peter Zandan, declared the Web a mass medium in *USA Today*. It took radio 28 years before there were 50 million listeners. It took television 13 years to garner 50 million eyeballs. It took the World Wide Web just five years.[2]

As with so much pertaining to the continual hype surrounding multimedia, clarification and analysis is in order. First, it is important to distinguish the World Wide Web from the Internet (not to mention the true characteristics of a mass medium).

As described in Chapter One, the roots of the Internet go back to 1968 and experiments by the Department of Defense to design a communications network to survive nuclear holocaust. The concept was simple: link supercomputers at different locations in the nation using leased long-distance lines. Over the intervening years, the network grew and was initially used by

academics to speed communication of research and make real time collaboration over great distance possible.

The Internet Goes Commercial

When invented by British Computer scientist Tim Berners-Lee, the World Wide Web brought several related enhancements to the Internet:[3]

• Point-and-click browsing using a mouse
• Colorful graphics and photographs
• Downloading of audio and video files

Seemingly overnight, nonprofits and corporate America alike were constructing World Wide Web "sites" to create a presence among affluent users of this new medium. Terms like

Information Superhighway, cyberspace and *surfing the net* became part of the vernacular. In his book, *Deeper,* John Seabrook describes the experience of surfing Cyberspace with a mouse:

> "The art to Web surfing seemed to be knowing how to skate like a waterbug across the surface tension of Webalicious sites, never lingering long enough in any one place to break through the crust, borne forward by the pursuit of media satisfaction, which always seemed to lie tantalizingly just beyond your feelers."[4]

Before long, the Web was becoming still more commercialized. It was not enough to simply have a site, or "home page." Advertising space began to appear as banner ads and animated GIFs scrolled and flashed at the top of home pages. A click of the mouse takes the skipping, fickle waterbug to yet another site, revealing the promise of what was only hinted at in the teasing tag line of the banner ad:

> "Enter our sweepstakes, and win a
> new Toyota…"
> "Click to download now…"
> "Search more than a gazillion
> recipes."
> "Order five CDs for only $19.95,"
> and on and on.

A Personal Mass Medium

Yet along with the big guns of corporate America, the World Wide Web was populated by a dazzling variety of amateur, highly personalized sites. Anyone with a PC and an on-line service provider could create, register, and post a World Wide Web page. "Welcome to 'Driftwood Kennels' Home Page… Ch. Driftwood Whirligig's next litter due this Spring…"

Kids built home pages to post school projects and artwork for gramps and grandma, living across the country, to view at their leisure. Artists and writers found a self-publishing and distribution tool in the World Wide Web.

And, of course, pornographers, and purveyors of racism and loopy political, religious, and social views of the left, right, and amusingly half-baked staked out their claims in the burgeoning "Wild West" territory of the World Wide Web.

All of which leads one to ask, what is this www-something-dot-com all about? Is it a mass medium? A diversion for geeks and nerds? A place to order "cool stuff" on-line? A serious research tool? A window to anonymous companionship bathed in the soothing glow of the electronic chat room? An aid to democratic government that provides instantaneous access to local, municipal, state, and federal agencies? A place for advertisers in search of eyeballs? A tool for companies to communicate with internal and external audiences? A mysterious place that doesn't really exist save for the ever-changing digital bits and bytes of a global village known as cyberspace? An aid to distance learning? An "information superhighway," or, as Clifford Stoll decreed, a lost highway offering the wayward soul nothing more than a mind-numbing elixir known as silicon snake oil? All this and much, much more! And whatever the World Wide Web is, has become, or will be, what are the implications for media writers?

A Targeted Mass Medium

Clearly, the World Wide Web has grown and will continue to grow at exponentially mind-numbing rates. As of this writing, however (early 1999), it is nowhere nearly as ubiquitous as television. Walter Mossberg points this out in a recent *Wall Street Journal* column on personal technology: "Nearly every U.S. home, in every economic class and neighborhood, has at least one TV set, and often several …but only about 27 percent of American homes boast an on-line connection."[5]

Equally significant, especially to content providers and designers, the user experience of the Web provides its "magic" as a medium. And that special brand of "magic" mitigates against the Web ever becoming a mass medium similar to radio or television, no matter how many homes are eventually hooked into it. As Mossberg and others point out, the Internet is not a broadcast but a narrowcasting medium, offering smaller but more dedicated audiences content and services tailored to their specific needs and interests.

"Even in an era of declining network television viewing," Mossberg writes, shows like *Seinfeld* can draw 25 or 30 million households—more than the total of Internet-connected homes—simultaneously for a solid half-hour. But the biggest consumer gateway to the Internet, America Online, can accommodate only about 800,000 of its 13 million members at any one time."[6]

Equally compelling is that one does not sit around with friends munching popcorn while surfing the Internet. "Skating like a waterbug" tends to be a solo activity. When more than one person is involved in an on-line activity, it tends to be just that—an activity. People discuss a topic or issue in a chat room. Kids (or their fathers) play a cross-continental computer game on-line.

Web advertisers are still experimenting and inventing the rules of engaging minds, eyeballs, and, most important, the "click-streams" that translate into on-line sales, travel reservations, a stronger brand image, or publicity for a new product, rock star or movie release, one mouse click at a time.

Corporate Web Applications

In addition to advertising, traditional corporate communicators and trainers have found significant uses for Internet technology to get information where it is needed faster and to construct knowledge repositories that enhance employee performance, productivity, and customer service.

These corporate users have generated the Internet subcategories known as intranet and extranet applications. Intranets are "firewall" protected portions of an Internet site that is meant for internal communication with employees. Extranet "business-to-business" sites are also often

limited in access to customers, suppliers, business partners, and the like. Pharmaceutical companies may have sites that are for physician-only participation. Figure 12.1 illustrates the general correlation between applications and audiences for corporate and organizational Internet, intranet and extranet uses.

This is not meant to be an exhausting listing of audiences and applications. There is tremendous diversity within many of these major categories. Amazon.com and on-line banking applications are both examples of electronic commerce but differ greatly in their interface design, use of data base technology, and overall functionality.

A Web Site Navigational Model

Whether describing a public-oriented Internet site or even most intranet applications, Figure 12.2 depicts how information is introduced to and tends to move through a large corporate Web site over time. Here is how a user typically moves through the site.

Home Page

The very tip of the pyramid is the site's "Home Page" which serves dual functions:

1. Content communication
2. Content indexing (providing direct access to other sources of information)

Content Communication: First and foremost, the "home page" must clearly identify the company, organization or brand image to the user. In addition, the home page generally communicates bulletins or short informational "nuggets" on the most current, important news about corporate products, operations, people, places, and financial performance. Due to space limitations, however, the home page rarely functions as more than a "headline" service.

Navigation & Indexing: By contrast, as much as two-thirds of home page "real estate" is

Figure 12.1: Ways in which corporations use the Internet to narrowcast to specific audiences.

Internet Audiences	Intranet Audiences	Extranet Audiences
• General public • Business & trade press • Shareholders • Financial analysts • Consumers	• Employees • Association & organization members • Subscribers • Work groups	• Customers • Distributors • Suppliers • Business partners
Internet Applications	**Intranet Applications**	**Extranet Applications**
• Corporate image & branding • Product information • Electronic commerce • E-mail requests for information • Electronic fundraising • Public relations & publicity • Advertising • Customer service • On-line catalogues	• Employee communication • Training & testing • Recruiting • Project management • Knowledge management & sharing	• Customer service • Product information • Electronic commerce • E-mail requests for information • On-line catalogues • Subscription services

usually devoted to navigation or indexing. This indexing function plays a critical role by directing site visitors to specific topics to find detailed information, data, and site functionality.

The Mini-Page

More detailed information is often found or accessed in the second level of the pyramid— designated as the "mini-page." Typically this level includes separate content areas populated by information from company business units, product lines or services, corporate functions such as human resources, and other logical content groupings. Like home pages, the mini-page also serves as the "gateway" to accessing detailed category-specific information such as product specifications or geographic office locations.

Category Specific Content

As Figure 12.2 illustrates, the ratio of *content* to indexing becomes far greater at this level. There is also more opportunity for information to remain accessible to site viewers over time than is possible on the corporate home page, since this site "gateway" should be continuously updated.

Hot Content & Content Repository

"Hot content" refers to the most recently posted or most requested information within the site. As content is no longer relevant to most site visitors, it is replaced by newer, or "hotter," information.

Over time, "hot content" cools, moving into the "content repository" section. As "hot content" becomes cooler, it begins taking on characteristics similar to that of a historical, archival document retrieval function—the data is maintained on a "might be used" basis.

The "content repository" is also where one typically finds forms to request information and submit résumés electronically, as well as other e-mail functions designed to serve various user groups.

Indexing

The indexing function, depicted on the left side of the pyramid, appears at each and every level of Web-site content. This illustrates how identical information may be accessed through multiple paths—including hypertext links.

Equally important, indexing functionality allows site users to return from deep within the content repository to the level of a mini or even the home page. Specific content, therefore, can be accessed via a number of interactive routes—from the top, bottom, or any point in between.

How Sites Are Populated

At first glance, Figure 12.2 may suggest a central information repository managed by an all-knowing Webmaster. In reality, the larger and more complex the corporation or enterprise, the more likely information populating the site is pulled from multiple sources (Figure 12.3). These sources may also be functionally and geographically diverse.

- Product data and technical specifications may come from manufacturing locations, R&D centers, or divisional sales and marketing organizations.
- The treasury function may input corporate stock prices, earnings information or other financial news daily.
- New releases can be provided by both corporate public relations and/or business unit media relations staff.

Figure 12.2: Web Site Navigational Model (created and designed by Robert Schulte, Director of Innovation, VuCom newMedia).

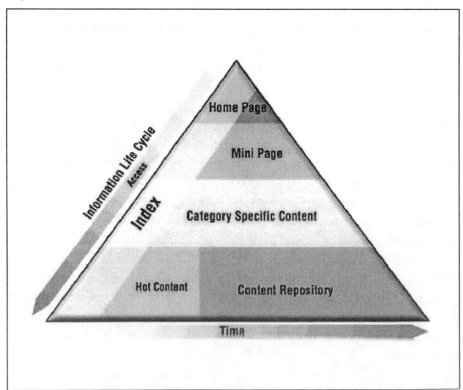

Figure 12.3: A variety of sources from differing areas of company operations provide input to populate a large site.

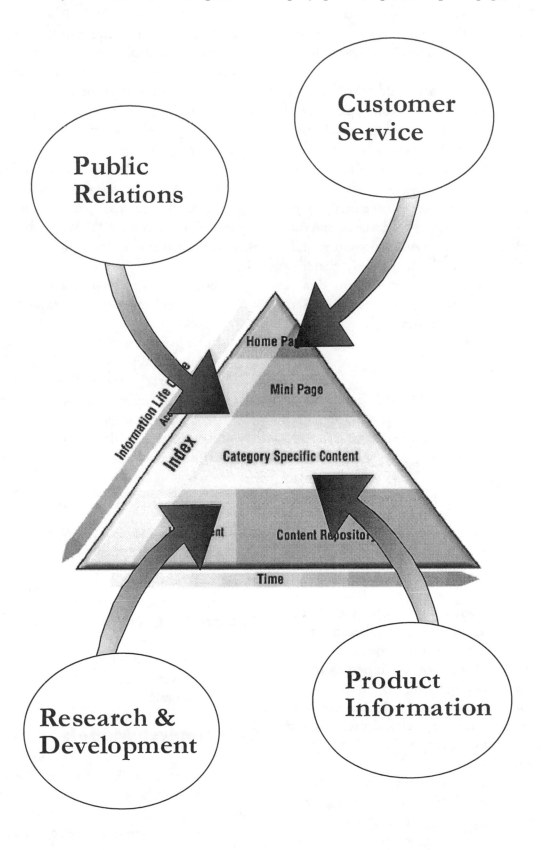

- Responses to consumer/customer questions, complaints, or technical support may come from the product area, scheduling, shipping, customer support, and technical or product support/service centers.

Some sites are designed so volatile information such as product availability, pricing, and order fulfillment is populated by operational data bases. Whenever a price change is made to the main system, it is automatically updated on the company Web site.

One of the primary functions of the "master Webmaster," then, is to design a site that will accommodate input from various sources while maintaining a consistent "look and feel," narrative style, and corporate identity. Often, this is accomplished by creating templates that allow users to input information such as news releases, product and price changes, etcetera.

Site Visitors as Input Source

Site visitors may also serve as input sources. Whenever a site seeks to gather demographic information from a user, allows site visitors to request information (whether fulfillment is by E-mail or snail mail), book reservations, purchase products or services, or interact with a sales representative—data is being input, collected, analyzed, manipulated, acted upon and filed by the company.

Thus, the two-way interactivity of a Web site encourages data collection and publication from a variety of internal and external sources.

Ideally, the more sources inputting timely, accurate information and data on a routine basis, the more functional and useful a site becomes—so long as the navigational model and user interface facilitate access to a wide range of users with diverse needs and interests.

By the same token, although templates help standardize "look & feel," they also encourage a rigid "one size fits all" mentality that can stifle imagination and creativity in narrative and graphic styles as well

as interactive experiences.

For the "master Webmaster" this poses a difficult balancing act between needs of site visitors and those responsible for site maintenance. The solution involves careful attention to information architecture. The discipline of "information architecture" provides intuitive access to information while providing for efficient content management over time.

All Web sites possess information architecture. Many, however, do not have a *planned* information architecture based on the information-seeking behavior of users. What benefits result from planned information architecture?

1. Sound information architecture helps users find and access information quickly and easily.
2. It helps users avoid looking for information that's not available.
3. It supports browsing through association and consistent design (grouping, labeling, indexing, and search systems).
4. And finally, good information architecture supports the goals of the sponsoring organization.

Three Significant Web Applications

The remainder of this chapter examines three specific high-profile Web-site applications:

1. Electronic commerce
2. Advertising
3. Training

E-Commerce Models

Selling over the Internet, known as E-commerce, offers a new and, for many companies, viable and significant distribution outlet. One of the Web's marketing strengths is that outgoing message and incoming response happen in the same medium. The Web can function simultaneously as on-line store, catalog, and ordering system.

Furthermore, in contrast to a 30-second radio or television commercial, the Web allows individual buyers to seek more and quite specific product information. They may also "skate like a waterbug" over product information that is of no immediate interest or personal relevance. In this way, a Web site serves as a "cybersales" representative— touting only those product features and benefits important to each specific buyer. You can window shop on-line and, when something snags your eye, put it in your electronic shopping cart with a mouse click, then charge it to your credit card.

Of course, not all products are suited to this E-commerce model—but many are, even those you might intuitively think do not lend themselves to it. Can you kick a tire or open the hood of an auto on-line? Maybe not physically. But you can learn all about the vehicle makes and models you're interested in on-line without having to pile into your old clunker, waste gas driving around town and be held hostage by the annoying car sales representative. You'll also find places where you can get financing and purchase that new car all on-line.

E-commerce systems range from simple, easily programmed E-mail forms allowing a buyer to place an order, to far more sophisticated on-line shopping models. The most advanced programs feature "add to shopping cart" functionality that tabulates a running total of items purchased, calculates appropriate shipping and tax, and keeps your address and credit card information on file, saving you the bother of completing an on-line form each time you wish to purchase.

Other types of buying and selling have also been adapted to the World Wide Web: on-line auctions, travel reservations, and buying clubs.

Advertising & Branding

In its short infancy, the World Wide Web has already spawned new types and forms of advertising. The most characteristic feature of Web advertising is that these are commercials you can "click." Rather than skating like a waterbug, Web advertisers seek to create a specific "click-stream" or path, enticing users to move from one site to another and within a site from page to page.

This is how the "banner" ad was born. A rectangular graphic element usually placed at the top of a home page, the banner is meant to tease the user to "click here" and "click now." The tease might be to enter a contest, win a prize, get information, see some "cool stuff," get a good deal, vote for something or someone, join an organization, go where no man or woman in cyberspace has gone before, and so on.

Placement of such banners on appropriate sites, as well as sales of banner space, are becoming as sophisticated in the reach, frequency and measurement options as those available to advertisers in traditional media.

When you get right down to it, however, there are only two options for the Web advertiser. As Jim Sterne points out in his insightful, exhaustive book on Web advertising, *What Makes People Click, Advertising on the Web*. "You can make a name for a company and forever tie it to the Internet in the minds of the public by taking the branding path, or you can do whatever it takes to get people to respond. So here are your choices:

- Branding
- Direct response

"The rest of your time will be spent differently, depending on which selection you make."[7]

Branding uses the Internet to pursue the traditional goals of public relations and corporate communications—let the public know about the great products you make, your company's commitment to quality, customer service, or its good citizenship as a steward of the environment, the community, or as patron of the arts. These are traditional, time-honored public relations goals.

Direct response, by contrast, adapts the traditional direct-marketer tools: direct mail, catalogs, or the "call now, operators are standing by now" style TV commercial to sell a product using the Web.

The Web brings two great innovations to direct marketing. The first is 24/7 accessibility. The on-line catalog is available at 3 A.M. and never gets accidently lost in the recycling pile. The on-line store stays open 24 hours, seven days a week, including holidays.

The second innovation was mentioned before but is so compelling it bears repeating: outgoing message and incoming response happen in the same medium. You can research the specs on that new stereo, comparison shop, then place the order, all in one Internet session. Or, you can be skimming like a waterbug, notice a banner ad, click, and before you know be placing an impulse order for a pound of chocolates.

Let's explore the implications, one at a time. As Jim Sterne points out, "A brand is not a positioning statement. It is not a marketing message. It is a promise. Made by a company to its customers and supported by that company ...a brand is something that lives apart from what the company plans because it is the culmination of all the interactions a marketplace has with the firm."[8]

If your goal is branding, you want company name and/or logo to show up as often as possible. If you are interested in direct response, you want to craft a call to action. You want people to "click here and now!" So you combine a mouse click with something the user gets in return:

- An offer
- A limited time offer
- Something for free
- The chance to enter a contest
- Something new
- Something so cryptic it'll entice the curious to check it out

What you seek to accomplish is to create a "click-stream" that eventually leads the user into your electronic commerce model and gets them to take action. Perhaps that first action is not yet a sale but does lead to getting the customer to provide some demographic information that gives you insight into how to target your marketing and sales promotion messages to that individual. Now you have a potential hook to get that user to come back to your site. Eventually, he or she may become an on-line buyer.

Whether your goal is branding or direct response, the strategies you employ will be no different from those that public relations and advertising professionals have used and refined for decades. Your tactics, however, will need to be adapted to the interactive multimedia potential of the World Wide Web. Copy will not only have to serve the traditional advertising functions but also be adapted to the specific requirements of the Internet—just as a copywriter will structure the same ad differently for print, television, and radio. The next chapter covers the craft of Web copywriting in more depth.

Education & Training

In addition to its commercial aspects, the World Wide Web has become a significant force in the "distance learning" evolution. Reputable colleges and universities have adopted the Web as a tool for reaching a new student population, giving rise to the "university without walls." It is especially suited to adult continuing education of all types. In this form, however, the Web is often more of a facilitation tool, allowing instructor to communicate readings and assignments, answer questions, and provide feedback to student work in progress.

Pharmaceutical companies have integrated patient education Web sites into their marketing mix, helping patients and families understand various disease states, offering insight into the pros and cons of differing treatments, and serving as a tool to answer medical questions directly over the Internet. In another medical context, the Web is used extensively for physician continuing medical education. Tutorials on the latest medical findings and clinical trials can be developed for Web delivery. Physicians can log on with specific passwords and, at the completion of their study, take a test via the Internet administered by the accrediting institution or organization.

Developing Internet training materials offers the potential to employ many of the interactive techniques and tools discussed in Chapters 9-11. Again, however, the integration of media, especially video, is restricted by the combined limitations of bandwidth and the specifications of the computer on the receiving end.

Corporate trainers have a distinct advantage when establishing technical specifications for designers and writers of interactive media for content delivered over a company-wide intranet, by possessing insight into bandwidth and computer specs at field locations. A media writer must always develop content, use of media, and interactivity with such specifications in mind. And when designing Web-based training applications for the general public, one is usually forced to design for the lowest common denominator at any point in time.

Summary

By the time this book is in your hands, new developments will have pushed Web technology to greater levels of sophistication, and its use will have expanded to an ever-widening global audience. Working in this interactive realm, therefore, requires becoming a keen and continual student of the Internet.

Corporate Web site development, which only a few years ago was something of a renegade activity done on an ad hoc basis by some ambitious information services geeks or corporate researchers, has now become a high-profile public relations, advertising, and training activity. In addition, electronic commerce, boosted by the on-line immediacy of outgoing message and incoming response taking place via the same medium, is changing the way many industries sell and fulfill customer orders.

As with other media writing applications discussed in Part II, success in these projects requires imaginative use of interactive technology to meet time-honored advertising, marketing, corporate image, and training goals. The next chapter offers a more detailed look at writing copy that will live as interactive screen text.

Footnotes

1. Jim Sterne, *What Makes People Click: Advertising on the Web*, (Indianapolis, IN: Que Corporation, 1997) p. 38.
2. Ibid, p. 3
3. (Seabrook, p. 161-2)
4. (Seabrook, pg. 163)
5. Walter S. Mossberg, "To Be a Mass Medium, the Web Must Be Freed from the PC," *Wall Street Journal*, Nov. 5, 1998, p. B1, col. 1.
6. Ibid.
7. Sterne, *What Makes People Click*, p. 329.
8. Ibid., p. 164.

CHAPTER 13

WRITING TEXT FOR THE SCREEN

> "Intelligence implies that one can dwell comfortably without pictures, in a field of concepts and generalizations."[1]
>
> Neil Postman

Although interactive and linear media share the same writing process, there are differing techniques, skills, and tools. On the surface, it might seem that interactive-media writing, with its great reliance upon text displayed on the computer screen, brings us "full circle" to the domain of print writing. It is a great (and frequently made) mistake, however, to assume that if one can write stimulating brochure copy or create an intriguing feature story, that there is no difference in writing copy for the computer screen. This chapter focuses on the unique aspects of writing text for multimedia and Web presentations.

To discover ways in which we might write text differently for the computer screen, a good starting point is to examine how people *read* the printed word on-line. How does reading/interacting with text on a computer screen *differ* from reading text on the printed page?

A Perfectly Good Display Device

First, consider the book or magazine as a display device. When reading a book, we have it open to a specific page. Psychologically, this communicates something about where we are in the text. We sense by the heft of the book and pages in our hand whether we are at the very beginning, somewhere in the middle, or closing in on the "final chase." It is sensory input we do not have when reading computer text.

When holding a magazine in our hand, we take in the entire page composition at once. Furthermore, with a magazine or brochure, two facing pages can be treated as a "spread," changing the "aspect ratio" from vertical to horizontal.

While reading a book you can write notes in the margin or highlight certain words of text for future reference. One may even pause to seek the meaning of a word in the dictionary or to simply reflect on the significance of an author's point. (Reading on-line, one always has the sense that the "clock is ticking.")

Highly portable, books and magazines travel well, making them easy to read anytime, anywhere—on the beach, on the bus to work, in bed, even on the "john" (leading to the journalist's rule: "no story so long it can't be read while on the throne").

Reading with the Mice

Notice, too, you don't read a book with a mouse in your hand and keypad before you. A mouse offers an experience that is impossible to simulate in print: "point, click, and see something happen." What happens, however, always remains within the fixed aspect ratio of the computer display. Scrolling may allow the reader to see more text—but the more one scrolls to reveal text, the more disorienting the experience. People reading text off a computer screen are reading from a reflected surface, at an uncomfortable distance, and with compromised resolution.

All this accounts for the need to print pages for editing text. One has a better sense of the spatial relationship between paragraphs and sections of text. It is easier to spot word or structural repetitions that may be separated by a few paragraphs. You can also read faster. In one study, researchers found reading from computer screens about 25 percent slower than reading from paper.[2]

Yet the mouse confers powers not available to print readers. Chief among these: hyperlinks. Hyper-linked text allows the user to follow a specific interest—drilling down into the content to the most relevant layer of depth and detail.

The mouse also confers the power to click on graphics, reveal rollover text, play animations, perform a "drop & drag" activity, see a video, or hear an audio clip. In this sense, text often competes with other media elements. We tire of reading text—so we click the button or icon that will deliver content via video or simply load the next Internet page, which, we hope, will have some especially appealing graphics or animation.

For all the functionality hypertext brings, it also encourages readers to scan the page. Research done by Jakob Nielsen and John Morkes for SunSoft Science Office found that 79 percent of test users always scanned any new Internet page they came across; only 16 percent read word-by-word.[3]

On the Internet, each page must compete for attention with hundreds of millions of others. Users can't be sure if this page is the one they need or whether some other page further along in the "click-stream" will be better.

In other research in which users were asked to perform the same tasks on five different versions of the same Web site, Nielsen and Morkes found "measured usability dramatically higher for the concise version (58% better) and for the scannable version (47% better). As a result, they offer several guidelines for Web-page writers of text:

- One idea per paragraph
- Highlight keywords (either by hypertext links or through typeface and color variations)
- Use lists with bullets rather than paragraphs with long lists imbedded within the copy

Other suggestions they offer include using the venerated inverted pyramid taught in journalism classes. By putting the most important information at the top of a newspaper story and the least important facts at the end, copyeditors can quickly shorten an article without fear of lopping off the point of the story. Nielsen and Morkes also encourage use of meaningful sub-headings.

Perhaps their most compelling advice to Web writers, however, is to use *half the word count,* or less, than conventional writing! Their academic research is confirmed by professional Web designers competing in the "Cool Site In a Day" competition. (See sidebar.)

Cool Site In a Day

Here's a strong confirmation of Morkes and Nielsen's scientific research from Web design practitioners...

While doing research on-line for this chapter, I happened upon a Web design competition described by Dale Dougherty, publisher of Web Review.[4] The idea of the competition was simple: two teams, one from the East Coast and another from the West Coast, would be given the same content and 24 hours to design a Web site (the "Cool Site in a Day" design competition).

Writes Dougherty: "I was confident these all-star design teams would create good-looking page layouts and elegant graphics, but how would they handle text?"

Each team was supplied printed materials from the nonprofit organization, Literacy Volunteers of America. They had to sift through the material and determine:

- What to use, and...
- How to present it on the Web

Speaking with team members, Dougherty received the following comments:

Said Leslie Harpold, an East team member from Fearless Media: "The information we started with needed serious reworking before it was suitable for the Web. It had to be rewritten in a voice that was more personal, direct, and conversational than most things in print."

"Our biggest job," commented East team captain Aliza Sherman, "was to reduce the amount of information down to what was most essential. We tried to identify the key phrases that the organization used." Sherman remarked that if the organization had created the Web site itself, the site might have contained a lot more information.

Both teams relied heavily upon words to get the illiteracy message out and to appeal for volunteers. They each incorporated personal stories of students being helped by the literacy programs. "Stories allow people to connect with each other," said Derek Powazek, the West team captain. "We wanted users to tell their own stories to each other as well."

For a sample page from these two sites, see Figures 13.1 and 13.2. The West, by the way, was judged the winning entry. You may draw your own conclusions.

The Media Equation

In their book, *The Media Equation*, Byron Reeves and Clifford Nass describe a series of experiments designed to answer the question: "How different are media and real-life experiences?"

"When we began our research," they write, "we believed that people might occasionally confuse media and real-life, but the confusion wasn't pervasive, and, most important, it was curable."[5] Following a series of experiments, their conviction changed dramatically. "People respond socially and naturally to media even though they believe it is not reasonable to do so and even though they don't think that these responses characterize themselves."[6]

In the very first experiments described in their book, they found, for instance, that "computers, in the way that they communicate, instruct, and take turns interacting, are *close enough* to human that they encourage *social* responses."[7] Taking turns is also a type of social interaction and key component of play. Writing text for a computer

Figure 13.1: One treatment of material from a Web page supplied by Literacy Volunteers of America for the "Cool Site in a Day" competition.

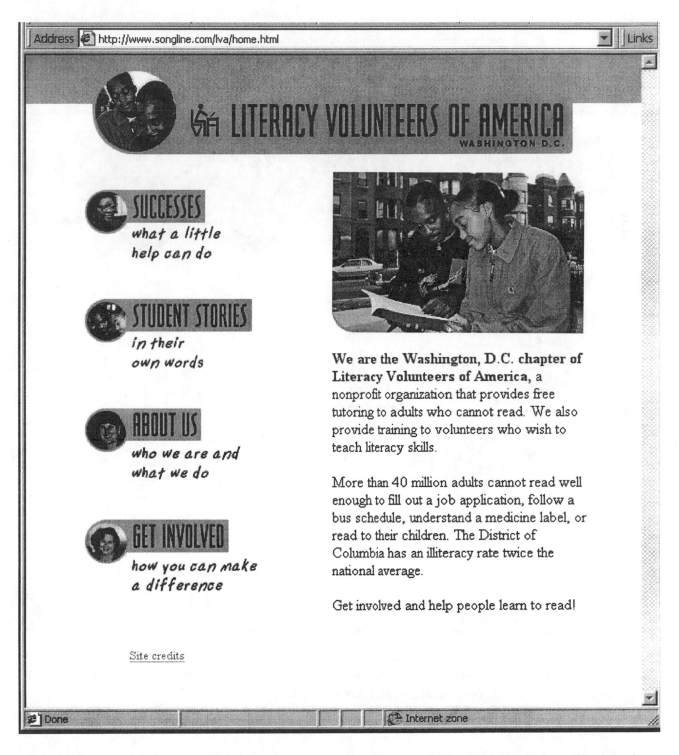

A page from the West's winning entry in the "Cool Site in a Day" competition. Notice the sparse use of text in the layout, the reliance upon stories, and how text along the side of the page is edited to work with the overall design. Provided by Literacy Volunteers of America, National Capital Area. Used by permision.

Figure 13.2: The same content as treated by the East team for the "Cool site in a Day" competition.

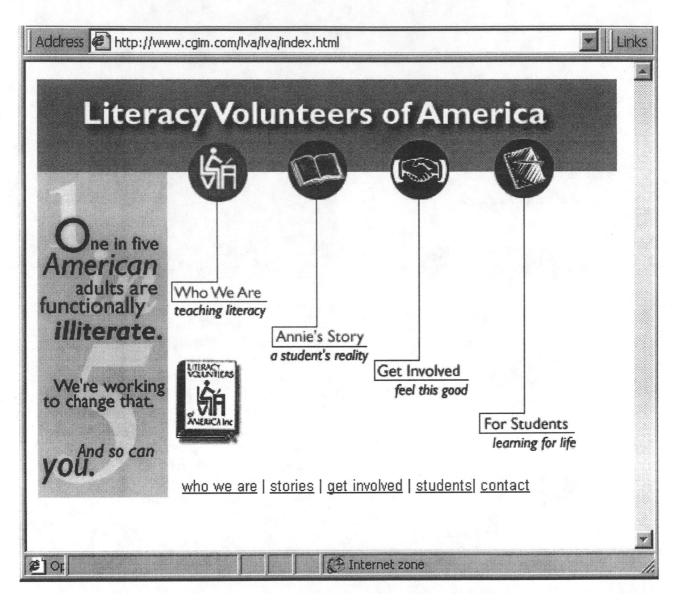

A page from the East's design also illustrates how text is edited for integration into the overall design and how use of stories can humanize and personalize content. Provided by Literacy Volunteers of America, National Capital Area. Used by permision.

screen, therefore, differs from writing text for a book or a brochure because, in a multimedia experience, people anticipate "taking turns interacting."

In addition, Reeves and Nass discovered that people in their experiments accorded computers politeness—just as they extend politeness to people in real-world social interactions. People respond "socially and naturally" to computers. This has great significance to those designing interactive digital multimedia experiences.

Reeves and Nass go so far as to postulate some suggestions for designing "polite" media based on the maxims of H. Paul Grice, a philosopher and psychologist. Grice viewed conversation as an exercise in which people try to be helpful. "Grice argued that all people feel that conversations should be guided by four basic principles that constitute the rules for polite interaction: quality, quantity, relevance, and clarity."[8]

Grice's principles or rules for polite human interaction:

- *Quality = Speakers should say things that are true.*

- *Quantity = Each speaker should contribute only what the conversation demands, not too much or too little.*

- *Relevance = What people say should clearly relate to the purpose of the conversation.*

- *Clarity = Contributions to an interaction should not be obscure.*

I believe this habitual taking turns throughout a conversation partially explains why experienced interactive digital media trainers develop screen formats that use short blocks of text while encouraging interaction via a Socratic teaching method with frequent interjection of questioning techniques. The best instructional designers and media writers are highly sophisticated in using question-and-response techniques as well as in incorporating meaningful "point and click" exercises to stimulate a dialogue with the learner.

Questions are used not simply to test comprehension. Many instructional designers employ questions to disseminate new information. Getting the answer "right" and moving on to the next screen is not the intent. Rather, the feedback to each possible answer (right or wrong) contains significant content or teaching points.

Note, for example, how the question in Figure 13.3, from a training program for beginning automobile company credit analysts, is used to convey important concepts about the characteristics of various co-signers. If you know nothing about the characteristics of co-signers, you learn *something* relevant and useful no matter which answer you select. Furthermore, a wrong answer merely encourages you to remain engaged in the dialogue on this topic. The feedback to the "correct" answer encourages the learner to click the alternate incorrect answers to learn more.

Likewise, in a training program for Michigan court clerks and support personnel that teaches principles for helping guide citizens to the appropriate court based on their legal issues, learners are encouraged to select all responses to the question: "What things should you consider before giving directions to a specific court?"

By contrast, one earmark of the inexperienced interactive writer's work is reliance on text-only screens punctuated by linear page-turn after page-turn. This "page-turner" mentality does not engage the audience in conversation, and the "point-and-click" technology soon becomes a mind-numbing, tedious activity.

Figure 13.3: Sample multiple-choice question with feedback.

Question Input Form

Question... To evaluate the value a co-signer brings to the equation you must determine their debt and their ability/willingness to contribute to the terms of the loan. Of the three types of co-signer, which is the best to get?	

Answer 1 Friend	Feedback 1 Worst. Friends break up. Friends can easily never see each other again.
Answer 2 Spouse	Feedback 2 Usually a spouse is a co-buyer because they are sharing the car. If a spouse is added because the primary buyer is marginal, the spouse can strengthen the deal. If the primary buyer is rated as poor, the spouse needs to be evaluated to see if he/she can handle taking over payments. The deal might be stronger if the spouse were the primary buyer.
Answer 3 Grandparent or parent	Feedback 3 You can't always count on a grandparent or parent to accept the responsibility of taking over payments on a child's car. Parents have been known to punish the child by saying "take the car back," when the child fails to manage his/her money. If the primary buyer is marginal, a grandparent or parent typically knows where the child can be located. That helps in the case of a suspected "skip hazard" or if you want the deal "collectable."

Figure 13.4: Your Guide to Accessing Michigan Courts Question Input Form

Question... What things should you consider before giving directions to a specific court?	
Answer 1 Do you fully understand what the person is asking?	Feedback 1 Absolutely. Most citizens are unfamiliar with the court system and court terminology. They rely on our guidance and assistance. Be sure you understand what they need before you direct them to a specific court.
Answer 2 Are you sure you are sending them to the right place?	Feedback 2 You may not be familiar with all the different parts of the court system. Giving incorrect directions could affect the person's ability to access the courts. Be sure you are sending them to the proper place
Answer 3 Your response may be mistaken for legal advice.	Feedback 3 Quite possibly. When you direct someone to a specific court, they may take your direction for legal advice.

Source: From "Your Guide to Accessing Michigan Courts," developed and produced by VuCom newMedia Learning for the Michigan Judicial Institute, Court Support Staff Training Consortium. Used by permission.

Socratic Questioning

Think of a recent meaningful conversation. Reflect on the role of questions in that conversation. Very likely there were lots of them—but the conversation was not a test. As Socrates is quoted as saying: "I have no answers, only questions."

In designing multimedia or Internet screen flow, we can use questions for the same reasons we use them in daily conversation or in a classroom.

- To gain feedback
- To check understanding
- To solve problems
- To stimulate thought
- To gain and keep attention
- To create a dialogue
- To check for understanding
- To involve participants
- To find out if there is a training need
- To draw on experience
- To direct the conversation
- To assist retention
- To check recall
- To create active learning

If the media writer fails to engage the audience in a conversation, then one must ask whether a printed text wouldn't be a more appropriate medium for the message.

Immediacy Versus Permanency

A carefully worded argument or thesis, as Neil Postman suggests, is far more suited to the experience of reading a well-reasoned, lively written book containing "the lineal, analytical structure of print."

"Language," writes Postman in *Amusing Ourselves to Death*, "makes sense only when it is presented as a sequence of propositions. Meaning is distorted when a word or sentence is, as we say, taken out of context." For instance interactivity, would simply get in the way of enjoying *Walden's Pond* for both its ideas and prose.

"Books," states Postman, "are an excellent container for the accumulation, quiet scrutiny, and organized analysis of information and ideas. It takes time to write a book and to read one; time to discuss its contents and to make judgments about their merit . . . a book is an attempt to make thought permanent and to contribute to the great conversation conducted by authors of the past."[9]

Time and technology are not hospitable to such a linear unfolding of ideas—marching from page 1 to page 510 in strict order. One does not engage in this type of discourse on the Internet. Chat-room conversations are more of the "passion hot" variety. It is free writing at its best. "Chatty," in a word.

The Internet, particularly the highly commercial World Wide Web segment of the Internet, offers a good laboratory in which to test this hypothesis because it provides access to significant amounts of text that do not contain opportunity for interactivity—unless you consider scrolling up and down interactivity. For most people, scrolling simply to reveal text is a nuisance.

I often use the Internet as a research tool, as do many writers. Once I locate what I'm seeking, a medical journal article about new work in brain chemistry, for example, I much prefer to print the article so it exists in analog form as "ink on dead trees," to quote Negroponte. From then on, I treat it as a traditional print or text-reading experience—not a digital interactive media experience.

Which brings me to a pet peeve: is anyone really reading the thousands of pages of outdated corporate news releases posted on the Internet? Or perhaps I have failed to appreciate that old news releases don't die but are immortalized on the Internet. The best corporate Web sites give visitors things to do.

On Goodyear's Web site, for example, you can learn about blimps and how they are designed. On the Gap's site, you can "drop and drag" various clothing items to create a wardrobe, then "click" to order it. These sites engage their audience in interactive dialogue—not in long blocks of text.

This is true also of purely informational CD-ROMs. A Picker International CD used for recruiting management information personnel employs a variety of activities on an interactive timeline that conveys company history milestones. Rollovers reveal text that quotes current employees on their challenging work. There's even a direct Internet link so that a prospective candidate can immediately access the company's job board posted on its Web site.

Such functionality goes beyond the mundane "point and click to get to the next screen" by engaging the viewer in a participatory experience. It allows users to enter a new world and reality and explore at their own pace based on personal interests.

Summary

So where does this leave the writer when it comes to creating text for the computer screen? There are those who argue that "good writing is good writing"—whether published in the *New Yorker* or on the World Wide Web. But if you were writing prose you expected people to read word for word, following "the lineal, analytical structure of print," would you publish that work on a medium where

79 percent of your readership always *scanned* any new page?

Writing text for the computer screen can be both well-written and appropriate for the medium. But such copy will consist of a more telegraphic, conversational, and scannable style, one that is linked closely to graphics, photos, and animations.

Footnotes

1. Postman, Neil, *Amusing Ourselves to Death, Public Discourse in the Age of Show Business,* 1985, (New York: Penguin Books), pgs. 69-70
2. Nielsen, Jakob, (1997) *How Users Read on the Web,* http://www.useit.com/alertbox/whyscanning.htm
3. Ibid., http://www.useit.com/alertbox/9710a.htm
4. Dougherty, Dale, (1997) *Don't Forget to Write,* http://webreview.com/97/10/10imho/index.htm
5. Reeves, Byron & Nass, Clifford, *The Media Equation, How People Treat Computers, Television and New Media Like Real People and Places,* 1996, (Cambridge, England: Cambridge University Press) pg. 26
6. Ibid., pg. 7
7. bid., pg. 22
8. Ibid., pg. 29
9. Postman, pgs. 69-70.

APPENDIX A

SHOOTING SCRIPT FORMATS

The Drafting Process

Drafting a linear shooting script differs from writing the treatment in the following ways. The shooting script:

1. Uses language of media production terminology
2. Uses one of two generally accepted shooting script formats
3. Contains detailed, specific and complete narration/dialog
4. Contains adequate and appropriate description of visuals that will appear on screen
5. Links visual and narrative cues in time, indicating a precise chronological sequence of events.

In so doing, the scriptwriter crafts detailed, specific instructions for the production team to follow in producing the program.

Sight and Sound in Time

When watching a linear-media program, you see a continuous evolution of spatial relationships between the camera (film, television, or still camera) and the subject. Concurrently, you hear a continuous mix of music, voices, and sound effects. To describe this chronological sequence of events and the relationship between sight and sound cues, the writer uses a special vocabulary—the language of media-production terminology.

Such terms and descriptions are the basic vocabulary of television, film, and multi-image production. The terminology is a functional shorthand, a way of communicating instructions on how to "make" the audiovisual production. (The shorthand codes in a shooting script function in a way similar to the abbreviations used in recipes to communicate quickly and efficiently what the cook must do to move from printed page to hot dish.)

The writer also sets down copy to be spoken with visuals; music to establish mood, time, or locale; and sound effects to punctuate on-screen action.

Figure A.1: Camera Shots

Long Shot (LS)

Medium Shot (MS)

Close-up (CU)

Extreme Close-up (ECU)

The Split-Page Format

The media writer continually orchestrates three raw materials. A shooting script simultaneously shows. . .

| spatial events, which describe the visual content of specific scenes and shots | and... | auditory information, which includes narrative copy, music, and sound effects. |

If we orchestrate visual and auditory cues side-by-side, as shown above, we have the classic split-page format generally used for television, multi-image, and multimedia shooting scripts (see Figure A.2).

Figure A.2: Split-Page Format Sample

VIDEO	AUDIO
Wide angle view of model office. Narrator moves toward TRIPS terminal.	**NARRATOR**: OUR NEW TRAVEL SERVICE OFFICE—MODERN, COMFORTABLE, SPACIOUS. THE OFFICE ITSELF SAYS "PRESTIGE, INTEGRITY, SECURITY, AND SERVICE."
ZOOM in to MS of Narrator and terminal.	THIS IS THE TRIPS TERMINAL. AND AS YOU CAN SEE, IT'S RIGHT AT HOME IN OUR NEW ENVIRONMENT.
CU on Narrator.	BUT WHAT IS TRIPS? TRIPS IS A MULTI-ACCESS RETAIL RESERVATIONS, AC-COUNTING, AND COMMUNICATIONS SYSTEM... AND TO CALL IT REVOLUTION-ARY IS AN UNDERSTATEMENT. THE TRIPS COMPUTER SYSTEM PUTS THE WHOLE WORLD OF TRAVEL INFORMATION LITER-ALLY AT YOUR FINGERTIPS.
ECU of hands on terminal keyboard.	IT'S AS SIMPLE AS A TYPEWRITER AND AS NEW AS TOMORROW.
ECU on computer screen displaying information.	IT'S A NEW WAY OF HANDLING INFORMA-TION...
Text on screen changes rapidly two or three times.	...ALL KINDS OF INFORMATION.
SPECIAL EFFECT as screen now displays artwork graphic of globe with animated net-work. MS on Narrator and terminal.	IT'S A NEW METHOD TO ENHANCE OUR WORLDWIDE DISTRIBUTION NETWORK... OUR WHOLE MARKETING EFFORT. IT'S A NEW TECHNIQUE TO EXPAND CUSTOMER SERVICE CAPABILITIES. TRIPS MAKES AVAILABLE, FOR THE FIRST TIME ANYWHERE, ALL OF OUR TRAVEL

CUT TO:	RESOURCES ON A MULTI-ACCESS TERMINAL:
MS of jet passenger carrier speeding down runway...	AIRLINES...
MS on exterior of exotic hotel...	
	HOTELS...
MS on tour bus and group boarding...	TOURS...
MS of car rental area in airport.	CAR RENTALS...
ECU on computer terminal with display.	OTHER TRS SYSTEMS...
MS on Narrator by terminal.	EVERYTHING—RIGHT HERE ON THIS ONE SCREEN.

Source: From "TRIPS: Your Selling and Servicing Partner," written by Allen Neil, directed by James G. Libby, produced by Video Marketing Group for American Express Travel Services. Used by permission.

Time is the glue that binds the two events together. Why this emphasis on time? In the pragmatic business of corporate and industrial video and film, the subject matter is highly specialized. Inexperienced writers often become entangled in the spider web of subject-matter expertise, placing far too little emphasis on the ultimate *viewing experience.*

When scripting chunks of informational copy, the writer must consider how the duration of audio events establishes the pacing of the visual content. One full page of narration, typed double-spaced on the right side of the page, equals about 60 seconds of screen time. For every page of narration, the viewer must also *see* something for 60 seconds! The left side of the page must be synchronized to the auditory cues on the right side of the page. Look again at Figure A.2.

Using a fundamental progression of "long shot" to "medium shot" to "close-up," the writer first establishes the scene with a wide-angle view, then calls for "close-ups" to illustrate specific copy points in greater detail. In this sequence of about 90 seconds, the writer calls for 12 different shots.

Furthermore, there's an integral relationship between shooting instructions on the left and the narrator's copy on the right. For instance, the writer clearly wants to see a "CU of hands on keyboard" at the precise moment when the narrator says: "It's as simple as a typewriter." Or, when the narrator states "all kinds of information," the writer calls for text on screen to "change rapidly two or three times."

The format is known as a "shooting script" because it provides sufficient detail for a production crew to execute the program from the written instructions describing what happens on the screen moment by moment. This script format links the synchronization between visual and auditory events occurring in time.

Cues for visual events need not be limited to narration or dialogue. The script excerpt in Figure A.3 shows how specific visual elements are linked to a music track.

Figure A.3: Linking Visual Elements to a Music Track

VIDEO	AUDIO
Multiple images of party fade in and out in various screen areas. Close-ups of activities such as a kid ripping open a present, playing pin-the-tail-on-the-donkey, and whacking a pinata.	MUSIC & SOUND EFFX: (Children's voices singing "Happy Birthday" mixed with party sounds and laughter.
Sequence culminates with full frame shot of birthday cake holding four candles. Use SPECIAL EFFECT to simulate flicker of candles. MATCH DISSOLVE	CROSS-FADE AUDIO…
Cake remains the same but there are now more candles—twenty to thirty.	MUSIC & SOUND EFFX: ("Happy Birthday" lyrics sung by more adult, middle-aged voices.)
MATCH DISSOLVE	CROSS-FADE AUDIO…
Cake remains the same, but is now ringed with candles—it is clearly the cake of a septuagenarian. As MUSIC establishes, shots of mature adults fade in and out of various screen areas.	MUSIC & SOUND EFFX: ("Happy Birthday" lyrics are now voiced by an elderly group of senior citizens… …as the lyric comes to its conclusion, we hear the sound effects of the celebration…) VOICE I: BE SURE TO MAKE A WISH! VOICE II: YOU'RE GONNA NEED SOME HELP BLOWING OUT ALL THOSE CANDLES…
SPECIAL EFFECT as candles on cake flicker, extinguish, and the screen FADES momentarily to BLACK.	SOUND EFFX: (Of breath blowing out candles followed by cheers, clapping and birthday salutations.)
As opening lyrics hit, images show mature men and women engaged in semi-athletic endeavors—biking, strolling in a park, playing golf and tennis, pitching ball to youngster, walking a dog, sailing a yacht. These are not decrepit seniors, but successful, active, upscale men and women who would not want to be slowed by arthritic conditions.	MUSIC: (While screen is in black, we hear the first strains of the show's theme song….)

Source: From "Happy Birthday," multi-image module written by William Van Nostran for The O'Hara Company. Used by permission.

This event-driven writing style distinguishes professional scriptwriters from the amateurs. Whenever the left side of the page lacks shot-by-shot detail, it's a dead giveaway the writer focused on narrative copy at the expense of visualization. This makes for neither good pictures nor good narration. As a result, narrative copy tends to be wordy and lengthy, more like a speech than commentary on pictures. Skilled scriptwriters search for the potential synergy between pictures and sound.

Pacing

As you move in tandem down the dual columns, be conscious of the "pacing" of the emerging text. Film and television involve a continuous evolution of spatial relationships between camera and subject, coordinated with a sequence of audio events. The rate at which those spatial relationships change is known as pacing.

Using our rule of thumb (one full page of narration, typed double-spaced on the right side of the page, equals about 60 seconds of screen time) when you've written a quarter page of narration, you know 15 seconds have elapsed. At the top of page 12, you know you're about 11 minutes into the program. Are you where you should be in terms of communicating critical content points? If your goal is a 15-minute script, are you about ready to "round third and head home?" This sense of time and energy is vital when generating a first draft.

The dual column shooting script helps you see the relationship between sight and sound events. The split-page format has evolved as a standard for many professional audiovisual productions. Most video and slide show scripts employ this format.

The Motion Picture Format

Film productions can be scripted in the dual column format, but many film producers are more comfortable with the motion picture format. Although this page layout still relies upon the use of production terminology (LS, MS, CU, etc.), the

relationship between picture and sound is expressed differently in the draft script. The American Express excerpt, shown in split-page format in Figure A.2, is displayed in a motion picture format in Figure A.4.

Figure A.4: Sample Motion Picture Format

1. INT: WIDE-ANGLE SHOT OF TRAVEL OFFICE. NARRATOR ENTERS AND MOVES TOWARD TRIPS TERMINAL.

NARRATOR
(Addressing camera.) Our new Travel Service
Office—modern,comfortable,spacious.
The office itself says "prestige, integrity,
security and service."

2. ZOOM IN TO TWO-SHOT OF NARRATOR AND TERMINAL.

NARRATOR
This is the TRIPS terminal. And as you
can see, it's right at home in our new
environment.

3. CLOSE-UP ON NARRATOR.

NARRATOR
But what is TRIPS? TRIPS is a multi-
access retail reservations, accounting and
communications system... and to call it
revolutionary is an understatement. The
TRIPS computer system puts the whole
world of travel information literally at your
fingertips.

4. EXTREME CLOSE-UP OF HANDS OPERATING KEYBOARD TERMINAL.

NARRATOR
It's as simple as a typewriter—and as new
as tomorrow.

5. EXTREME CLOSE-UP ON COMPUTER SCREEN DISPLAYING INFORMATION.

NARRATOR
It's a new way of handling information...

6. INFORMATION ON COMPUTER SCREEN CHANGES RAPIDLY TWO OR THREE TIMES.

NARRATOR
...all kinds of information. It's a new method
to enhance our worldwide distribution network...

7. MEDIUM SHOT ON NARRATOR AND TERMINAL.

NARRATOR
It's a new technique to expand our customer
service capabilities. TRIPS makes available,
for the first time anywhere, all of our travel
resources on a multi-access terminal:

8. EXT: MEDIUM SHOT OF PASSENGER JET ROARING DOWN RUNWAY.

NARRATOR
Airlines...

9. EXT: MEDIUM SHOT OF EXOTIC HOTEL ENTRANCE.

NARRATOR
Hotels...

10. EXT: MEDIUM SHOT OF TOUR BUS AND GROUP.

NARRATOR
Tours...

11. EXT: MEDIUM SHOT OF AIRPORT CAR RENTAL AREA.

NARRATOR
Car rentals...

12. INT: EXTREME CLOSE-UP ON TRIPS COMPUTER SCREEN WITH DISPLAY.

NARRATOR
Other TRS systems...

13. NT: MEDIUM SHOT OF NARRATOR BY TERMINAL.

NARRATOR
Everything—right here on this one screen.

Source: From "TRIPS: Your Selling and Servicing Partner," written by Allen Neil, directed by James G. Libby, produced by Video Marketing Group for American Express Travel Services. Used by permission.

Relationships between picture and sound in the motion-picture format are also delineated by typography and margin settings. Each camera shot is numbered. Narration, music, and sound effects are described below and within each shot. Changes in location are indicated by the shot description—"INT." for interior shots, "EXT." for exteriors.

As we said earlier, clients and subject-matter experts often cannot visualize a program. With the split-page format, the client and subject-matter expert may simply ignore the left side of the page, thinking the "important" material appears in narration or dialogue.

The motion picture format does make it more difficult to ignore visuals. However, it is probably no less bewildering to readers with little or no media background. Both script formats require visualization skills to "project" words on the page into sights and sounds on the "mental" screen.

Storyboards and Renderings

When you want absolute certainty that the client's perception of visual images matches your intent, the surest format is to storyboard.

In advertising agencies, storyboards are standard practice for television commercials. Storyboarding is an ideal way to communicate the

For lengthy television or film presentations (20 to 30 minutes or more), storyboarding may prove impractical. If the creative concept involves dramatic vignettes or documentary-style interview or action footage, the relationship between what the storyboard shows and what the actual footage offers may be quite different. A lengthy talking head scene of four minutes doesn't really require a storyboard to present the gist of the visual content. Or when the visual material is familiar to everyone and consists of real-life objects, it's

Figure A.5: Sample Production Storyboard

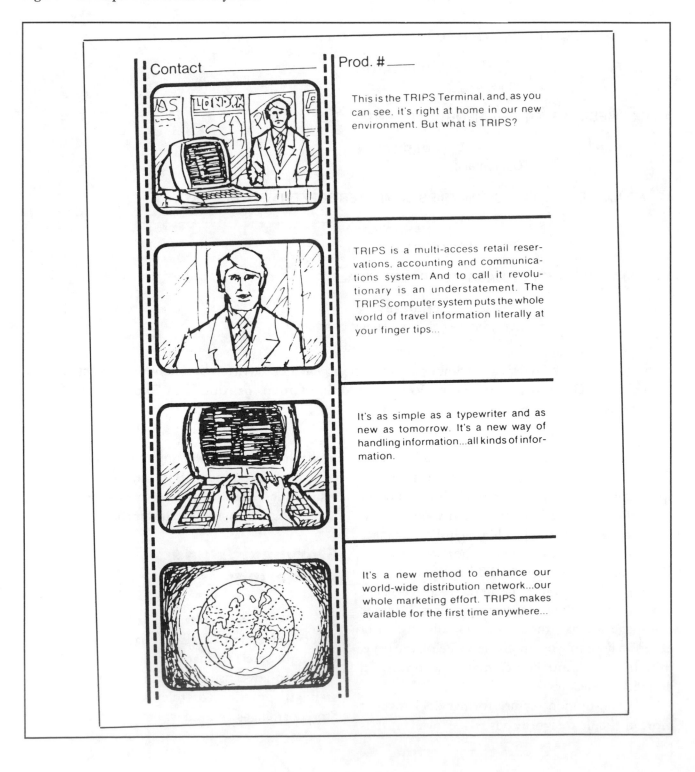

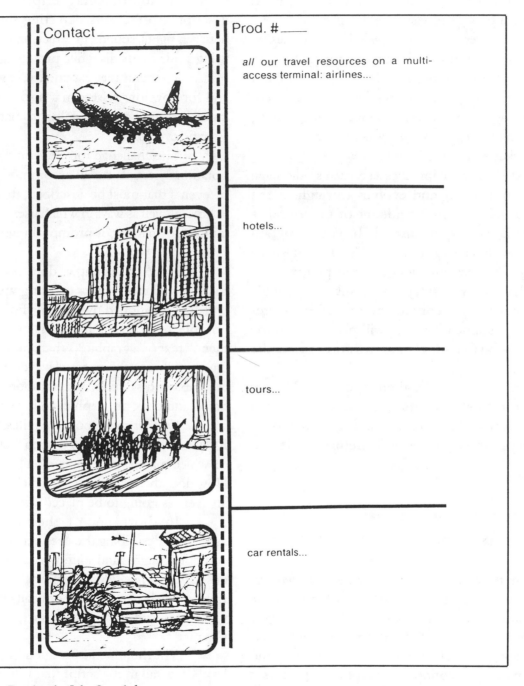

Source: Drawings by John Onuschak.

the visual material is familiar to everyone and consists of real-life objects, it's sufficient to write "CU on hands operating keyboard." It doesn't take great imaginative powers to visualize the shot.

However, there may be selected scenes or passages in a script that do cry out for some form of visualization. For many media scripts, a selection of sketches, illustrations, or "renderings" to augment the shooting script is an effective way to help clients, subject matter experts, producers, and directors visualize key elements.

If your script involves a stylized studio stage set, which changes and evolves throughout the program, then an artist's rendering of the set and its main variants is quite useful. If your program involves abstract subject matter (such as financial information or certain scientific concepts), you may wish to have an artist storyboard symbols or graphic treatments of key content points. If computer graphics or animated scenes will play a role in the script, the artist may want to storyboard the sequence.

As a basic rule, then, use the split-page format for most video projects. Use the motion picture format when you're scripting a film project or when you feel it will be more useful in the review process than a split-page draft.

Multimedia Production Script Formats

In the early days of corporate video, writers, producers, and directors were often frustrated or bewildered by clients incapable of visualizing a program when confronted with a two-column video production script. If only we had known how the gap between perception of the printed page as a viewing or user experience would widen with the advent of interactive media.

Furthermore, because multimedia is not a monolithic industry as was the case in the formative days of broadcast television, no "standardized" industry-accepted script format has yet emerged. Our multimedia scriptwriting definition also reveals that there are typically many more elements for the writer to include in the script:

"A multimedia script is the written description of events depicting the relationship between sights, sounds, graphics, animation, and text using a mix of media while providing users control over which events they experience, in what sequence, and for how long. Users may also make choices or input information that will automatically prompt specific events."

The challenge for the writer is to develop a notation system that will accommodate the variety of events that must be described, their relationship in time, as well as ways in which users control events, input information, or prompt things to happen on screen.

How, for example, does one indicate that the user will receive new text or graphics when the cursor is positioned over a specific screen area—a hot zone or "rollover" functionality? Is a "pull-down menu" text or a graphic? What about an active time line that allows users to scroll backward and forward, read text and see photos corresponding to various dates, and click on graphics to hear a video clip?

Furthermore, most Web sites, kiosks, or CD-ROMs include a variety of screen "templates," each of which may contain its own built-in functionality. How does the writer indicate which screen template an event is going to be placed within?

In short, one of the more challenging aspects of describing the user experience is that in, addition to sights and sounds, there is also a need to describe *functionality*. Functionality also includes flow—which is most economically communicated via a corresponding flow chart, as described in Chapter 11.

The multimedia production team requires a level of detail in the script that is likely to be more than the client, subject matter experts and other non-technical script readers require. The script readers identified earlier still include client, subject matter experts, producer, and possibly, though not always, a video director. In multimedia, an art director and software programmer are usually essential. Additional graphic designers and animators, as well as other programmers who bring all media elements together using an appropriate authoring package, often support the art director and lead programmer. Without a detailed, accurate flow chart that is coded to the events described in the script, the vast majority of interactive scripts are rendered useless to the production team.

When clients and other nontechnical script readers confront this level of detail, it is all too often overwhelming, short-circuiting mental visualization of the user experience.

This is one reason why design documents and prototypes are invaluable aids in the multimedia production environment. Scripts simply do not provide a sufficient sense of the actual user experience to allow clients and others to provide relevant feedback and develop a comfort level necessary to expend the funds needed to commit enthusiastically to full-scale production. Furthermore, prototypes allow for feedback from target audience members who can comment from the potential user's perspective. Their reaction to a prototype can influence subtle but significant

Figure A.6: Design Overview, Storyboards and Script Excerpts from "Play Away, Please"

A. DESIGN OVERVIEW

The purpose of this document is to provide a detailed account of "Play Away, Please," and suggest the experience a typical user might have. It is to be read in conjunction with other design documents, namely:

- Storyboard
- Structure chart
- Video treatment

General Characteristics

The exhibit is designed for viewing by a general public (golfers and non-golfers) of all ages. There are five principle topics:

- Swing Styles
- Course Architecture—Design Your Own Hole
- Match Play—Test your Knowledge
- USGA News
- Classic Eras

Each topic has a brief audio (or audio and video introduction) played from the videodisc. The topics are described below.

Visual and audible feedback is used to indicate which of several choices has been made and to indicate the "current" state of the program. This is generally achieved by changes in color for words and other symbols.

If a viewer does not touch the screen, a prompt is given to encourage interaction. Generally, two prompts are given. Then the program changes to its "cover screen." The time interval of prompts and "timeouts" varies from section to section, but will generally be relatively brief, in consideration of the museum environment and "traffic flow."

Cover Screen

A video "loop" plays continuously on the screen. The title "Play Away, Please," "Narrated by Steve Melnyk," and the instruction "Touch screen to begin" appear throughout. A touch anywhere on the screen causes display of the "main menu" and an audio.

Introduction

During the introduction, graphics and text for the main menu (Tee Off!) appear. The "Tee Off!" symbol appears in the lower left corner during the narration. It is not touch-sensitive in this case.

When the main menu is called from the cover screen, touch-sensitive "targets" do not become active until the audio introduction is complete.

Tee Off! (Main Menu)

This graphics screen is displayed as rapidly as possible whenever the Tee Off! symbol in the lower left corner is touched. Targets are active for each topic as soon as possible.

Principle Topics

Swing Styles

A video introduction shows slow-motion swings and places Palmer and Nicklaus side-by-side at the top of the screen and black below. Their names are added below their pictures. Audio continues as the "speed control" is displayed and explained. The wood-grain background and brass nameplates are added. Finally, the two take their swings simultaneously.

Touching any nameplate causes the previous nameplate to be "un-highlighted," and the new nameplate is highlighted. The golfers fade to black, and the names below the pictures are replaced by the new names. Fading up from black, then freezing for one second, the appropriate new pair of golfers is displayed, and they take their swings. The point of synchronization between the two golfers is always the moment of the club striking the ball. At the end of the swing they freeze. Touching the same nameplate again causes the swing to be repeated, with no change to the names.

The speed control allows the viewer to see the swing at normal speed or various slow speeds. Speed is changed by touching a point along the "speed bar." "Repeat Swing" causes the swing to be repeated.

"Solo Shots" shows a still frame of a golfer at the end of a swing. The golfer's name is highlighted on the left side of the screen. Any of the names can be touched, causing display of that player taking a swing.

Names are arranged alphabetically, from top to bottom. "Other Players" displays a new set of names, continuing the alphabetical order. When the last "page" of names is listed, "Other Players" causes the name display to "swap" to the first set of names.

Course Architecture

A video introduction shows scenes of several golf courses around the world. Graphics cover the video and show a set of icons that can be used to design a fanciful hole. Instruction is heard on the use of the symbols. When an icon is touched, it is redrawn with an outline designating it as the "current symbol." This symbol is then placed on the landscape by touching the screen. The icon area cannot be drawn over. "Start New Hole" causes the landscape to be cleared. "Instructions" causes the introductory explanation about the use of the symbols to be repeated.

The "Skip ahead" button shown during the video introduction causes audio to be muted as graphics for "Design a Hole" are displayed.

Match Play

A video introduction shows scenes of various awards ceremonies. Graphics (the scorecard, etc.) appear at the bottom of the screen. At the end of the introduction a graphic appears, to allow indication of "one player" or "two players." When this is answered, the first of nine quiz questions appears.

The questions consist of approximately 9 silent motion video segments and 27 still photos. They are presented sequentially, so that viewers playing multiple games are unlikely to encounter the same question twice.

Questions and choices for answers, are displayed in either a multiple-choice or true/false format. There are four answers for each multiple-choice question. Questions appear as text overlaid on video.

When a question is asked, each player must touch an answer, in turn, as indicated by illumination of a name on the scorecard. After the second player answers, score is registered for both players (in the case of a single player, only "Player 1" is illuminated). If both players are correct, polite applause is heard. If both are incorrect, a crowd "sigh" is heard (for a single player, no sounds are heard). At the end of the game (except for a tie?) video fades to black and robust applause is heard.

The option is then presented to:

1. Print the questions and answers
2. Play another game
3. Explore other parts of the program

If the "print" option is chosen, the questions and answers, with the correct answer identified, are printed out. The printout also includes the USGA name and adress and an invitation to visit the museum store.

"Play another game" removes the above buttons. Sound is heard, asking the number of players, and a graphic allows the indication of the answer. When the answer is given, the game proceeds as before.

"Explore other parts of the program" causes display of the "Tee Off!" menu. This third choice might simply be offered implicitly through the "Tee Off!" button in the lower left corner.

USGA News

A royal-blue background is displayed, featuring the USGA seal in a low-contrast "water-mark" fashion. Text is written over the background, describing championship results, current news, upcoming events, etcetera. The text display consists of a single font in one color.

The text is drawn from a file prepared by USGA personnel.

Classic Eras

A timeline is displayed, portraying five groups of famous players. Touching any group causes the timeline to fade to black, followed by a fade up on a video clip of that era. The viewer may return to the timeline by touching "Other Eras" or by waiting for the end of the clip. At the end of the clip, video fades to black and then fades up on the timeline.

Figure A.7: "Play Away, Please" Structure Chart

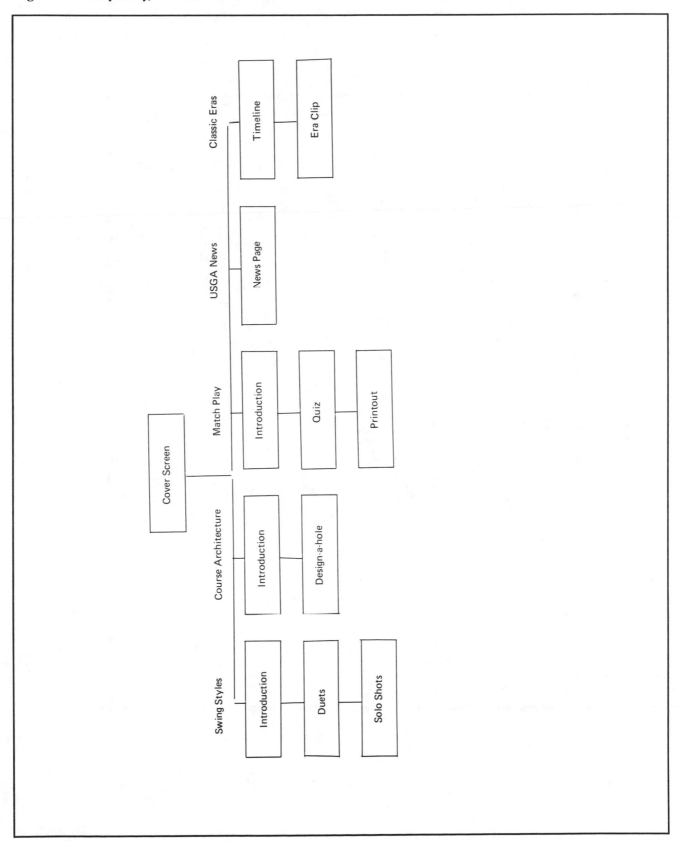

Figure A.7: "Play Away, Please" Storyboards

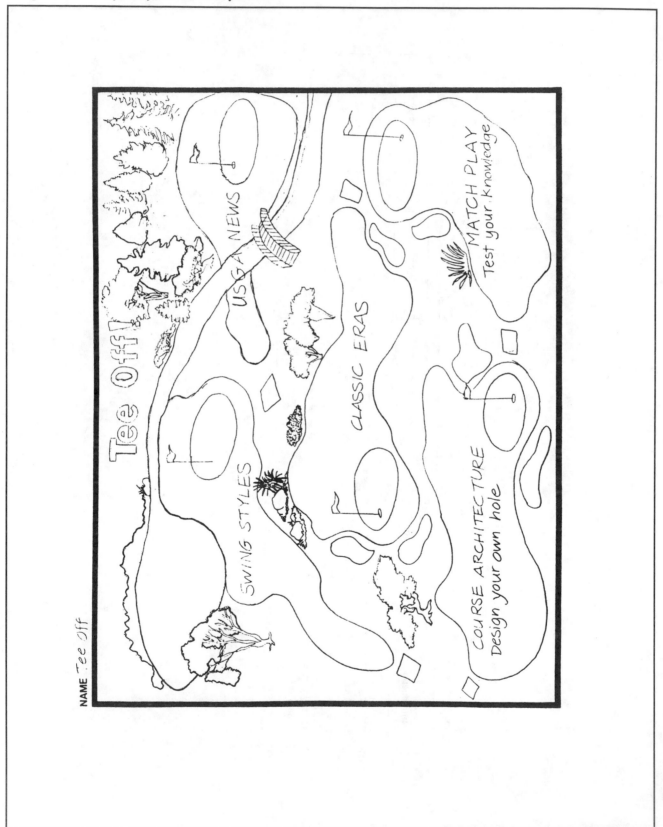

Figure A.7: "Play Away, Please" Storyboards (cont.)

Figure A.7: "Play Away, Please" Storyboards (cont.)

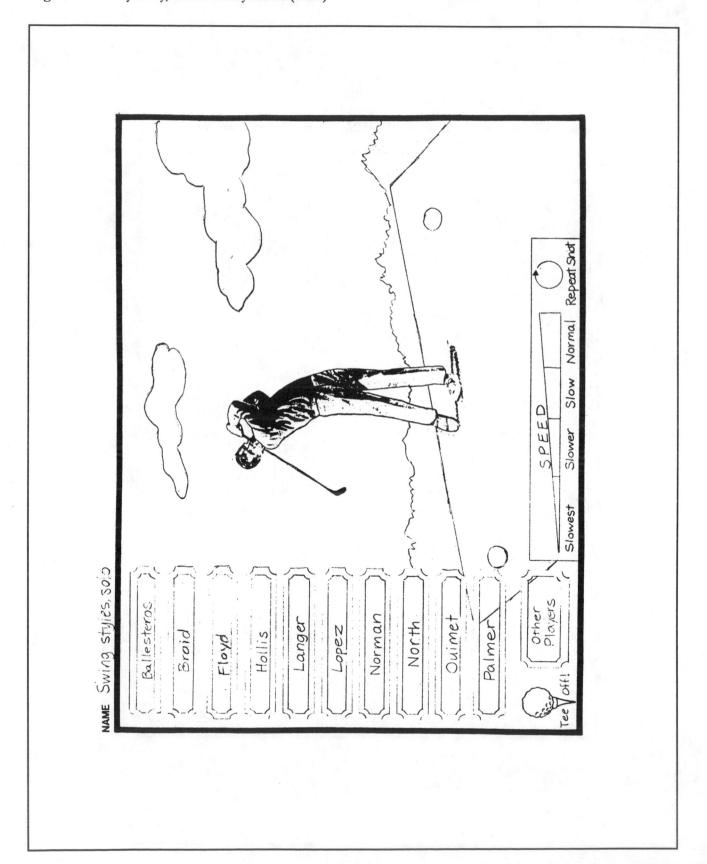

Figure A.7: "Play Away, Please" Storyboards (cont.)

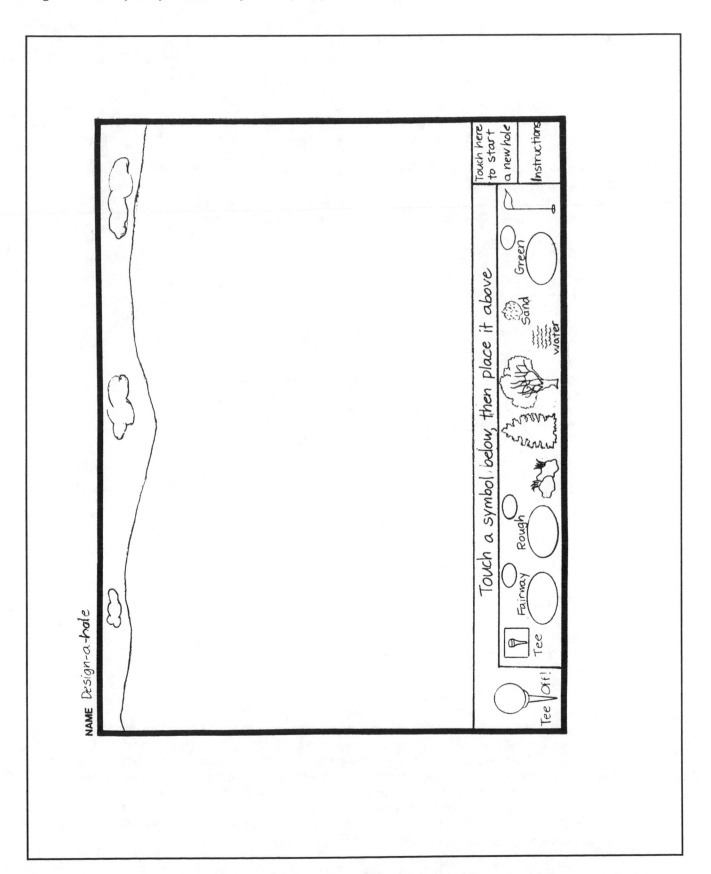

Figure A.7: "Play Away, Please" Storyboards

NARRATION: PLAY AWAY, PLEASE

Intro to Main Menu

Welcome to "Play Away, Please."

This exhibit features games, news photographs, and historic motion picture footage, all under your control. Explore them by touching one of these fairways. You'll see the topic and a new display. Touch words and other symbols to guide the presentation.

Feel free to interrupt; touch the screen at any time. Return to these fairways by touching the ball in the lower left corner.

So, go ahead.

As we say at all USGA championships, "Play away, please."

Narration for "Classic Eras"

Each of golf's major eras is remembered for a famous group of players. See them at their best.

Narration for "Swing Styles"

(Bobby Jones traced slow-mo)
Swing styles have changed over the years, with the introduction of new equipment and balls and today's manicured golf courses.

(Full frames shrink and squeeze side-by-side, 4 sec.)
Here you can compare the great players of this century.

(Speed control appears, 5 sec.)
Use the speed control for a closer look, or to repeat a swing.

(Wood-grain plaques and names fill in, 6 sec.)
Watch for placement of feet relative to the ball, turning of the hips and height of the backswing.

(They swing together, 2 sec.)
Give it a try.

All right.

Play away, please.

Narration for "Course Architecture"

Just as the Industrial Revolution changed the characteristics of golf equipment, the twentieth century brought changes in golf course design and construction techniques. As land became more precious, designers had to alter the terrain rather than rely upon the natural features. But whatever the landscape, certain elements appear in all courses. One of golf's great pleasures is the variation in design among thousands of courses in the world today.

These elements are derived from characteristics of the Scottish seacoast. St. Andrew's shows off the natural landscape—exposed land and bunkers. Golfers playing the nine holes "out" share double greens with other golfers playing back "in."

Dramatic cliffs and foggy weather mark Pebble Beach in California. The short seventh hole with its isolated green, is merely warm-up for the chasm one encounters on the eighth.

Bobby Jones was co-designer, with Scottish architect Alister Mackenzie, of Augusta National. There is no real rough, only trees and shrubbery along wide fairways leading to large undulating greens. Perennial site of the Masters tournament, the course boasts beautiful foliage and immaculate grounds.

Shinnecock Hills, Long Island, is reminiscent of St. Andrew's. Both are "links" courses, having been reclaimed from dunes and near the ocean. Shinnecock Hills is one of the few such courses in the United States.

Narration for "Design a Hole"

You are the architect now. Join Alister Mackenzie, Donald Ross, and A.W. Tillinghast. Try your hand at designing a golf hole.

Everything you need is at the bottom of the screen.

Touch one of these symbols, and place it on the landscape above.
You only need to touch the symbol once, but you can use it many times.
Slide your finger to fill in large areas.
You can always clear the screen by touching "Start New Hole."

Play away, please.

Prompts

Go ahead. Make a selection.

Just touch the screen to indicate your choice.

Touch the screen to operate this exhibit.

Remember, you can also slide your finger across the screen.

Take a swing at it.

Take a shot at it.

Stop putting around. Touch the screen.

Please make a choice, or let others play through.

Can't you make up your mind?

Congratulations.

Source: From "Play Away, Please," written by Carol Strohecker, produced by Brian Raila and Gabriel Savage Docterman of Digital Techniques, Inc. Used by permission.

changes in the next iteration.

Interactive Production Script Formats

The interactive script formats illustrated below show the same content using two differing notation systems. Some background on the project and screen templates will help to fully correlate information on these scripts with events the user experiences. The script is one small instructional module from a series of seven interactive CD ROMs created to train Chrysler Financial credit analysts on the basics of analyzing and investigating applications using the A.C.E. System—a computerized tool for analyzing and investigating the creditworthiness of an applicant.

Figure A.14: There are four basic screen templates:

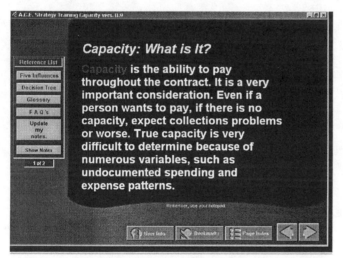

1. **Banner Page:** a screen used at the beginning of each lesson.

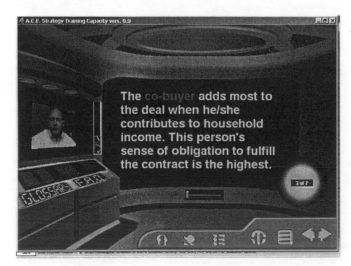

2. **The Learning Room:** a screen using object animation to reveal text in several areas: a main screen, a narrator's screen that is also used to play video clips, and a scrolling marquee. The screen also has video controls built into the screen design. This page may also include an optional event: a drop-down screen introducing an upcoming A.C.E. Screen Page.

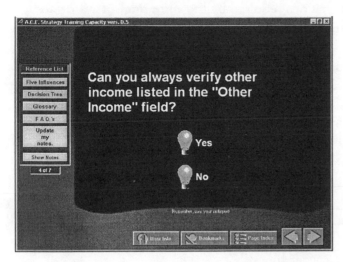

3. **Basic content page:** generally a text-only screen that often incorporates multiple-choice questions, rollovers, and other interactive tools. May sometimes include a video clip, usually as part of the response to multiple-choice questions.

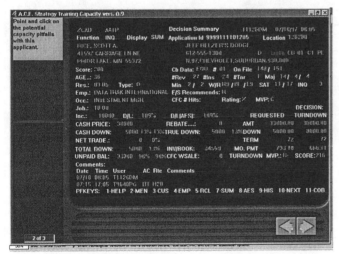

4. **A.C.E. screen pages:** pages that are used to display data about the applicant, dealer, and potential "deal" as taken from the consumer's application and information drawn from credit bureau reports. Commentary on the data, questions, and responses to mouse clicks in data fields are also displayed to the left of the actual A.C.E. screen data.

Source: From "A.C.E. Training Strategies," Dr. Karen Cowan, executive producer, Duane Mattson, content expert, developed and produced by VuCom newMedia Learning for the Training and Development Department of Chrysler Financial Services, LLC. Used by permission.

The script format shown as sample A.15 uses a form to communicate how various entries correspond to each screen template. It is a text-based representation of information and/or events associated with each screen. Page names correspond to page designations required by the authoring software package.

An essential aspect of multimedia production, especially when complex branching is involved, is to be able to track previous and next-page information. This allows users to access the next or last page simply by clicking a "Forward" or "Back" button. Note also the designation of previously edited and identified video and audio clips to permit the software programmer to include appropriate media excerpts as events within selected screens.

Figure A.15: Input Forms used by writer

EVALUATING THE APPLICATION (B)

BASICBANNER PAGE	
Page Name	Evauateappbanner
TOC	Evaluating the Application
PrefacePage	
Index Title	
NextPageName	3 4 evaluateapp1
PreviousPageName	home
PreviousPageTransition	None Zoom Push Wipe
NextPageTransition	None Zoom Push Wipe

BANNER TEXT	
Notes	
Board/Wall	To succeed as a Credit Analyst, you must become proficient at evaluating the credit application. To do this you first profile a customer, or build a story. This ensures that you are considering all relevant data. Building a story consists of using data on the application to construct a picture of the applicant that is both realistic and believable. During this process, you identify the areas of concern on the app and seek to clarify or resolve those issues.

Figure A.15: Input Forms used by writer (cont.)

3 4 evaluateapp1 (C)

BASICCONTENTPAGE PAGE	
Page Name	3 4 evaluateapp1
TOC	Story Building
PrefacePage	
VideoClipName (no ext.)	
AudioClipName (no ext.)	
Index Title	
NextPageName	3 4 evaluateapp 2 (QC)
PreviousPageName	Evaluateappbanner
PreviousPageTransition	*None Zoom Push Wipe*
NextPageTransistion	*None Zoom Push Wipe*

TEXT	
Notes	
Board/Wall	People are creatures of habit and, therefore, behave in predictable patterns. Storybuilding, or profiling, ensures that you link critical information to predict the performance of one applicant based on the behavior patterns of large populations.

ANIMATION SEQUENCE		
From	**To**	**Location**

Figure A.15: Input Forms used by writer (cont.)

3 4 evaluateapp 2 (QC)

QUESTION BASICCONTENTPAGE PAGE	
Page Name	3 4 evaluateapp 2 (QC)
TOC	Where Do You Look?
PrefacePage	
VideoClipName (no ext.)	
AudioClipName (no ext.)	
Index Title	
NextPageName	
PreviousPageName	
Question Widget	FI DD MZ HZ TF YN MC
PreviousPageTransition	None Zoom Push Wipe
NextPageTransistion	None Zoom Push Wipe

TEXT	
Notes	
Board/Wall	In addition to the Summary screen, where else would you look to build a complete customer story or profile?

ANIMATION SEQUENCE		
From	**To**	**Location**

Figure A.15: Input Forms used by writer (cont.)

QUESTION CHOICE / RESPONSE / WIDGET PARAMETERS			
Choice	Collateral Screen		
Response	Yes. Even though much of the information is on the Decision Summary screen, you may need to go to the Collateral screen to get more information.		
Correct / Incorr		**Answer Weight**	
Transparent (YN)		**Enabled (YN)**	
Play Media Clip		**Branch To**	
Case Sensitive (YN)		**Match Order (YN)**	
Sounds Like (YN)		**Ignore Punc. (YN)**	

Credit Bureau Report

QUESTION CHOICE / RESPONSE / WIDGET PARAMETERS			
Choice	Credit Bureau Report		
Response	Yes. Even though we have a summary of credit bureau information on the Summary screen, you may need to go to this report for the details that complete your customer profile.		
Correct / Incorr		**Answer Weight**	
Transparent (YN)		**Enabled (YN)**	
Play Media Clip		**Branch To**	
Case Sensitive (YN)		**Match Order (YN)**	
Sounds Like (YN)		**Ignore Punc. (YN)**	

Employment Screen

QUESTION CHOICE / RESPONSE / WIDGET PARAMETERS			
Choice	Employment Screen		
Response	Yes. You may need to go to this screen to determine the composition of total income. This would help you complete your profile or picture. Example: income shows $6,000 but Employment Screen indicates this includes the wife's salary of $3,000, but the wife is not on the contract. This could affect your story and ultimate decision.		
Correct / Incorr		**Answer Weight**	
Transparent (YN)		**Enabled (YN)**	
Play Media Clip		**Branch To**	
Case Sensitive (YN)		**Match Order (YN)**	
Sounds Like (YN)		**Ignore Punc. (YN)**	

Figure A.15: Input Forms used by writer (cont.)

3 4 evaluateapp 3 (S)

BASICSPACEROOM PAGE	
Page Name	3 4 evaluateapp 3
TOC	
PrefacePage	
VideoClipName (no ext.)	Story1
AudioClipName (no ext.)	
Index Title	
BranchTo (in script)	3 4 evaluateapp 4
PreviousPageName	3 4 evaluateapp 2 (QC)
PreviousPageTransition	*None* Zoom *Push* *Wipe*
NextPageTransistion	*None* Zoom *Push* *Wipe*
MarTitle	The story helps you look at patterns and relationships of data.
Learn Button; change buttonclick to	2

TEXT	
NarrationBalloon	Watch this one-minute thirty-second video on projecting the future.
ACE Monitor	
Notes	
Board/Wall	Storybuilding allows you to judge the believability of the data. It helps you build a template to sift through the data and determine what is important. It assists you in determining an applicant's performance and the degree of risk. You do this by comparing the applicant's profile to the performance profile of others in similar situations.

ANIMATION SEQUENCE		
From	**To**	**Location**

Figure A.15: Input Forms used by writer (cont.)

3 4 evaluateapp 4 (C)

BASIC CONTENT PAGE PAGE	
Page Name	3 4 evaluateapp 4
TOC	Can They? Will They?
PrefacePage	
VideoClipName (no ext.)	
AudioClipName (no ext.)	
Index Title	
NextPageName	3 4 evaluateapp 5
PreviousPageName	3 4 evaluateapp 3
PreviousPageTransition	*None* Zoom *Push* Wipe
NextPageTransistion	*None Zoom Push* Wipe

TEXT	
Notes	
Board/Wall	Throughout the process, the fundamental questions that you ask are: "Can they pay?" and "Will they pay?"

ANIMATION SEQUENCE		
From	*To*	*Location*

Figure A.15: Input Forms used by writer (cont.)

3 4 evaluateapp 5 (QC)

QUESTION BASICCONTENTPAGE PAGE	
Page Name	3 4 evaluateapp 5 (QC)
TOC	
PrefacePage	
VideoClipName (no ext.)	
AudioClipName (no ext.)	
Index Title	
NextPageName	3 4 evaluateapp 6
PreviousPageName	3 4 evaluateapp 4
Question Widget	FI DD MZ HZ TF YN MC
PreviousPageTransition	None Zoom Push Wipe
NextPageTransistion	None Zoom Push Wipe

TEXT	
Notes	
Board/Wall	Assume all the following is found on an application submitted by a 27-year old. Which of the choices does not fit the pattern?

ANIMATION SEQUENCE		
From	To	Location

Figure A.15: Input Forms used by writer (cont.)

In bureau for 6 years

QUESTION CHOICE / RESPONSE / WIDGET PARAMETERS			
Choice	In bureau for 6 years		
Response	This is possible for a 27-year old. People become credit active around 21-years of age.		
Correct / Incorr		Answer Weight	
Transparent (YN)		Enabled (YN)	
Play Media Clip		Branch To	
Case Sensitive (YN)		Match Order (YN)	
Sounds Like (YN)		Ignore Punc. (YN)	

With present employer for four years

QUESTION CHOICE / RESPONSE / WIDGET PARAMETERS			
Choice	With present employer for four years		
Response	This fits the pattern of a 27-year old person.		
Correct / Incorr		Answer Weight	
Transparent (YN)		Enabled (YN)	
Play Media Clip		Branch To	
Case Sensitive (YN)		Match Order (YN)	
Sounds Like (YN)		Ignore Punc. (YN)	

Limited, but good credit.

QUESTION CHOICE / RESPONSE / WIDGET PARAMETERS			
Choice	Limited, but good credit.		
Response	This is entirely possible, but not always the case. A 27-year old can have extensive credit as well as limited credit. The key is good credit.		
Correct / Incorr		Answer Weight	
Transparent (YN)		Enabled (YN)	
Play Media Clip		Branch To	
Case Sensitive (YN)		Match Order (YN)	
Sounds Like (YN)		Ignore Punc. (YN)	

Figure A.15: Input Forms used by writer (cont.)

Limited, but good credit.

QUESTION CHOICE / RESPONSE / WIDGET PARAMETERS			
Choice	Limited, but good credit.		
Response	This is entirely possible, but not always the case. A 27-year old can have extensive credit as well as limited credit. The key is good credit.		
Correct / Incorr		Answer Weight	
Transparent (YN)		Enabled (YN)	
Play Media Clip		Branch To	
Case Sensitive (YN)		Match Order (YN)	
Sounds Like (YN)		Ignore Punc. (YN)	

Making $8,000 a month

QUESTION CHOICE / RESPONSE / WIDGET PARAMETERS			
Choice	Making $8,000 a month		
Response	Probably not. This is not the usual case for someone who is 27-years old. This requires more investigation.		
Correct / Incorr		Answer Weight	
Transparent (YN)		Enabled (YN)	
Play Media Clip		Branch To	
Case Sensitive (YN)		Match Order (YN)	
Sounds Like (YN)		Ignore Punc. (YN)	

Figure A.15: Input Forms used by writer (cont.)

3 4 evaluateapp 6 (QC)

QUESTION BASICCONTENTPAGE PAGE	
Page Name	3 4 evaluateapp 6 (QC)
TOC	
PrefacePage	
VideoClipName (no ext.)	
AudioClipName (no ext.)	
Index Title	
NextPageName	3 4 evaluateapp 5
PreviousPageName	3 4 evaluateapp 7
Question Widget	FI DD MZ HZ TF YN MC
PreviousPageTransition	None Zoom Push Wipe
NextPageTransistion	None Zoom Push Wipe

TEXT	
Notes	
Board/Wall	Assume all of the following information is found on an application submitted by a 50-year old. Which of the choices does not fit the pattern?

ANIMATION SEQUENCE		
From	**To**	**Location**

Figure A.15: Input Forms used by writer (cont.)

Two years on the job

QUESTION CHOICE / RESPONSE / WIDGET PARAMETERS			
Choice	Two years on the job		
Response	This does not fit the usual pattern for a 50-year old person. They are usually employed at the same location for more than two years. This requires investigation.		
Correct / Incorr		Answer Weight	
Transparent (YN)		Enabled (YN)	
Play Media Clip		Branch To	
Case Sensitive (YN)		Match Order (YN)	
Sounds Like (YN)		Ignore Punc. (YN)	

$10,000 per month income

QUESTION CHOICE / RESPONSE / WIDGET PARAMETERS			
Choice	$10,000 per month income		
Response	Again, this does not fit the usual pattern of a 50-year old person who has recently changed jobs, especially someone who has a marginal credit history. These two facts do not usually add up to a $10,000 per month income.		
Correct / Incorr		Answer Weight	
Transparent (YN)		Enabled (YN)	
Play Media Clip		Branch To	
Case Sensitive (YN)		Match Order (YN)	
Sounds Like (YN)		Ignore Punc. (YN)	

20 years with marginal credit history

QUESTION CHOICE / RESPONSE / WIDGET PARAMETERS			
Choice	20 years with marginal credit history		
Response	This is not what you would expect if the $10,000 per month income is accurate. This needs investigation.		
Correct / Incorr		Answer Weight	
Transparent (YN)		Enabled (YN)	
Play Media Clip		Branch To	
Case Sensitive (YN)		Match Order (YN)	
Sounds Like (YN)		Ignore Punc. (YN)	

Figure A.15: Input Forms used by writer (cont.)

The applicant is an accountant

QUESTION CHOICE / RESPONSE / WIDGET PARAMETERS			
Choice	The applicant is an accountant		
Response	This is possible, but given the other information, you should investigate whether the person is a CPA. Regular staff accountants do not usually make $10,000 per month.		
Correct / Incorr		**Answer Weight**	
Transparent (YN)		**Enabled (YN)**	
Play Media Clip		**Branch To**	
Case Sensitive (YN)		**Match Order (YN)**	
Sounds Like (YN)		**Ignore Punc. (YN)**	

3 4 evaluateapp 7 (QC)

QUESTION BASICCONTENTPAGE PAGE	
Page Name	3 4 evaluateapp 7 (QC)
TOC	
PrefacePage	
VideoClipName (no ext.)	
AudioClipName (no ext.)	
Index Title	
NextPageName	3 4 evaluateapp 8
PreviousPageName	3 4 evaluateapp 6
Question Widget	FI DD MZ HZ TF YN MC
PreviousPageTransition	None Zoom Push Wipe
NextPageTransistion	None Zoom Push Wipe
TEXT	
Notes	
Board/Wall	Assume all of the following information is found on an application submitted by a 45-year old. Which of the choices does not fit the pattern?
ANIMATION SEQUENCE	

From	To	Location

Figure A.15: Input Forms used by writer (cont.)

Twenty years on the job

QUESTION CHOICE / RESPONSE / WIDGET PARAMETERS			
Choice	Twenty years on the job		
Response	This is possible. It fits a pattern for a 45-year old person.		
Correct / Incorr		Answer Weight	
Transparent (YN)		Enabled (YN)	
Play Media Clip		Branch To	
Case Sensitive (YN)		Match Order (YN)	

$7,000 per month income

QUESTION CHOICE / RESPONSE / WIDGET PARAMETERS			
Choice	$7,000 per month income		
Response	Depending on the occupation, this is believable. Especially when you consider the other supporting information such as good credit history and a sizeable down payment on the vehicle.		
Correct / Incorr		Answer Weight	
Transparent (YN)		Enabled (YN)	
Play Media Clip		Branch To	
Case Sensitive (YN)		Match Order (YN)	

20 years and good credit history

QUESTION CHOICE / RESPONSE / WIDGET PARAMETERS			
Choice	20 years and good credit history		
Response	Given the other variables, it fits the pattern.		
Correct / Incorr		Answer Weight	
Transparent (YN)		Enabled (YN)	
Play Media Clip		Branch To	
Case Sensitive (YN)		Match Order (YN)	

Figure A.15: Input Forms used by writer (cont.)

25% down—48 months for a Durango

QUESTION CHOICE / RESPONSE / WIDGET PARAMETERS			
Choice	25% down—48 months for a Durango		
Response	This fits the pattern of someone who has progressed in age and income, but who doesn't want to take on more debt than necessary.		
Correct / Incorr		**Answer Weight**	
Transparent (YN)		**Enabled (YN)**	
Play Media Clip		**Branch To**	
Case Sensitive (YN)		**Match Order (YN)**	

3 4 evaluateapp 8 (S)

BASICSPACEROOM PAGE	
Page Name	3 4 evaluateapp 8
TOC	
PrefacePage	
VideoClipName (no ext.)	Story3
AudioClipName (no ext.)	
Index Title	
BranchTo (in script)	3 4 evaluateapp 9
PreviousPageName	3 4 evaluateapp 7
PreviousPageTransition	None Zoom Push Wipe
NextPageTransistion	None Zoom Push Wipe
MarTitle	The same set of variables for two applicants can result in two different stories.
Learn Button; change buttonclick to	3
TEXT	
NarrationBalloon	In watching this one-minute, 30-second video, Duane explains why you shouldn't take information at face value.
ACE Monitor	
Notes	
Board/Wall	Separating the data to get to "Can they pay?" and "Will they pay?" involves assessing the applicant's pattern of behaviors.

ANIMATION SEQUENCE		
From	**To**	**Location**

Figure A.15: Input Forms used by writer (cont.)

3 4 evaluateapp last (C)

BASICCONTENTPAGE PAGE	
Page Name	3 4 evaluateapp last
TOC	
PrefacePage	
VideoClipName (no ext.)	
AudioClipName (no ext.)	
Index Title	
NextPageName	home
PreviousPageName	3 4 evaluateapp 8
PreviousPageTransition	None Zoom Push Wipe
NextPageTransistion	None Zoom Push Wipe

TEXT	
Notes	
Board/Wall	When you receive a credit application, the data intertwines to form a story that will assist you in making good credit decisions. You cannot take one fact and make a decision. You must consider all relevant data points as you connect the dots to build a story. You then analyze whether the story is believable and project the probability of the customer paying throughout the length of the contract.

ANIMATION SEQUENCE		
From	To	Location

The following alternative script format takes the same content and functionality, but employs a more visual way of depicting the flow by customizing software designed for creating technical drawings. Again, it's vital to understand the screen templates to interpret the writer's intent.

Figure A.16: Input forms used by writer

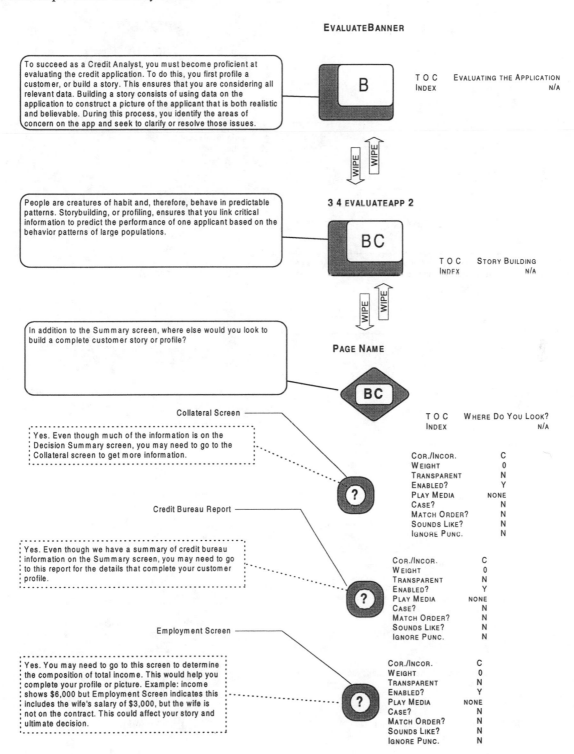

Figure A.16: Input forms used by writer (cont.)

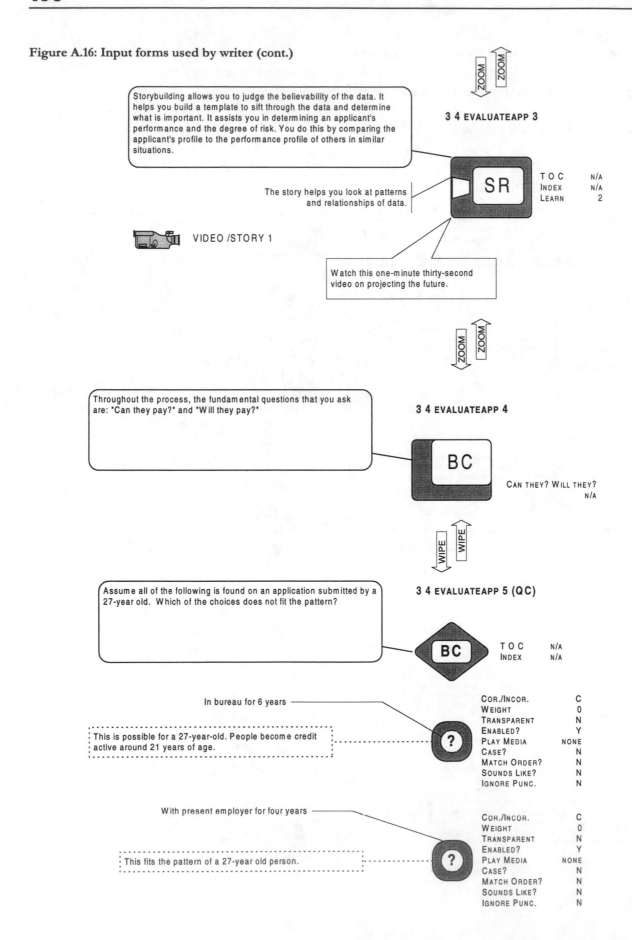

Storybuilding allows you to judge the believability of the data. It helps you build a template to sift through the data and determine what is important. It assists you in determining an applicant's performance and the degree of risk. You do this by comparing the applicant's profile to the performance profile of others in similar situations.

ZOOM   ZOOM

3 4 EVALUATEAPP 3

The story helps you look at patterns and relationships of data.

SR   TOC   N/A
        INDEX   N/A
        LEARN   2

VIDEO /STORY 1

Watch this one-minute thirty-second video on projecting the future.

ZOOM   ZOOM

Throughout the process, the fundamental questions that you ask are: "Can they pay?" and "Will they pay?"

3 4 EVALUATEAPP 4

BC

CAN THEY? WILL THEY?
                    N/A

WIPE   WIPE

Assume all of the following is found on an application submitted by a 27-year old. Which of the choices does not fit the pattern?

3 4 EVALUATEAPP 5 (QC)

BC   TOC   N/A
        INDEX   N/A

In bureau for 6 years

This is possible for a 27-year-old. People become credit active around 21 years of age.

?

COR./INCOR.	C
WEIGHT	0
TRANSPARENT	N
ENABLED?	Y
PLAY MEDIA	NONE
CASE?	N
MATCH ORDER?	N
SOUNDS LIKE?	N
IGNORE PUNC.	N

With present employer for four years

This fits the pattern of a 27-year old person.

?

COR./INCOR.	C
WEIGHT	0
TRANSPARENT	N
ENABLED?	Y
PLAY MEDIA	NONE
CASE?	N
MATCH ORDER?	N
SOUNDS LIKE?	N
IGNORE PUNC.	N

Figure A.16: Input forms used by writer (cont.)

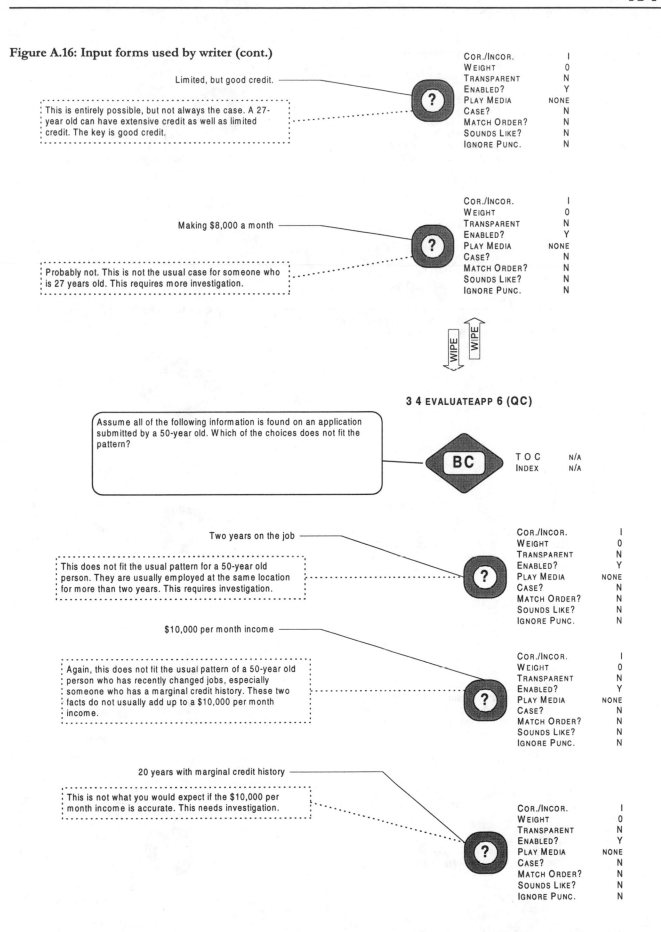

Limited, but good credit.

This is entirely possible, but not always the case. A 27-year old can have extensive credit as well as limited credit. The key is good credit.

COR./INCOR.	I
WEIGHT	0
TRANSPARENT	N
ENABLED?	Y
PLAY MEDIA	NONE
CASE?	N
MATCH ORDER?	N
SOUNDS LIKE?	N
IGNORE PUNC.	N

Making $8,000 a month

Probably not. This is not the usual case for someone who is 27 years old. This requires more investigation.

COR./INCOR.	I
WEIGHT	0
TRANSPARENT	N
ENABLED?	Y
PLAY MEDIA	NONE
CASE?	N
MATCH ORDER?	N
SOUNDS LIKE?	N
IGNORE PUNC.	N

WIPE WIPE

3 4 EVALUATEAPP 6 (QC)

Assume all of the following information is found on an application submitted by a 50-year old. Which of the choices does not fit the pattern?

BC

| T O C | N/A |
| INDEX | N/A |

Two years on the job

This does not fit the usual pattern for a 50-year old person. They are usually employed at the same location for more than two years. This requires investigation.

COR./INCOR.	I
WEIGHT	0
TRANSPARENT	N
ENABLED?	Y
PLAY MEDIA	NONE
CASE?	N
MATCH ORDER?	N
SOUNDS LIKE?	N
IGNORE PUNC.	N

$10,000 per month income

Again, this does not fit the usual pattern of a 50-year old person who has recently changed jobs, especially someone who has a marginal credit history. These two facts do not usually add up to a $10,000 per month income.

COR./INCOR.	I
WEIGHT	0
TRANSPARENT	N
ENABLED?	Y
PLAY MEDIA	NONE
CASE?	N
MATCH ORDER?	N
SOUNDS LIKE?	N
IGNORE PUNC.	N

20 years with marginal credit history

This is not what you would expect if the $10,000 per month income is accurate. This needs investigation.

COR./INCOR.	I
WEIGHT	0
TRANSPARENT	N
ENABLED?	Y
PLAY MEDIA	NONE
CASE?	N
MATCH ORDER?	N
SOUNDS LIKE?	N
IGNORE PUNC.	N

Figure A.16: Input forms used by writer (cont.)

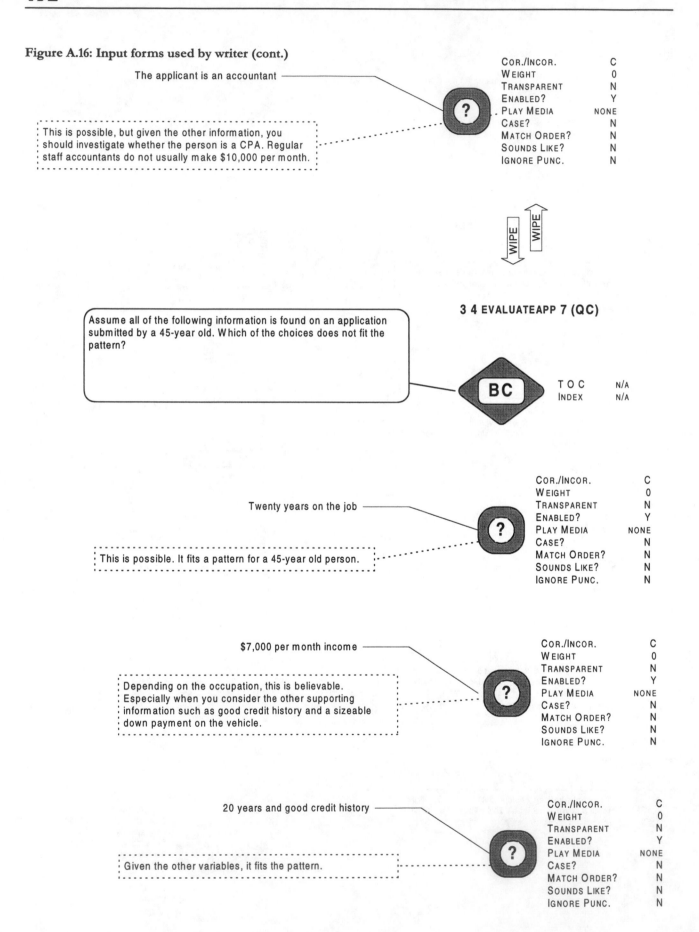

The applicant is an accountant

COR./INCOR.	C
WEIGHT	0
TRANSPARENT	N
ENABLED?	Y
PLAY MEDIA	NONE
CASE?	N
MATCH ORDER?	N
SOUNDS LIKE?	N
IGNORE PUNC.	N

This is possible, but given the other information, you should investigate whether the person is a CPA. Regular staff accountants do not usually make $10,000 per month.

WIPE   WIPE

Assume all of the following information is found on an application submitted by a 45-year old. Which of the choices does not fit the pattern?

3 4 EVALUATEAPP 7 (QC)

BC

| T O C | N/A |
| INDEX | N/A |

Twenty years on the job

COR./INCOR.	C
WEIGHT	0
TRANSPARENT	N
ENABLED?	Y
PLAY MEDIA	NONE
CASE?	N
MATCH ORDER?	N
SOUNDS LIKE?	N
IGNORE PUNC.	N

This is possible. It fits a pattern for a 45-year old person.

$7,000 per month income

COR./INCOR.	C
WEIGHT	0
TRANSPARENT	N
ENABLED?	Y
PLAY MEDIA	NONE
CASE?	N
MATCH ORDER?	N
SOUNDS LIKE?	N
IGNORE PUNC.	N

Depending on the occupation, this is believable. Especially when you consider the other supporting information such as good credit history and a sizeable down payment on the vehicle.

20 years and good credit history

COR./INCOR.	C
WEIGHT	0
TRANSPARENT	N
ENABLED?	Y
PLAY MEDIA	NONE
CASE?	N
MATCH ORDER?	N
SOUNDS LIKE?	N
IGNORE PUNC.	N

Given the other variables, it fits the pattern.

Figure A.16: Input forms used by writer (cont.)

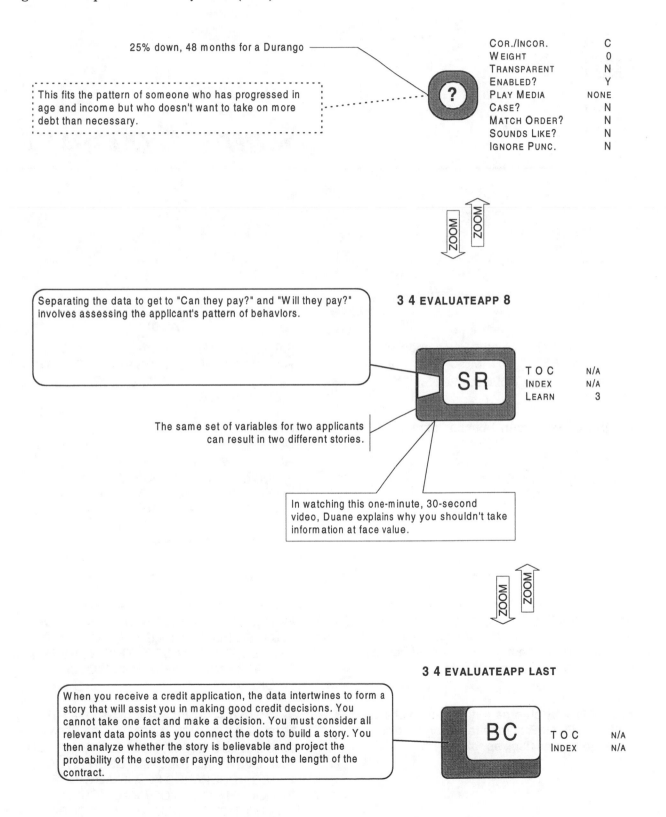

25% down, 48 months for a Durango

This fits the pattern of someone who has progressed in age and income but who doesn't want to take on more debt than necessary.

Cor./Incor.	C
Weight	0
Transparent	N
Enabled?	Y
Play Media	NONE
Case?	N
Match Order?	N
Sounds Like?	N
Ignore Punc.	N

ZOOM ZOOM

Separating the data to get to "Can they pay?" and "Will they pay?" involves assessing the applicant's pattern of behaviors.

3 4 EVALUATEAPP 8

SR

T O C	N/A
Index	N/A
Learn	3

The same set of variables for two applicants can result in two different stories.

In watching this one-minute, 30-second video, Duane explains why you shouldn't take information at face value.

ZOOM ZOOM

3 4 EVALUATEAPP LAST

When you receive a credit application, the data intertwines to form a story that will assist you in making good credit decisions. You cannot take one fact and make a decision. You must consider all relevant data points as you connect the dots to build a story. You then analyze whether the story is believable and project the probability of the customer paying throughout the length of the contract.

BC

T O C	N/A
Index	N/A

APPENDIX **B**

SCRIPT EXAMPLES

Script Example B.1: Advertising the Structure

Excerpt 1:

VIDEO	AUDIO
MS on Jack by the chroma-key screen. It contains a FREEZE FRAME of a track and field event—runners going around a track.	JACK: WE CAN LEARN A LOT ABOUT HANDLING OBJECTIONS FROM SPORTS. CONSIDER, FOR INSTANCE, TRACK AND FIELD EVENTS
CLOSE UP on screen as action of race begins.	GARRY AND I HAVE ALWAYS BEEN PROPONENTS OF HAVING A SALES TRACK TO RUN ON. WHEN YOU'RE PREPARED; WHEN YOU KNOW YOUR LINES SO THEY'RE NATURAL AS BREATHING—THEN YOU'RE LIKE THE TRACK STAR WHO'S PREPARED AND CONDITIONED FOR RUNNING THE BIG RACE.
MS on Garry, who is now seen in main stage area. Abstract style artwork suggests a stadium or arena. Several hurdles are positioned in front of cyc to provide an area for Jack and Garry to move from point to point. In this establishing shot, Garry refers to hurdles behind him.	GARRY: BUT WHAT HAPPENS TO THE RUNNER WHO SUDDENLY FACES AN UNEXPECTED OBSTACLE—SUCH AS A HURDLE? IF THAT RUNNER HAS NEVER TRAINED FOR HURDLES—HE OR SHE WILL BE THROWN OFF STRIDE. THEIR RHYTHM AND CONFIDENCE WOULD BE BROKEN.
MS on Jack by chroma-key screen. It shows FREEZE FRAME of race featuring hurdles. Footage rolls as Jack speaks.	JACK: BUT—SUPPOSE THAT SAME RUNNER HAS TRAINED INTENTLY TO RUN A RACE INVOLVING HURDLES. THEN, EACH AND EVERY HURDLE HAS BEEN ANTICIPATED—PREPARED FOR IN ADVANCE THROUGH HOURS OF PRACTICE AT TAKING THE HURDLE WITHOUT BREAKING STRIDE.

MS on Garry by hurdles.

GARRY: IN THE NEXT FEW MINUTES, WE'RE GOING TO PROVIDE YOU TECHNIQUES FOR RUNNING A SALES TRACK THAT HAS THE HURDLES IN PLACE. THOSE HURDLES STAND FOR THE SALES RESISTANCE AND INEVITABLE OBJECTIONS YOU SHOULD ANTICIPATE DURING EACH AND EVERY SALES PRESENTATION. BY TRAINING TO RUN ON THIS SALES TRACK—YOU'LL BE CONDITIONED TO THE RESISTANCE AND TAKE OBJECTIONS RIGHT IN YOUR STRIDE.

DIFFERENT ANGLE, featuring Jack as he walks into main stage area, joining Garry.

JACK: BY DEVELOPING TECHNIQUES FOR TAKING OBJECTIONS IN STRIDE, YOU'LL BEGIN TO DEVELOP THE CONFIDENCE WHICH WILL LEAD TO AN ATTITUDE THAT WELCOMES OBJECTIONS AS VALUABLE FEEDBACK FROM YOUR PROSPECT. BEFORE GETTING INTO SPECIFIC TECHNIQUES FOR OBJECTION HANDLING— LET'S DEFINE WHAT WE MEAN BY SALES RESISTANCE AND OBJECTIONS.

Excerpt 2:

DIFFERENT ANGLE on Jack with two hurdles next to him. He flips down placards that read "Insincere" on one hurdle, "Genuine" on the second.

TO HANDLE AN OBJECTION EFFECTIVELY, YOU MUST UNDERSTAND WHAT KIND OF OBJECTION YOU'RE FACING. OBJECTIONS FALL INTO TWO GENERAL CLASSIFICATIONS: INSINCERE OBJECTIONS AND GENUINE OBJECTIONS.

Isolate Garry by the "Insincere Objection" hurdle. He flips down the second placard under the hurdle, with the text: "Sales Resistance."

GARRY: THE INSINCERE OBJECTION IS KNOWN AS SALES RESISTANCE, SINCE IT IS NOT REALLY AN OBJECTION THAT CAN BE ANSWERED. GENERALLY, THE INSINCERE OBJECTION IS ILLOGICAL. IT'S EXPRESSED THROUGH ALIBIS, EXCUSES, OR STALLS. THE PROSPECT GIVES FICTITOUS REASONS TO HIDE THE REAL, GENUINE OBJECTIONS.

HERE ARE SOME EXAMPLES OF INSINCERE OBJECTIONS:

DISSOLVE TO:

SPECIAL WIPE EFFECT matting close-ups of lips from each voice in black and positioning them in various screen areas.

VOICE I: I'M REALLY TIED UP AT THE OFFICE RIGHT NOW. I JUST DON'T HAVE TIME TO TALK ABOUT INSURANCE NOW…

VOICE II: YOUR PLAN HAS A LOT OF MERIT. BUT I'D LIKE TO SLEEP ON IT…

VIDEO	AUDIO
DISSOLVE TO: CU on Jack.	VOICE III: I'M INSURANCE POOR AS IT IS—I CAN'T IMAGINE NEEDING MORE… JACK: THE INSINCERE OBJECTION, OR SALES RESISTANCE, IS NOT MOTIVATED BY LOGIC. THE PROSPECT OFFERS FICTITIOUS REASONS OR EXCUSES. QUITE OFTEN, THE INSINCERE OBJECTION MASKS THE REAL, GENUINE OBJECTION.

Source: From *How You Handle Objections*, from the Kinder Brothers & Associates Professional Profile Video Series, written by William Van Nostran; directed by John P. Kenlon; created and produced by Kinder Brothers & Associates and The Prudential Audio Visual Communications Division. Used by permission.

Script Example B.2: Unadvertised Structure

VIDEO	AUDIO
FADE UP ON: The program opens in a hallway by an elevator door. A male in his mid-thirties (Hank Conroy) dressed in shirt and tie, carrying a lot of paperwork, paces back and forth, hitting the "call" button impatiently. As the door opens, he gets in and briefly acknowledges a female employee (Liz Talbot), who also carries a handful of papers. The doors close… SUPER: **The Ups and Downs of Materials Management** DISSOLVE TO: REVERSE ANGLE from within elevator as doors open. Two additional male employees get on. One of these is an installer (Phil Fisher) in shirt and tie, carrying a briefcase with his tools. A portly 50 year-old, he's a cigar-chomping type. The second is a locker person (Jeff Collins) in casual, functional clothes. The door closes again on these faces. SUPER: "An Orientation to Materials Management Operations"	MUSIC: (Vamp theme plays under, creating a rhythmic cadence to punctuate the action.) PHIL FISHER: GOIN' UP? HANK CONROY: C'MON IN.

MS outside elevator doors as a warehousing person (Larry Nichols) is waiting for the elevator.

He goes in and the doors close behind him. Before the doors open again, however, the lights flicker and the elevator bounces up and down. The riders look to one another in awe…

They try hitting the floor buttons again in a futile attempt to make the elevator continue on—up or down.

SPECIAL EFFECT

PAGE TURN or WIPE to indicate passage of time. Hank is listening to the building superintendant's voice over the elevator intercom.

MUSIC & SOUND EFFX: (The music screeches to an abrupt conclusion. Elevator noise goes off. There's a brief moment of silence.)

LARRY NICHOLS: OOH… I DON'T LIKE THE FEEL OF THAT…

HANK CONROY: …DOOR DOESN'T WANNA OPEN.

LIZ TALBOT: I THINK WE'RE BETWEEN FLOORS.

HANK CONROY: IT'S NOT GONNA BUDGE, IS IT?

JEFF COLLINS: (Checks his watch.) GREAT—I'VE GOT FIFTEEN MINUTES 'TIL I'M DUE BACK TO MY LOCKER.

HANK CONROY: LET'S EVERYBODY STAY CALM, AND WE'LL BE JUST FINE.

PHIL FISHER: IF I MIGHT MAKE A SUGGESTION—GIVE THAT EMERGENCY PHONE A TRY.

BUILDING SUPER: (Off-camera and filtered.) I'LL GET RIGHT ON THE CASE. BUT YOU'D BEST SIT TIGHT IN THERE. NO TELLIN' HOW LONG IT MIGHT TAKE TO FIX THE PROBLEM.

JEFF COLLINS: (Checks watch again.) NOW I'VE GOTTA BE BACK TO MY LOCKER IN TEN MINUTES.

LIZ TALBOT: (Not really believing it.) HEY— THEY'LL HAVE US OUTTA HERE IN NOTHING FLAT.

PHIL FISHER: DON'T JUMP TO CONCLUSIONS. TAKE IT FROM ME—YOU CAN NEVER PREDICT EXACTLY HOW LONG IT'S GONNA TAKE TO MAKE REPAIRS.

LARRY NICHOLS: WELL, IF THAT'S THE CASE, MIGHT AS WELL GET TO KNOW ONE ANOTHER. I'M LARRY NICHOLS FROM MATERIALS MANAGEMENT…

At this point, they begin to introduce them-selves...

MONTAGE of shots on mouths and hands intercut with wider shot of group as they all try to shake hands reaching across one another, hampered by the lack of space.

MONTAGE OF VOICES: (They all start talking at once, shaking hands, and introducing themselves. With the lack of space in the elevator, it becomes a hub-bub of conversation and takes on a comedic air. We hear only snatches of the interchanges...)

I THOUGHT YOU LOOKED FAMILIAR...

YOU MEAN YOU WORK IN THE MATERIALS MANAGEMENT WAREHOUSE?

THAT'S A REAL COINCIDENCE, ISN'T IT?

HANK CONROY: WELL, ALL I'VE GOT TO SAY IS THEY'D BETTER GET US OUTTA HERE OR THEY'RE GONNA HAVE A WORK SLOW DOWN IN MATERIALS MANAGEMENT.

PHIL FISHER: I DON'T BELIEVE THIS. OF ALL THE DEPARTMENTS TO GET STUCK WITH, I HAVE TO PUT UP WITH YOU MATERIALS MANAGEMENT FOLKS.

LARRY NICHOLS: WE ALL TRY TO DO THE BEST JOB WE CAN.

PHIL FISHER: (Full of self-righteousness.) YOU MATERIALS MANAGEMENT PEOPLE SURE CAN MAKE OR BREAK MY DAY. IF I DON'T GET THE RIGHT MATERIALS EVERY SINGLE MORNING, I WIND UP TAKIN' THE HEAT FROM THE CUSTOMER.

LIZ TALBOT: LOOK—THERE'S A LOT THAT GOES INTO GETTING MATERIALS AND EQUIPMENT TO EVERY LOCKER AROUND THE STATE DAY AFTER DAY...

HANK CONROY: WHILE WE'RE STUCK HERE TOGETHER, MIGHT BE WORTH-WHILE TO FIND OUT WHAT WE ALL DO IN MATERIALS MANAGEMENT.

PHIL FISHER: (Getting in another jab.) I DON'T HAVE ALL DAY, YOU KNOW.

LIZ TALBOT: HOWEVER LONG WE'RE STUCK HERE, I SHOULD WARN YOU. I'M A LITTLE CLAUSTROPHOBIC.

The men react outwardly to this admission.

Source: From "The Ups & Downs of Materials Management," written by William Van Nostran, produced and directed by Kim Cloutman, for SNET Corporate TV Center. Used by permission.

Script Example B.3:Unadvertised Structure

Excerpt 1:

VIDEO	AUDIO
FADE UP ON:	RADIO SOUNDTRACK: (Mix sounds of highway traffic going by with sound of Ray Charles Maxwell House commercial growing louder. As car passes by, lyric is filtered to simulate automobile radio sound.)
WIDE SHOT on highway early in the morning. A few cars go by. Then, as soundtrack comes up, isolate on midsize sedan. We follow it as the car goes by camera position. Then…	
CUT TO interior of car as Rich Sullivan sips coffee from Styrofoam™ cup while humming along.	(Mix sound of Rich Sullivan chiming in with Ray Charles, followed by typical morning drive time chatter, such as:) …COMIN' UP ON EIGHT-FIFTEEN HERE AT KTZ. IF YOU'RE JUST LEAVIN' FOR WORK—BETTER GRAB THAT UMBRELLA. CHANCE OF AFTERNOON SHOWERS. (Pull under.) IN A MINUTE HERE, WE'LL GO TO THE PHONES AND SEE IF WE CAN GIVE AWAY SOME FREE CD's. BUT FIRST, YOU GOTTA LISTEN FOR OUR COUNTRY QUIZ PERFORMER OF THE DAY. AND HERE SHE IS NOW… (etc., as song continues under.)
During Narrator's speech, insert ECU on open briefcase beside Rich in car. Show special promotion materials covering unopened Benechoice booklet mailing.	NARRATOR: (Voice-over.) MEET RICH SULLIVAN—A MAXWELL HOUSE SALES REP. RICH'LL BE IN AND OUT OF MORE SUPERMARKETS IN THE NEXT EIGHT HOURS THAN MOST OF US SEE IN A MONTH. MAXWELL HOUSE INSTANT'S GOT A SPECIAL PROMOTION COMING UP. SO YOU CAN BET RICH SPENT A FEW HOURS OVER THE WEEKEND GETTING READY TO PERSUADE STORE MANAGERS TO STOCK UP IN ADVANCE. RICH ALSO INTENDED TO SPEND TIME WITH HIS GF BENECHOICE BOOKLET THIS WEEKEND— DIDN'T YOU RICH?
DIFFERENT ANGLE, from rear seat as Rich pulls into supermarket lot.	
Rich addresses Narrator from rearview mirror.	RICH SULLIVAN: (To camera.) LISTEN… I PLANNED TO SKIM IT. BUT WHEN I GOT ASKED TO GO SAILING—WELL, MY PRIORITIES GOT REARRANGED.
Rich gets out of car with briefcase and goes to trunk for sample case.	NARRATOR: FOR A GUY IN RICH'S SHOES, IT'S EASY TO PUT BENEFIT PLANNING ON THE "BACK BURNER." HE'S TWENTY-EIGHT AND SINGLE. NOT A SOUL TO LOOK AFTER EXCEPT HIMSELF—AND A LONG LIST OF SUPERMARKET MANAGERS.

Closes trunk and walks toward supermarket.

RICH SULLIVAN: (To camera.) MAYBE I'LL LOOK THIS BENECHOICE STUFF OVER WHEN I GRAB A SANDWICH AT NOON…

DISSOLVE TO:

NARRATOR: (Skeptically.) SURE, RICH. WE'LL CATCH UP TO YOU LATER…

Howard Richardson in office. He stands at desk, getting items out of briefcase and arranging stacks of papers. We catch a glimpse of Benechoice booklet and worksheet showing penciled entries.

NOW *THIS* GUY'S A COMPLETELY DIFFERENT STORY: HOWARD RICHARDSON. HE'S A MANAGER IN THE PET FOODS DIVISION. HE'S IN HIS MID-FORTIES…

Howard puts suit coat on and gathers up materials to take with him.

HOWARD RICHARDSON: (To camera.) HEY, THAT'S NOT SO BAD. I STAY IN SHAPE.

NARRATOR: (Continuing right on.) …AND HE AND HIS WIFE HAVE *THREE* TEENAGERS…

TIGHT on family photo, three kids grinning through braces.

HOWARD RICHARDSON: (Glances at family photos.) NOW YOU'RE TALKIN' MAJOR PROBLEMS…

WIDER as Howard exits office and moves to area where Roberta Scott, a young African-American, is organizing for the day ahead.

NARRATOR: NEED I SAY MORE? HOWARD'S SPENT HOURS ANALYZING *HIS* CHOICES UNDER GF's NEW FLEXIBLE BENECHOICE PROGRAM.

Roberta puts bag on desk and we see Benechoice booklet in a side pocket.

HOWARD'S SECRETARY, ROBERTA SCOTT IS ALSO TRYING TO REACH A DECISION ON HER OPTIONS. LIKE HOWARD, ROBERTA'S MARRIED. SHE'S IN HER LATE TWENTIES WITH NO CHILDREN.

Howard starts to exit, then turns back for line about glasses.

HOWARD RICHARDSON: HERE'S THE ADDITION TO THE PACKAGING STUDY. I'M OFF TO HENRY'S STAFF MEETING. SEE YOU LATER. SAY—YOU GET NEW GLASSES?

ROBERTA SCOTT: HARDLY. THESE ARE *OLD* GLASSES. LENS FELL OUT OF MY GOOD ONES ON THE BEACH THIS WEEKEND. GOOD THING I HUNG ONTO THESE…(She squints.) I THINK.

DIFFERENT ANGLE as Roberta calls after Howard as he is heading down corridor.

BEFORE YOU GO, MR. HORNBEIN ASKED IF I COULD SCHEDULE YOU FOR A MEETING TOMORROW AT TWO-THIRTY. THAT'S OKAY, ISN'T IT?

HOWARD RICHARDSON: SHOULD BE. BOOK IT.

MS on Roberta working at desk.

NARRATOR: ROBERTA—DON'T FORGET TO SCHEDULE SOME TIME FOR *YOURSELF* TODAY.

ROBERTA SCOTT: (To camera.) TIME FOR *MYSELF?* IN THIS DEPARTMENT? YOU'RE A REAL BLUE-EYED OPTIMIST, AREN'T YOU?

NARRATOR: (A bit of a nag.) YOU REACH ANY DECISIONS ON BENECHOICE? YOU'RE RUNNING OUT OF TIME.

ROBERTA SCOTT: HONEY, I'M RUNNIN' OUTTA *MOTIVATION* TO READ ABOUT BENEFITS. DOESN'T QUITE GRIP YOU LIKE STEPHEN KING'S LATEST SPELL-BINDER.

NARRATOR: WITH THE LUCK YOU'VE HAD WITH EYEGLASSES LATELY—YOU OUGHTA BE SPELLBOUND BY THE SECTION ON REIMBURSEMENT ACCOUNTS.

DISSOLVE TO:

ROBERTA SCOTT: (Resigned.) OKAY, I HEAR YOU. LET MET GET THROUGH MY MORNING COFFEE, FIRST.

MS on Terri Felton walking through entrance to Dover Plant. Condense action to pick her up at desk, on phone. We see photo of her son displayed in work area.

NARRATOR: FINE—GIVES ME A CHANCE TO INTRODUCE ONE MORE PERSON— TERRI FELTON. SHE'S A CUSTOMER SERVICE REPRESENTATIVE IN HER MID-TWENTIES. SHE'S RECENTLY GONE THROUGH A DIVORCE. GOT HER HANDS FULL RAISING HER YOUNG SON, BEN. THINK THAT'S BENNY ON THE PHONE NOW...

CU on Terri.

TERRI FELTON: (Delivered à la Bob Newhart. Terri has a slight edge to her voice.)...BENNY, YOU PUT *WHAT* IN THE GOLDFISH TANK? (Beat.) THAT'S WHAT I THOUGHT YOU SAID. BENNY, WHERE'S MRS. LEVITT? (Beat.) CLEANING OUT THE GOLDFISH TANK. BENNY, I'VE TOLD YOU PLEASE NOT TO CALL MOMMY AT WORK UNLESS

IT'S A REAL EMERGENCY. NOW TELL MRS. LEVITT I'LL CALL AROUND LUNCH-TIME. AND, PLEASE, NO MORE EXPERIMENTS…

VIDEO	AUDIO
Puts down phone, starts going about her business…	NARRATOR: TERRI—YOU REALIZE YOU COULD NOW BE PAYING MRS. LEVITT WITH TAX-*FREE* DOLLARS?
…then turns to camera.	TERRI FELTON: TAX-FREE DOLLARS? SOUNDS LIKE SOMETHING FOR THE "HIGH ROLLERS." (Leans forward and delivers next line half confidentially, half jokingly. With a twinkle in the eye.) JUST BETWEEN THE TWO OF US—I'M NOT EXACTLY IN THE FIFTY-PERCENT TAX BRACKET.
Camera PUSHES IN.	
Now she listens to Narrator.	NARRATOR: LET ME PUT IT THIS WAY— RECENT CHANGES IN TAX LAWS, COMBINED WITH GF's NEW BENECHOICE PROGRAM, MAKE IT POSSIBLE FOR YOU TO STRETCH YOUR DOLLAR FURTHER— NO MATTER WHAT YOUR SALARY.

Excerpt 2:

VIDEO	AUDIO
MS on Rich Sullivan eating a burger in diner. His Benechoice booklet's propped up in front of him by a Coke glass.	RICH SULLIVAN: (Interior monologue.) IF I UNDERSTAND THIS RIGHT—USING BEFORE-TAX DOLLARS FOR THE LONG-TERM FEATURE OF THE THRIFT-INVESTMENT PLAN'S A LOT LIKE AN I.R.A…
	NARRATOR: I'VE BEEN LOOKIN' ALL OVER TOWN FOR YOU. WHERE'VE YOU BEEN?
	RICH SULLIVAN: HEY—I'VE BEEN OUT WHERE THE RUBBER MEETS THE ROAD, YOU KNOW? NOW, I WAS THINKING ABOUT OPENING AN I.R.A. AT MY BANK. MAYBE THE LONG-TERM FEATURE OF THE THRIFT-INVESTMENT PLAN'S A LOT LIKE AN I.R.A…
	NARRATOR: YES, IT CAN BE BETTER THAN AN I.R.A. IT'S ALL THERE IN YOUR BOOKLET.
	RICH SULLIVAN: HIT ME WITH THE HIGH-LIGHTS.

VIDEO	AUDIO
Rich looks to placard advertising dessert special.	NARRATOR: SEE THAT PLACARD?
	RICH SULLIVAN: STRAWBERRY SHORTCAKE?
Placard rotates to become graphic display area for TIP highlights.	SOUND EFX: (As placard rotates magically.)

Source: From "Benechoice," written by William Van Nostran, directed by James G. Libby, produced by William Hoppe for General Foods Corp. Used by permission.

Script Example B.4: Matters of Style

Excerpt 1:

VIDEO	AUDIO
TWO SHOT on both.	
	FEMALE NARRATOR: GOOD REASONS TO TAKE THE ENTIRE ISSUE OF SEXUAL HARASSMENT SERIOUSLY. BUT THEN THE QUESTION BECOMES: "WHAT CONSTITUTES SEXUAL HARASSMENT AT WORK?"
	MALE NARRATOR: NOW WE'RE GETTING TO THE CRUX OF THE PROBLEM. SURE, THERE'S A TYPE OF BEHAVIOR THAT IS BLATANT HARASSMENT. FOR INSTANCE, I CAN ENVISION THE SORT OF GUY WHO MIGHT…
	FEMALE NARRATOR: (To camera.) THIS I WANT TO SEE!
	MALE NARRATOR: OH, YOU NOT ONLY GET TO SEE IT, JENNIFER—YOU GET TO LIVE IT…
SPECIAL VIDEO EFFECT, similar to dream or other imagined event. It should be obvious television "convention."	MUSIC & SOUND EFX:(Theme and effects to clearly establish transition to fantasy sequence.)
Effect takes us through to scene set in office done in same "pop-up" art style.	
ECU on *Wall Street Journal* cover. ZOOM OUT to reveal Male Narrator reading at desk. His dress parodies the well-heeled executive: three-piece pinstripe suit, flower in lapel, gold cuff links and tie tack. He's also given a touch of gray at the temples. Both Narrators obviously "play-act" these scenes.	

MALE NARRATOR: (To himself, after a groan.) WHY DO I ALWAYS LISTEN TO THAT IDIOT BROKER? (He puts newspaper down in disgust, then speaks through his intercom.) MISS PENNEYPINCH.

FEMALE NARRATOR: (Off-camera.) YES, MR. LETCHWORTH?

MALE NARRATOR: (With a leer and un-abashed lilt in his voice.) DICTATION TIME, MISS PENNEYPINCH!

MS on entrance of Female Narrator. She is attired in a tight-fitting sweater dress, giving her a buxom appearance. Overly made up, she sports a blonde wig and cracks chewing gum. She plays this scene as a cross between Pamela Anderson and Marilyn Monroe. She moves to chair in front of desk.

FEMALE NARRATOR: (Entering through doorway with steno pad.) IS THIS TO BE INTERCOMPANY CORRESPONDENCE OR A LETTER TO THE OUTSIDE WORLD?

MALE NARRATOR: THE DOOR, MISS PENNEYPINCH … I CAN'T CONCENTRATE WITH THE DOOR OPEN.

FEMALE NARRATOR: BUT YOU KNOW WE GET SO MUCH MORE DONE WITH THE DOOR OPEN, MR. LETCHWORTH … MAYBE JUST AJAR A BIT?

MALE NARRATOR: (Fixated on her.) MY DEAR, YOU'RE LOOKING FAR TOO LOVELY TODAY TO EVEN THINK OF LEAVING THE "JAR" "ADOOR"… (realizing his flub.) UH … DOOR AJAR. (He closes door firmly. Then stalks about her as he begins to dictate.) MEMO TO R.O. HAMILTON …SUBJECT: SEVERE INVENTORY SHORT-AGES … THE RECENT RASH OF INVEN-TORY SHORTAGES, COMMA… (He loses train of thought, fixating on her again. She looks up.) READ BACK WHAT YOU HAVE SO FAR…

DIFFERENT ANGLE. As she reads, he leans over her and places arm around her. He's obviously not listening.

FEMALE NARRATOR: TO R.O. HAMILTON… SUBJECT: SEVERE INVENTORY SHORT-AGES… THE RECENT RASH OF INVEN-TORY SHORTAGES, COMMA…

MALE NARRATOR: (Fondling her shoulder.) MISS PENNEYPINCH, THAT PERFUME… YOU KNOW WHAT IT DOES TO ME? (He nuzzles.)

FEMALE NARRATOR: (To the audience, breaking into her Narrator persona.) JEEZ, WHAT A TRITE COME-ON... (She rises, and refers to steno pad.) I THINK YOU LEFT OFF IN THE MIDDLE OF A SENTENCE, MR. LETCHWORTH...

MALE NARRATOR: (Trying to compose himself.) I DID? OH, YES... I WAS SAYING THAT YOUR PERFUME BRINGS OUT THE BEAST IN ME... (He pursues, she moves away, but it puts her in front of sofa.)

FEMALE NARRATOR: (Reading from pad.) YOU REALLY WANT MR. HAMILTON TO KNOW THAT "THE RECENT RASH OF INVENTORY SHORTAGES, COMMA, BRINGS OUT THE BEAST IN ME?

MALE NARRATOR: PUT THAT ASIDE. (Taking pad and pencil from her.) I'M TALK-ING ABOUT YOU AND ME, MISS PENNEYPINCH. WE CAN MAKE SUCH BEAUTIFUL MUSIC TOGETHER. (He leans into her, forcing her to plop onto the sofa.)

FEMALE NARRATOR: BUT WHAT ABOUT THE DUET YOU HAVE WITH—*MRS.* LETCHWORTH?

MALE NARRATOR: (He leans over her and kisses her neck.) COMPARED TO YOUR LOVELINESS, MRS. LETCHWORTH'S A WORN-OUT TUNE... AN OLD REFRAIN...

FEMALE NARRATOR: (To camera.) I JUST HOPE MOTHER NEVER SEES THIS... (She breaks free of him, rises, gathers her compo-sure, and emphatically says:) MR. LETCHWORTH, SHOULDN'T WE GET DOWN TO BUSINESS?

MALE NARRATOR: WELL PUT, MISS PENNEYPINCH. (With a sense of intimida-tion.) I HOPE YOU REALIZE YOUR CONTIN-UED EMPLOYMENT HERE DEPENDS ON MY PERSONAL ESTIMATE OF YOUR PERFORMANCE?

FEMALE NARRATOR: (Intimidated.) YES, I'M WELL AWARE OF THAT, MR. LETCHWORTH.

MALE NARRATOR: GOOD. BECAUSE IF YOU'RE GOING TO PLAY IN MY ORCHES-TRA—YOU'D BETTER PICK UP THE TEMPO!

FEMALE NARRATOR: MR. LETCHWORTH… I DON'T KNOW WHAT TO SAY…

MALE NARRATOR: ACTIONS SPEAK LOUDER THAN WORDS, MISS PENNEYPINCH… (He pursues with renewed vigor.)

VIDEO	AUDIO
SPECIAL VIDEO EFFECT to highlight the transition… DISSOLVE TO: MS on Narrators in studio setting, seated on stools in foreground. They are dressed as seen at the outset.	MUSIC & SOUND EFX: (Transitional theme to reality.)

Source: From "Sexual Harassment: Fact or Fiction?" written by William Van Nostran, directed by James G. Libby, produced by William J. Benham for AT&T Corporate Television. Used by permission.

Script Example 5.5 Matters of Style—Excerpt B

Excerpt 2:

VIDEO	AUDIO
Scene in open office area where Cindy works with other programmers. Cindy is wrapping up a phone conversation at her desk as George comes over to her.	GEORGE: (Quite sincere.) CINDY…JUST WANT TO LET YOU KNOW THAT, FOR THE NEW KID ON THE BLOCK, YOU'RE DOING JUST FINE. THIS PROGRAMMING'S FIRST-RATE.
	CINDY: WHAT A RELIEF. I SURE SPENT ENOUGH TIME ON IT… RUINED LAST WEEKEND, IN FACT.
	GEORGE: JUST ONE LITTLE AREA NEEDS TO BE REWORKED SOME…
	CINDY: OH, WONDERFUL—HOW BADLY DID I REALLY MESS UP?
He pulls up a chair and places an arm around her as they pour over her work.	GEORGE: IT'S NOT A MISTAKE, ACTUALLY. JUST A LITTLE PECULIARITY IN OUR APPROACH TO DATA TRANSFER. YOU SEE… OUR COMPUTERS ARE SET UP TO PROCESS INCOMING SERVICE RE-QUESTS LIKE THIS…

CLOCK WIPE EFFECT:	DIFFERENT ANGLE on Cindy's area. Shot features Jack in foreground straightening his desk before going home. Cindy is bent over stack of computer printouts.

CINDY: FIVE O'CLOCK ALREADY? WHAT A WEEK!

JACK: YOU'RE NOT KIDDIN'. I'M GETTIN' OUTTA HERE ON TIME FOR ONCE. I'M GONNA CRASH IN FRONT OF THE TV— DON'T CARE WHAT'S ON. YOU READY TO LEAVE?

CINDY: I'M JUST GOING TO FINISH UP A FEW THINGS.

JACK: OKAY. HAVE A GOOD WEEKEND…

GEORGE: CINDY! YOU LOOK AS BEAT AS I FEEL. SOME WEEK, HUH?

CINDY: WELL, AT LEAST IT MAKES YOU APPRECIATE THE WEEKENDS.

GEORGE: AT THIS MOMENT, I'M JUST LOOKING FORWARD TO GETTING OVER TO RYAN'S. HEY—WHY DON'T YOU C'MON OVER, AND I'LL BUY YOU A COCKTAIL?

CINDY: NO, REALLY. I'VE GOT TO GET HOME…

GEORGE: HEAVY DATE, OR WHAT?

CINDY: A LOT LESS EXCITING, I'M AFRAID.

Hand on arm; trying to be sympathetic

GEORGE: LOOK. JUST 'CAUSE ONE GUY TURNS OUT TO BE A LOUSE DOESN'T MEAN WE'RE ALL BUMS. ONE DRINK. (Beat.) IT'LL MAKE MY WEEK…

CINDY: (Relenting, but hardly enthusiastic.) OH, ALL RIGHT. BUT JUST FOR A FEW MINUTES. THEN I'VE GOT TO GET GOING. SERIOUSLY, I DO HAVE SOMETHING PLANNED.

Source: From "Sexual Harassment: Fact or Fiction?" written by William Van Nostran, directed by James G. Libby, produced by William J. Benham for AT&T Corporate Television. Used by permission.

Treatment Example B.6: Sample Linear Video Treatment

PROGRAM: Ohaus Toploader (A precision scale used for accurate weighing of small items.)

We FADE UP on an extreme wide angle shot of the Ohaus GT Toploader balance in a stark studio environment. The GT Toploader is bathed in a white light with a hard cyc sweeping behind and around it. Lighting gels give the cyc a diffuse color wash.(1)

The camera begins a slow PUSH IN. The MUSIC is an electronic style theme, slightly active and growing, but not too fast.(2) The Off-Camera Narrator sets the stage…

"Introducing the GT series: affordable, versatile, state-of-the-art electronic toploaders from Ohaus. The GT Series balances combine all the high-tech features you want with the solid, sensible design you expect from Ohaus…"(3)

As this opening narration continues, highlighting key features, the long PUSH IN to the balance continues. At the same time, we INTERCUT near subliminal shots showing the GT Toploader in the same studio environment with a wide range of items appearing on the scale.(4)

When the PUSH IN finally concludes, the camera settles on a shot of the GT balance framed to the right of the screen. The lighting is quite dramatic, giving the scale a handsome, high-tech look.(5)

Now we begin a short sequence in which the narration highlights the diverse environments in which the GT Series of toploaders can perform.

"The GT Series of toploaders is equally at home in the scientific lab… the electronic lab… the school lab… the manufacturing plant… the test kitchen… or the medical lab.

"Ohaus GT balances will prove themselves time and again, no matter where you use them…"(6)

During this segment, the screen shows a series of carefully timed DISSOLVES in which various props appear beside the balance to visually depict the differing environments. For instance, when we mention scientific lab, a group of test tubes and beakers appears next to the balance. (One of the beakers might contain dry ice to animate the frame with rising vapors.)(7)

When we mention electronic lab, the test tubes will DISSOLVE off as the picture is transformed into a tableau featuring the balance with various electronic components.(7)

The Narrator mentions "school lab" and the scene DISSOLVES into a shot featuring the scale with a grouping of textbooks and slide rule. When we talk about the manufacturing plant, a miniature conveyor belt appears by the GT balance with small cartons moving along the belt and off the lower left frame. In each instance, the transition includes a change in the colored gels used to illuminate the cyc to intensify the effect of the same scale appearing in different environments.(7)

Next, we transition to a segment which demonstrates key features and benefits of the Ohaus GT Series precision toploaders. For this sequence, the GT balance is positioned in the center of the frame, the CAMERA looking down on the scale at a slight angle.(8) Once again we use a series of DISSOLVES as a variety of objects magically appear on the scale, each chosen to demonstrate a specific application—from taring and basic weighing to batching, check weighing, parts counting and animal weighing.(9)

The narration provides commentary on the GT balance's performance in each application. Through these diverse applications we also demonstrate the function of key features:

- easy-to-use FillGuide
- the Over/Under Indicator
- the Movable FineRange
- the Metric, non-metric and three custom units
- and Parts Counting.

Throughout, the large digital display read outs appear as an INSET (10) in the picture showing the interaction between the item being weighed and the functional display. During this segment, some shots of the GT precision balance will be taken from overhead, looking directly down on the balance. Once again, each change in the item being weighed will be accompanied by a change in the lighting effect on the background cyc.(11)

For the program close, the electronic MUSICAL (12) bed picks up in tempo. The narration provides additional general information about the Ohaus GT Series—stressing versatility, quality, accessories, cost-effectiveness, and the company's warranty and service commitment.

During this narrative segment, the screen will now go to a series of fast-paced cuts in sharp contrast to the DISSOLVES the audience has been seeing. Each cut will feature the GT balance weighing various items as seen previously and shots of the balance with the props symbolizing the many environments the GT balance can call "home."(13)

The final shot of the program is a reverse of the slow PUSH IN used to open the presentation. During this shot, the Narrator is telling the viewer…

"For a closer look at the Ohaus GT Series of balances, contact your local dealer representative or call Ohaus direct. Ask for a demonstration. Or, let an Ohaus specialist help you select the right balance for your needs."

Final titles and credits appear over the slow PULL BACK to the opening shot. Then we…(14)

FADE TO BLACK

NOTES

In this visuals-and-voice treatment, the writer must describe the sights and sounds that will unfold on the screen as a chronological sequence of events. This video treatment for a brief program depends largely on props and staging, lighting, camera lenses and angles, and camera movement to create the stylized visual look of a relatively simple, low-budget concept. A limbo studio space is used to showcase the product as props symbolizing a variety of applications appear "magically" on cue.

1) The writer begins by describing the opening shot, clearly placing the action in a studiosetting, while describing the visual "look" in terms of light and texture.
2) The writer describes camera action in non-technical terms and suggests how music accompanies the action.
3) Sample narrative copy establishes the tone or "voice," which is slightly on the clinical side.
4) Use of a subliminal editing technique is described as a component of the unfolding on-screen viewing experience.
5) Again, the writer not only describes the action, but also suggests the visual "look and feel" in terms of staging and lighting.
6) The narration for these scenes can be conveyed quite succinctly…
7) …the accompanying visuals, however, require more detail to flesh out. Notice that although the treatment is specific , it's also suggestive. (The reference to dry ice to create vapors, for example.) From a production perspective, the effect of various props appearing beside the balance requires a "locked off" camera shot so the scale and background remain in the identical position with only the props changing around it. The director will understand this is what's required. Less technical script readers would only be baffled by technicaljargon such as "locked off shot."
8) Here, the specific framing of a shot is important in visualizing the action that follows, so the writer includes this specific information in the treatment.
9) Details relating to the specific content of this segment should be provided in the content outline. Here, the writer summarizes action to focus primarily on the overall function of the visuals in a general way.

10) Information about digital display read-outs is an important element, so the writer describes how this will be integrated into the action.

11) Since this is a highly stylized concept, the writer suggests how lighting might heighten visual impact.

12) Music plays a functional role in establishing a faster pace as the short program draws to a close.

13) Not all content points need detailed narrative description in the treatment. Here, content is alluded to, as well as a change in the overall pacing of the program.

14) The writer has given thought to closing the program by reversing the camera action and visualization described in the opening.

Source: From "Ohaus Toploader," written by William Van Nostran for the Ohaus Company. Used by permission

Treatment Example B.7: Sample Linear Video Treatment 2:

PROGRAM: You're Hired! The Nuts and Bolts of Job Hunting

Open on shot of female TV news reporter outside plant delivering a field report. "So, as of next week, employees at this 60-year-old plant will be looking for new jobs. As the gates close for good, one has to wonder, where will the new jobs come from? This is Brenda Devlin—Channel 6 News."

Segue to groups of employees coming out of the plant. We catch bits and pieces of their conversation. Their glib joking masks the inner turmoil.(1) "Hey, Bobby—there's your chance to be on TV."

"Well, I don't know about the rest of you. But I feel like I've earned a good, long vacation."(2)

"Yeah—we paid into unemployment all these years. 'Bout time we took a little somethin' out…"(2)

Follow two of these employees to a car as they share a ride. One, Nick Conti, is in his mid-thirties. The other, somewhat older, looks around, shakes his head and comments. "I can remember the first time I came through these gates."(2)

"Somewhere along the way, I got the notion I might just work here 'til I won the lottery, kicked the bucket or retired. Never dreamed it would all just end like this."(2)

They commiserate, talking about how all the rumors have come to pass.

They're about to drive off when Manny asks Nick: "You worried about gettin' work, Nick?"(2)

"Why worry? Like my dad used to say: 'anyone willing to work can find work. Simple as that.'"(2)

They drive off as opening titles and credits appear over a dinner scene in the Conti's home. Nick's wife, Linda, is seen fussing at the kids: "Stacey, put some of those brussel sprouts on your plate."

There's tension in the air. Nick trys too hard to act as though everything's normal. But around the table—there's this feeling a bomb might go off. The kids are eager to finish and be dismissed. (3) Left alone, Nick and his wife Linda talk. Nick still seems overly confident about finding work.(4)

Cut to (5) television station as the News Reporter, Brenda Devlin, talks with her News Director.

"I want to follow the story beyond the plant closing. Look at the people-side of the story. Report on how their lives are effected. What obstacles they encounter looking for work. Some are going to pick themselves up, go out and find work. Others will flounder. What'll make the difference? I want to show just what it takes to find a job in today's economy."(6)

The News Director expresses concern over her workload, then reluctantly gives her a go-ahead to follow the story.

Cut to a classroom setting as a woman leads a Job Search Group in discussion. She's a dynamic speaker, very much in charge. "Looking for a job *is* a full-time job…" As she delivers her "pep talk," we PAN around the room at faces listening intently. Many are familiar from the opening scene—including Manny. But Nick is not among them. "It's just like selling a product—only you're the product. Now, before we get into your workbook, let's talk a little about what you and your families will experience emotionally…"(7)

Her speech continues voice-over, while the action shifts to scenes at the local Unemployment Office. We focus on shots of various individuals waiting on lines and completing the paperwork needed to collect compensation. Here, Nick is among the group. We see him with some cronies. Many are among those in the Job Search class. The segment ends with a brief exchange between Nick and another laid-off worker: "You sign up for that Job Search class, Nick?"

"Aw, who needs it?" Nick responds. "They're just tryin' to make us feel better about bein' on the street. I didn't need help findin' my last job. I know what it takes."

Cut to the Reporter interviewing the Job Search Group Leader as background for her story."So what will make the difference between those who land good jobs quickly and those who don't?"

"Attitude and technique?"

"Technique? I don't follow."

"Basic job-hunting skills. Think about it. Nobody teaches you how to organize and conduct a job campaign. Most people are rank amateurs at it. And I'm talking about simple little things—like knowing how to use the phone to your advantage…"(7)

Cut to shot of Nick at pay phone in coffee shop. We listen in as he makes the cardinal sin of asking bluntly: "Do you have any openings?" We see him react as the voice on the other end responds, "Sorry. We're just not hiring now."(7)

Cut back to Reporter and Group Leader as she continues making points about job-hunting skills. "You have to use a system so you know how many phone calls you should be making each day. You've gotta keep records for follow-ups and referrals. Of course, before you even begin looking, you should know how you're going to sell yourself to an employer…"

We segue to classroom shot as the Group Leader is now working with the class. "So you're going to start by taking an inventory of your skills. Things you know how to do well. From this, we'll develop a way to present yourself to an employer positively. You'll learn how to capitalize on your strengths and minimize weaknesses."(7)

As the group begins to work, we DISSOLVE to Nick in an office being interviewed by a rather intimidating supervisor, a real no-nonsense type. "So just what makes you think you'd be able to do a good job for us?"

Nick's thrown off-balance by the bluntness of the question. He responds tentatively, "Well—I really need this job…" After a few seconds of silence, the interviewer comes back with another question. "It's a lot less money than what you're used to making. How do I know you won't stay here a couple of months and then up and quit when you find something better?"(7)

Cut back to classroom as Group Leader is going around the room for respnses. "Okay, Marilyn—how would you answer that question?"(7)

We hear Marilyn give her structured response. "Well, one way of handling that is to say, 'In my old job, I had to travel a lot farther. Since this is closer to home—I'm willing to work for slightly less to begin with since I'll be paying less to commute."(7)

We cut back to Nick, still floundering. "Well… you see… if I come to work here.. I wouldn't really be looking anymore…"(7)

We cut back to the reporter talking with the Group Leader as she makes another point: "The folks who don't go about it right, often find themselves dead in the water. They're depressed to begin with—then they start facing a lot of rejection…"97)

Cut to another shot of Nick on phone in his kitchen. We watch his reaction as the voice on the other end says, "I'm sorry, Mr. Conti. The position's been filled already. You should've called about that interview on Monday. But we'll keep your application on file…"(7)

He hangs up. His wife, making a sandwich, senses without asking that it's another blind alley.

Cut back to Reporter and Group Leader as she continues on. "They're not prepared for the isolation. Pretty soon, it affects them at home…"97)

Cut to TIGHT SHOT of Nick. His wife is clipping his hair.

"Hold still, Nick."

"How can I hold still when you keep askin' questions."

"I just want to know if they said when they'd get back to you?"

"They didn't say much of anything definite."

"Well, didn't you ask 'em?"

Nick jumps up and throws down the sports section of the newspaper. "Dammit—you know so much about gettin' a job, why don't *you* go quit your part-time work at day care and get somethin' full-time, and I'll stay home with the kids. Cook and wash and gossip with Corrine."(9)

Notes

This treatment of a dramatization is meant to motivate displaced blue-collar workers to take job search skill-training seriously. In addition to describing action in each scene, a treatment for a dramatization should suggest character, dialogue and how dramatic vignettes relate to or illustrate key learning points.

1) Here the writer sets the scene and describes the action involved on the day of a plant closing. A TV Reporter provides exposition.

2) Some sample dialogue conveys a sense of style and communicates character. From the beginning, it is clear this production involves a "slice of life" reality style in the vein of a docudrama.

3) In just a few sentences, the writer conveys the sense of tension among family members, which is the sole function of the scene.

4) It's not necessary to flesh out each and every scene in a treatment. Here, the writer describes the action with broad brush strokes. (In the actual draft script, this scene seemed superfluous and was omitted.)

5) Reference to transitions suggests a fast-paced, docudrama style.

6) We begin to see that the TV Reporter in the opening scene will become an important character and storytelling device.

7) Juxtaposition of Job Search Group Leader scenes with vignettes of Nick committing job search mistake provides a structural framework for contrasting good and poor job search techniques.

8) Action of haircut provides a context for the dialogue that follows. The writer had to defend this stage business in a production-planning meeting. Is the wife giving the husband a haircut simply a bit of stage action? No, the haircut has symbolic value. Raising issues such as: Is the wife doing the haircut because they're trying to live on a tight budget? Or, has she always done this? Is Nick especially concerned about his appearance because he's going on interviews? The action has symbolic value and was kept in the production. It is an example of how visuals communicate in ways that narration and dialogue cannot.

9) Conflict is the essence of dramatic action. Here the stress of job hunting begins to tell on family relationships.

Source: From "You're Hired! The Nuts and Bolts of Job Hunting,"™ written by William Van Nostran, created and produced by Karli & Associates and The Prudential, Audio Visual Communications Division. Used by permission.

Script Example B.8: Integrating Music into the Script

VIDEO	AUDIO
	SHIRLEY COOPER/INSTRUCTOR: MAKING THE TRANSITION FROM A LONG PERIOD OF UNEMPLOYMENT TO THE WORLD OF WORK IS THE KIND OF MAJOR CHANGE THAT CAN PROVE STRESSFUL.
	WHAT DOES STRESS FEEL LIKE? SOME PEOPLE EXPERIENCE STRESS PHYSI-CALLY—SOME MENTALLY AND EMOTION-ALLY. IN SOME WAYS, IT'S A LITTLE LIKE A ROLLER COASTER RIDE…
MOS FOOTAGE of roller coaster ride. Begin with sequence of roller coaster going slowly toward the top.	SOUND EFX & MUSIC: (Mix of carnival music and sounds of roller coaster and riders.)
	SHIRLEY COOPER/INSTRUCTOR: FIRST THERE'S THE ANTICIPATION OF THE SLOW, STEEP CLIMB UPWARD…
SLO-MO of roller coaster reaching the peak…	THEN THERE'S THAT BRIEF MOMENT WHEN YOU SEEM SUSPENDED IN TIME AT THE VERY TOP—STOMACH FULL OF KNOTS.
	AND THEN, THE EXCITEMENT OF FREE FALL—GRAVITY TAKES OVER.
Then normal action as it descends. INTER-CUT reactions of riders.	AND FINALLY, THE EXHILARATION OF MAKING IT SAFELY TO THE END OF THE RIDE.
CU on Shirley Cooper.	SOME OF THE STRESSES YOU EXPERI-ENCE TRAVELING TO THE WORLD OF WORK MAY MAKE YOU FEEL LIKE YOU'RE ON A ROLLER COASTER.
INTERCUT MOS footage of roller coast with almost subliminal shots of Laura, Eduardo and James Scott as seen previously.	USUALLY, THE PERIODS *CLOSEST* TO THE ACTUAL CHANGE ARE THE MOST STRESSFUL, LIKE THAT FIRST DAY OF CLASS… THE FIRST INTERVIEW… THE FIRST DAY ON THE JOB…
	ANTICIPATING THE CHANGE IS LIKE GOING UP THE ROLLER COASTER—THE CLOSER TO THE INSTANT OF CHANGE—THE GREATER THE FEAR.

Source: From "The Choice is Yours,"™ written by William Van Nostran, directed by Walter Schoenknecht, created and produced by Karli & Associations and The Prudential, Audio Visual Communications Division. Used by permission.

Script Example B.9: Audiocassette Script

Excerpt A

MUSIC: (Energetic upbeat rock logo theme hits full for five seconds and is gone.)

ANNOUNCER: W-K-G-F! ALL SALES RADIO! ONE HUNDRED PERCENT ON YOUR DIAL AND SERVING THE WORLDS OF… (Echo) GENERAL FOODS (Echo out.)… WITH MUSIC AND ENTERTAINMENT THAT SELLS IT LIKE IT IS!

MUSIC: (Musical notes G-F-F-G, al la NBC chimes.)

SOUND: (Hovering helicopter, interior perspective; FADE UP and UNDER.)

HOST: (Speaking over copter effect.) WELCOME TO WKGF. I'M YOUR HOST, (actor's name), AND I'LL BE BRINGING YOU THE (AHEM) OVERVIEW TO HELP YOU PROFIT FROM THIS SERIES OF SIX PROGRAMS DESIGNED TO HELP YOU GO FAR ON THE ROAD TO SALES PROFESSIONALISM.

SOUND: (Copter UP briefly, then UNDER.)

HOST: TODAY, ON WKGF, YOU'LL BE TUNING IN TO CHARLIE "THE COLD" CALL'S CALL-IN SHOW TO GET SOME REAC-TIONS FROM OUT THERE ON THE ROAD…

DR. RUTH WILL BE ADVISING YOU ON "GOOD SALES"…

YOU'LL HEAR THE LATEST CHAPTER IN THE ADVENTURES OF AMERICA'S FAVORITE SALES REP ON WKGF's AWARD-WINNING SOAP OPERA, "AS THE WORLD SELLS,"… FOL-LOWED BY EXCITING SPORTS ACTION AS PETE SAMPRAS FACES IVAN LENDL AT THE GF OPEN…

AND, CLOSING WKGF'S BROADCAST DAY, DR. FAIRLEIGH LUCID WITH SOME THOUGHTS TO REFLECT ON.

SOUND: (Copter UP and UNDER.)

HOST: NOW FROM UP HERE, YOUR SITUATION LOOKS VERY GOOD. UP AHEAD, JUST OVER THE HORIZON, I CAN SEE AN EVEN BRIGHTER FUTURE. THERE IS SOME COM-PETING TRAFFIC ALONG THE WAY… A POSSIBLE ROAD BLOCK OR TWO, BUT LET'S SEE IF WE CAN HELP YOU GET AHEAD OF THE ONE AND STEER CLEAR OF THE OTHER. YOU'RE DOING FINE, AND WE'RE GOING TO KEEP YOU ON THE MOVE!

SOUND: (Copter UP.)

HOST: OH, I SEE IT'S TIME NOW FOR YOUR FAVORITE CALL-IN SHOW. OVER TO YOU CHARLIE!

SOUND: (Copter UP and OUT followed by bright, strident phone ring.)

CHARLIE: (Nasal, sniffily, chronic cold.) THANKS, (host's name). CHARLIE "THE COLD" CALL HERE, READY TO POP OPEN A CAN OF WORMS. WHADDA YOU SAY WE TAKE A COUPLE OF QUICK CALLS, OKAY? YOU'RE LIVE.

REP ONE: (Filter.) NO OFFENSE, BUT IF YOU REALLY WANT TO HELP ME FIND A BRIGHTER FUTURE...

CHARLIE: YEAH?

REP ONE: (Filter.) ...TELL ME HOW TO GET MY CUSTOMERS TO LISTEN TO ME. ONE WON'T HEAR ME OUT, ANOTHER JUST WALKS AWAY, OR THEY MAKE UP THEIR MINDS BEFORE I FINISH! AND ONE OTHER THING...

CHARLIE: TALK TO ME.

REP ONE: (Filter.) WHAT DO YOU DO WITH CUSTOMERS WHO GIVE PREFERENTIAL TREATMENT TO THE COMPETITION IN RETURN FOR PREMIUMS AND FREE TICKETS AND STUFF LIKE THAT, HUH?

CHARLIE: HOW ABOUT GIVING THEM BETTER SERVICE THAN THE COMPETITION?

Excerpt B

SOUND: (Phone rings.)

CHARLIE: THINK WE HIT A NERVE HERE, ALL RIGHT, ALL RIGHT. YOU'RE ON THE AIR... WHAT'S BUGGING YOU, PAL?

REP TWO: (Filter.) WHILE THE JOB CAN BE FUN AND EXCITING...

CHARLIE: HERE IT COMES!

REP TWO: (Filter.) WELL, LET'S FACE IT, WE DO HAVE OUR SHARE OF UNCOOPERATIVE CUSTOMERS AND TOUGH VOL-UME OBJECTIVES TO MEET. WE HAVE TO SELL MORE AND FASTER, AND NOW YOU'RE GOING TO TELL US SOMETHING ELSE WE SHOULD BE DOING?! GIMME A BREAK.

CHARLIE: OKAY, OKAY. THIS IS YOUR CAN OF WORMS, (host's first name), SO IT'S BACK TO YOU.

SOUND: (Copter UP and OUT.)

HOST: I HEAR YOU, CHARLIE. AND YOU DOWN THERE—I CAN SEE THAT YOU'RE CAUGHT BETWEEN THE PROVERBIAL ROCK AND A HARD PLACE, BUT I THINK WE CAN EASE THAT SITUATION, TOO. OH—WAIT A MINUTE—I CAN SEE THERE ARE SOME GF CUSTOMERS HEADING FOR THEIR TELEPHONES. COULD THERE BE ANOTHER SIDE TO THIS STORY, CHARLIE?

SOUND: (Phones ringing madly. FADE IN and UNDER.

CHARLIE: CAN YOU HEAR THOSE PHONES, (host)? THE SWITCHBOARD'S TURNED INTO A CHRISTMAS TREE. (On phone.) YOU'RE LIVE…

CUSTOMER ONE: (Filter.) YOU WANT THE OTHER SIDE OF THE STORY? TALK ABOUT NOT LISTENING—YOU SALESPEOPLE NEVER LISTEN TO MY OBJECTIONS, NEVER ANSWER MY QUESTIONS—JUST KEEP TALKING, TALKING, TALKING…

SOUND: (Phone rings.)

CHARLIE: GET IT OFF YOUR CHEST.

CUSTOMER TWO: (Filter.) CAN'T YOU TEACH THEM SOMETHING BESIDES THOSE WORN-OUT PREPARED SPEECHES? I GOT ENOUGH CANNED GOODS ALREADY. WHEN ARE THEY GOING TO TALK TO *ME*—ABOUT *MY* STORE? ON TOP OF THAT, THEY COST ME TIME AND MONEY TRYING TO SELL ME STUFF I CAN'T USE.

Excerpt C

ANNOUNCE: (Phone rings.) NOW, HERE TO ANSWER THOSE EMBARRASSING QUESTIONS AND PUT YOUR MIND AT EASE IS SALES THERAPIST DR. RUTH BESTTIMING WITH HER PRIZE-WINNING PROGRAM, "GOOD SALES!" WHAT'S UP, DR. RUTH?

DR. RUTH: YOUR SALES, I HOPE. (Giggles.)

ANNOUNCE: YOU HEARD, DR. RUTH, THE CONFLICTING POSITIONS OF THE SALES REPS AND THEIR CUSTOMERS?

DR. RUTH: SURE. IT'S A VERY NATURAL CONFLICT—VERY NATURAL.

ANNOUNCE: SO, WHO'S RIGHT AND WHO'S WRONG?

DR. RUTH: AS IS USUAL IN THESE CASES, EVERYONE IS A LITTLE BIT RIGHT AND A LITTLE BIT WRONG. BUT, REALISTICALLY, SINCE THE SALES REP TYPICALLY INITIATES THE CONTACT, HE OR SHE SETS THE TONE. AND, IN MY EXPERIENCE, AN OVERLY AGGRESSIVE "SELLING" TONE OFTEN STIMULATES THE PROBLEM.

ANNOUNCE: BUT A SALES REPRESENTATIVE HAS TO BE AGGRESSIVE, TAKE CHARGE, MAKE THINGS HAPPEN.

DR. RUTH: THERE ARE AS MANY WAYS TO MAKE A SALE AS TO MAKE LOVE—MAYBE MORE. AND WHAT WE ARE TRYING TO DO HERE ON "GOOD SALES" IS HELP ALL YOU SALES REPRESENTATIVES OUT THERE DISCOVER THAT YOU HAVE MORE ALTERNATIVES THAN YOU THINK. BUT YOU WILL HAVE TO THINK ABOUT WHAT MOTIVATES YOU TO SELL... EXAMINE YOUR ATTITUDES TOWARDS YOUR CUSTOMERS... AND ASK YOURSELF WHAT IS YOUR ROLE AS A SALES REPRESENTATIVE.

ANNOUNCE: DO TELL, DOCTOR.

DR. RUTH: FIRST OF ALL, SOMETIMES THE PERCEPTION OF "SELLING" CAN CONTRIBUTE TO OUR DIFFICULTIES.

ANNOUNCE: REALLY?

DR. RUTH: THINK ABOUT IT. "SELL!" CAN BE CONSIDERED A CONFRONTATIONAL WORD. ONE HUMAN BEING INDUCING ANOTHER HUMAN BEING TO BUY SOMETHING, SOMETIMES WITH NO REGARD AS TO WHETHER THEY NEED IT OR NOT. DO YOU LIKE THAT?

ANNOUNCE: NO.

DR. RUTH: WHAT DO *YOU* DO IF YOU FEEL SOMEONE IS MANIPULATING YOU LIKE THAT?

ANNOUNCE: I RESIST.

DR. RUTH: AH! YOU SEE? AUTOMATICALLY A HOSTILE ENVIRONMENT IS CREATED AND A HOSTILE ENVIRONMENT IS CONDUCIVE NEITHER TO LOVE NOR GOOD SALES.

ANNOUNCE: OH, TOO BAD. BUT STAY TUNED FOR TODAY'S EPISODE OF "AS THE WORLD SELLS." I THINK YOU'LL FIND IT VERY MUCH ATTUNED TO OUR DISCUSSION. GOODBYE FOR NOW AND GOOD SALES!

MUSIC: (Theme UP to conclusion.)

Excerpt D

MUSIC: ("Soap" theme on organ IN, then PULL UNDER.)

SOAP ANN: AND NOW, "AS THE WORLD SELLS..."

MUSIC: (Theme UP FULL and UNDER.)

SOAP ANN: ON OUR LATEST EPISODE, ANDY DOOLEY, UP AND COMING YOUNG SALES REP, DEMONSTRATED HIS ABILITY TO GRASP EVEN THE MOST TECHNICAL ASPECTS OF THE THEORY OF SELLING. BUT COULD HE PUT THEORY INTO ACTION? WE JOIN HIM NOW ON HIS FIRST CALL OF THE DAY...

SOUND: (Supermarket BKD; checkout counter dominant; bags being packed. Footsteps approach.)

ANDY: (Fading IN.) AH, THERE YOU ARE, MR. CANON. HAVE I GOT SOME GOOD NEWS FOR YOU TODAY!

CANON: (Hurried and hassled.) YOU'RE TAKING EARLY RETIRE-MENT? (Calling out.) OPEN UP NUMBER SIX! (Normal.) EXCUSE ME, I'M BUSY.

SOUND: (Two pairs of footsteps walking, one trying to keep up with the other.)

ANDY: YOU'LL WANT TO KNOW WHAT'S NEW ABOUT FROSTY FUDGE.

CANON: I KNOW WHAT'S NEW ABOUT FROSTY FUDGE—WHEN DID *YOU* FIND OUT? (Off mike.) URSULA, DON'T STACK THE PAPER TOWELS MORE THAN FOUR LEVELS HIGH, PLEASE. ONLY YOU CAN HELP PREVENT AVALANCHES.

JAMES, LEAVE THE BOTTLES AND BAG FOR A WHILE AT NUM-BER SIX. THANK YOU.

ANDY: SO YOU KNOW WE'VE ADDED TWO NEW FLAVORS?

CANON: YES. YOUR COMPETITION TOLD ME.

SOUND: (Shopping cart wheels in; footsteps stop.)

CUSTOMER: ARE YOU THE MANAGER, SIR?

CANON: YES MA'AM, CAN I HELP YOU?

CUSTOMER: I CERTAINLY HOPE SO. THERE'S NO MORE SANKA.

CANON: AISLE TWO, MA'AM... THE END OPPOSITE THE CHECK-OUT.

CUSTOMER: THAT'S WHERE IT *USED* TO BE.

ANDY: THERE'S ROOM IN YOUR FREEZER FOR TWO FACINGS OF THE STRAWBERRY...

CANON: THERE'S NO ROOM. (To customer.) I'LL FIND IT FOR YOU, MA'AM.

CUSTOMER: I SHOULD HOPE SO! I CAN'T DRINK ANYTHING ELSE! IMAGINE BEING OUT OF SANKA!

Excerpt D

SOUND: (Copter UP then UNDER.)

HOST: THE TRAFFIC ON THE ROAD TO SUCCESS IS PRETTY HEAVY NOW. TO STAY ON THIS ROAD AND KEEP UP TO SPEED CALLS FOR TOP NOTCH SKILLS IN FOLLOWING THE SALES MOTION. YOU'VE HEARD ABOUT THE SALES MOTION AND ARE PROBABLY WONDERING WHAT IT'S ALL ABOUT. WELL, LET'S SWITCH YOU NOW TO COURTLY FOREST HILLS AND COLORFUL JEAN PAVLOVA COVERING THE SAMPRAS-LENDL MATCH AT PARALLEL PARK IN WESTCHESTER.

SOUND: (Copter UP and OUT; CROSS FADING to tennis hits, polite "Awww" from crowd, followed by decorous applause. Game continues.)

FOREST: SAMPRAS TAKES THE FIRST GAME AND THE SERVE GOES TO LENDL. WHAT SHOULD WE BE LOOKING FOR IN THIS MATCH, BILLIE JEAN?

BILLIE: THE SALES MOTION.

FOREST: PARDON?

BILLIE: YEP. TO ME, TENNIS IS THE ALMOST PERFECT METAPHOR FOR THE SALES MOTION.

FOREST: (Feigning interest.) REALLY.

BILLIE: THE SALES MOTION, AS YOU KNOW, FOREST, IS THE BASIC DYNAMIC OF THE SALES SITUATION.

FOREST: BUT, TENNIS…

BILLIE: …IS A CONSTANT FLOW OF UNPREDICTABLE ACTION— AND ALTHOUGH IT ALWAYS FOLLOWS THE SAME RULES, IT NEVER HAPPENS EXACTLY THE SAME TWICE, RIGHT?

FOREST: WELL, YES…

BILLIE: JUST LIKE THE PRO OUT THERE, THE SALES REP HAS TO BE FLEXIBLE, READY FOR ANYTHING… PREPARED TO RESPOND. THAT'S THE SALES MOTION.

FOREST: TENNIS IS DIFFERENT…

BILLIE: OH, YES, FOREST. THERE'S A *BIG* DIFFERENCE. IN THE SALES MOTION, THE OTHER PARTY IS NOT YOUR OPPONENT BUT YOUR PARTNER. YOU HAVE TO WIN TOGETHER.

FOREST: STILL, BILLIE JEAN…

BILLIE: STILL-MOTION STUDIES HAVE SHOWN THERE ARE FOUR DISTINCT STAGES TO THE SALES MOTION. DID YOU KNOW THAT, FOREST.

FOREST: NO. (Lowering voice.) AH, LENDL'S ABOUT TO SERVE.

BILLIE: (Lowering voice.) THE SERVE IS LIKE THE FIRST STEP— THE "ATTENTION" STAGE OF THE SALE MOTION IN WHICH THE SALES REP CAPTURES THE CUSTOMER'S ATTENTION.

Source: From "The Sales Motion," written by Ed Schultz, produced by Jack Gagliardo, directed by William Rogers for General Foods Corp. Used by permission.

Script Example B.10: Audiocassette Script

MUSIC: (An Up-tempo Dixieland jazz theme hits full. We let the infectious rhythm play full for a few seconds, then PULL UNDER.)

NARRATOR: THAT'S A MUSICAL THEME SET TO THE BEAT OF A NATURAL RHYTHM...

AND HERE'S ANOTHER NATURAL RHYTHM WITH A STRONG BEAT...

SOUND EFX: (Musical theme segues into the steady pulsing of a strong, regular heartbeat.

NARRATOR: AND HERE'S ANOTHER NATURAL RHYTHM—THE FLOW OF THE PROCAINAMIDE DETAIL...

SALES REPRESENTATIVE: ...PROCAINAMIDE IS A NATURAL CHOICE AS FIRST-LINE THERAPY SINCE IT OFFERS: VERSATILITY BY TREATING BOTH VENTRICULAR AND ATRIAL ARRHYTHMIAS; COMPATIBILITY WITH DIGOXIN; (Pull under.) DEPENDABILITY OF MAINTAINING THERAPEUTIC DOSING LEVELS ALL DAY AND ALL NIGHT...

NARRATOR: RECENTLY, HOWEVER, THE NATURAL RHYTHMS OF THIS DETAIL ARE NOT BEING HEARD ON A REGULAR BASIS IN DOCTOR'S OFFICES AND HOSPITALS AROUND THE COUNTRY.

WE'RE GIVING COMPETITION THE OPPORTUNITY TO DROWN OUT OUR MESSAGE BY PLAYING INFERIOR THEMES...

SALES REPRESENTATIVE: ...DOCTOR, FOR YOUR PATIENTS WITH EITHER ATRIAL OR VENTRICULAR ARRHYTHMIAS, WILL YOU PRESCRIBE PROCAINAMIDE AS FIRST-LINE THERAPY?

AUDIO MIX: (Mix of voices detailing competitive products comes in on top of Sales Rep. The resulting babble drowns out the company Sales Representative.)

"QUINIDINE FREQUENTLY RESULTS IN GREATER THAN 90 PERCENT REDUCTION IN VENTRICULAR ECTOPY..."

"...DISOPYRAMIDE HAS PROVEN EXTREMELY EFFICACIOUS IN STABILIZING VENTRICULAR ARRHYTHMIAS..."

"...THIS DRUG'S RELATIVELY LONG THIRTEEN-HOUR HALF-LIFE MAKES IT SUITABLE FOR TWICE-DAILY DOSING, IMPROVING PATIENT COMPLAINCE..."

"...PROPRANOLOL IS INDICATED FOR TREATING BOTH SUPRAVENTRICULAR AND VENTRICULAR ARRHYTHMIAS..."

SOUND EFX: (At this point, a cacophony of dissonant themes, with audio effects to simulate wow and flutter, overpowers the company detail.)

MUSIC: (Establish bossa-nova or other soothing rhythmic beat, then PULL UNDER.)

NARRATOR: IN THIS PROGRAM, WE'LL PRACTICE THE NATURAL RHYTHMS OF THE PROCAINAMIDE DETAIL TO GENERATE THE STRONG, STEADY BEAT OF CONTINUED MARKET SHARE FOR THE PRODUCT. IT'S A BEAT THAT'S IRRESISTIBLE WHEN THE ENTIRE SALES FORCE PLAYS THE SAME THEME TO PERFEC-TION...

MUSIC: (Return to Dixieland main theme.)

NARRATOR: WE ASKED BOB TOBIN, PROCAINAMIDE PRODUCT MANAGER, TO PUT THE NEED FOR INCREASED DETAILING INTO PERSPECTIVE...

BOB TOBIN: (Key points:
• Introduction of generics and new products have created a more competitive environment.
• Fact remains, however, that when you analyze features and benefits compared to competitive strengths and weaknesses, procainamide still merits market leadership position.

NARRATOR: WHAT IS THE GOAL OF INCREASED DETAILING?

BOB TOBIN: Key points:
• Make certain cardiologist is fully aware of the competitive benefits procainamide offers.
• One-on-one detailing is crucial because only the sales represen-tative can address the specific concerns or issues which might make cardiologist or internist prescribe a competing product.

Source: From "The Beat," written by William Van Nostran, directed by David P. Emmerling for The O'Hara Company. Used by permission.

GLOSSARY

Actuality audio: Audio recorded on location to capture the sounds and ambiance of an environment. Generally, this is unscripted audio, used more as a sound effect than to convey content. Examples: sounds of an airport terminal, hospital lobby, or playground.

Assimilation: The first phase of the writing process. It includes research but also involves the synthesizing necessary to make a subject one's own. The writing products that result from assimilation are objectives, audience profile, and content outline.

Audience profile: Description of the intended audience and relevant information regarding the communication environment and viewing situation.

Bandwidth: The volume of digital information that can pass through the available communication device. Low bandwidth causes a "bottleneck" in the transmission of large data files. This is why it often takes time to download high-quality graphics, video, or audio files over the Internet. (see figure 2.1)

Bombardment: Use of multimedia capabilites of interactive media to present the message through a variety of stimuli: text, graphics, audio, video, animation, etcetera. Often, several stimuli will appear within the same screen or event.

Branching: Interactive media term describing the decision tree created by the program designer to give the user the sense of controlling the flow of material.

Camera directions: These terms originated in motion-picture production and were adopted by the fledgling television industry. Some are also used conceptually to describe special effects in multimedia production and computer animation.

The media writer uses the following terms to describe the *distance* between camera and subject:

> LONG SHOT (LS)
> MEDIUM SHOT (MS)
> CLOSE UP (CU)
> EXTREME CLOSE-UP (ECU)

To describe *movement* of the camera in relation to the subject, the writer uses terms such as:

> PAN RIGHT/LEFT—A horizontal rotation of the camera along a fixed axis parallel to the ground.

> TILT UP/DOWN—Vertical movement of the camera on a fixed axis perpendicular to the ground.

> DOLLY—Physically moving the camera closer to or farther from the subject.

> TRUCK—Physically moving the camera left or right on a horizontal plane, parallel to the subject.

> ZOOM IN/OUT—Changing the focal length of the lens to make the subject appear larger or smaller.

Caricature: A portrayal that seizes upon certain individual qualities of a person through exaggeration or distortion. Related to "comedy of humours"—a type of realistic comedy developed in the late sixteenth century by Ben Johnson and George Chapman—which depicted persons whose behavior is dominated by a single characteristic, whim or humor.

Character generator: An electronic titling system to superimpose text or numbers over a video picture. Text is entered using a keyboard and then electronically superimposed over another video image.

Characterization: The creation of imaginary persons so credible they exist for the viewer as real within the context of the program.

Character narrations: Narrative information conveyed as a monologue in which the narrator assumes the identity of a character.

Chunking: Technique used by instructional designers to categorize content in small, discrete units that become elements of the overall interactive design. To develop an interactive flowchart, for instance, the designer must organize content into specific categories, or "information packets."

Client: The person who "commissions" a media presentation. Generally, the client has a business "problem" or organizational need that can best be met by a media presentation or combination of media working in consort. Usually, the client also holds the "purse strings" and approves the budget.

Computer animation: Generating and manipulating frames of animation by computer. Frames may range in sophistication from simple object or two-dimensional animation to highly complex three-dimensional modeling animation with lifelike detail.

Concept: A single idea or premise that shapes style, format, content and structure into a unified, interesting, and aesthetically pleasing whole. Once a concept is set, parameters for aesthetic and production considerations are established. Also: A storytelling theme used to provide a warm, human touch to the cold facts that constitute the content. Often, the media writer's most important contribution to a project is a strong, viable concept.

Content outline: Description of the points that will be covered in a media presentation with no reference to visualization, format, interactivity, or style.

Creative product: A creative result that is original, appropriate, and of high quality. We cannot call something creative unless we classify it as both original and appropriate. If we do not see it as original, it may count as fine craftsmanship but not as creative. If we do not see it as appropriate, its originality simply makes it "off the wall." In addition, an original, appropriate creative concept must be executed in a craftsmanlike manner so as to result in a product of high quality.

Creativity: The process of bringing something new into being; having the quality of something created rather than imitated.

Cyclorama (cyc): A curved curtain or wall, usually white, used as a studio background to suggest unlimited space. Lights with colored gels can vary the intensity and shade of the cyc.

Dialogue: Conversation of two or more people as reproduced through a script. Gives the impression of naturalness without being a verbatim record (a semblance of reality, not reality itself). Good dialogue varies in diction, rhythm, phrasing, sentence length, etcetera, according to the character of the speakers.

Digital media: Media that is delivered via bits and bytes, typically using a computer and software programs as a means of displaying and interacting with the content by user commands. The Internet is one form of digital medium. The CD-ROM and digital video disc (DVD) are both methods used to record and provide access to digital media files.

Distance learning: Learning facilitated by technology to offer users access to instructors or content by overcoming a space or time barrier. Examples would be instruction via a teleconference or Web site or other facilitating technology. Provides a "classroom without walls" type of learning model.

Drafting: Third stage in the writing process following sssimilation and rehearsal. In drafting, the writer's primary goal is to generate a rough first draft script. In the drafting phase it is often helpful to suspend critical thinking and use "free writing" techniques to flesh out scenes. The writer's product is a first draft shooting or production script.

Dramatization: Any situation in which there is conflict between two or more characters.

Dramatization usually means communicating all content through dialogue and action. Dramatic vignettes, however, can also be freely intermixed and combined with other narrative formats.

Digital effects: Electronic manipulation of video images, graphics, or animation using computer hardware and software designed specifically for television and computer graphic production. Some simple, standard digital effects include "page turns," "flips," and "wipes."

Docudrama: Strictly speaking, a docudrama is a dramatization of an actual event that combines elements of documentary film production and style with dramatic restagings using actors/actresses to capitalize on the entertainment value of characters in dramatic situations. The term is also used more loosely to suggest any dramatization done in a documentary style.

Flow chart: A chart used in interactive-media design to map and illustrate the branching possibilities available to users interacting with the finished program.

Freeze frame: Technique of taking a single video or film frame and "freezing" the action to create a still-picture image on video or film.

Fully developed character: A realistic portrayal of an individual that reveals a variety of complex, sometimes contradictory motivations. Usually the individual's reaction to a situation cannot be predicted easily .

Functionality: The use of various computer capabilities to enhance the user's access to information or overall experience. A pull-down menu is a common, simple type of functionality. Linking key words of text to a glossary is yet another type of functionality. Offering a user the capability to enter data or "drop and drag" screen elements are both examples of differing types of functionality. An important consideration in program design is determination of what user functionality is most important to meet the objectives of the application.

HDTV (High-definition television): A new video production/display system with pictures composed of 1,125 scan lines compared to the traditional 525 scan-line picture. This produces an electronic image with the resolution and definition of 35mm motion pictures. With HDTV, the familiar three-by-four video aspect ratio gives way to something new: a picture that stretches the horizontal aspect ratio to something approximating 35mm motion-picture projection.

Hypermedia: Defined words or images that, when clicked, open other pages or documents. The most typical example is an underlined, highlighted word or phrase in a Web page (known as hypertext) that will "jump" the user to related information when clicked. This allows each user to create his or her own pathway through a document seeking only the relevant data.

Instructional design: The part of an educational system focusing on the design and delivery of content based on how people learn and how learning can be facilitated through technology. An instructional designer establishes educational objectives for the system, then designs media interactions to accomplish those objectives.

Interactive digital media: Involves use of random-access capabilities of the videodisc in combination with computer software in which the viewer appears to control what happens next. The interactive television viewer affects the outcome by selecting a specific sequence of events, using a keypad, touch-screen, mouse, or other interface mechanism.

Nontraining applications include video catalogues, informational kiosks, and exhibitions. When used as a "teaching machine," instruction is nonlinear and individualized, allowing a learner to create his or her own path through the content. Trainers can also receive printouts of each learner's test results for analysis or to demonstrate subject-matter mastery.

Interface design: The design of how a user communicates or interacts with a comptuer. Interaction designers focus on the flow of information, dialogue between user and computer, relationship of input to output, stimulus-reponse, and feedback mechanisms. The key to achieving a high degree of usability is to focus design efforts on the intended user of the system.

Interruptive video: A videotape presentation with stop points built in. Although similar to interactive video, the stopping points are often used in training situations to allow participants to discuss or test their knowledge of material presented so far. The interruptive program remains a linear presentation.

Kiosk: A free-standing computer, often employing touch-screen technology for the interface that is usually available to users in public places such as museums, trade shows, exhibitions, or college campuses.

M.O.S.: An abbreviation for footage shot without audio. Tradition has it the term comes from early motion picture days when a German director working in America would call for shots "mit out sound!" Also known as "wild footage" or "B-roll footage."

Multi-image: Display of two or more images *simultaneously.* The viewing audience responds to several presentational symbols often presented in rapid succession. A videowall presentation usually employs multi-image techniques.

Multimedia: Has come to imply use of text, graphics, animation, audio, and video for delivery of information using a computer interface, giving the user some control over the sequence of events and access to media or content.

Navigation: How content is organized or "chunked" to capitalize on the interactive experience. Navigation is often expressed on paper in the form of a flow chart.

Objectives: Expressions of the client's expectations for a media presentation. Objectives should be expressed in terms of communication/training outcomes.

Point of view, or P.O.V.: Used to indicate that the camera is positioned to represent the viewpoint of a character or individual in the program. (It's analogous to writing in the first person.) The technique is also used to create a sense of viewer involvement when screen action is shot as though the viewer is on-scene observing through the camera lens.

Presentational style: Dramatic writing in which the writer intentionally shatters the illusion of reality with dialogue in which actors "break character" to address the audience. May also be created or enhanced through striking use of stylized scenery, acting, costumes, or music.

Program format: A generic method of presenting information for linear media presentations. These include:

- Talking head
- Talking head with props
- Visuals and voice
- Interview
- Drama
- "Apples and Oranges"

Digital interactive media such as Web sites, CD-ROMS, and the like can also integrate significant amounts of text and graphics into a presentation.

Prototype: Developing an incomplete yet partially functional representation of a target system for testing purposes. Prototyping is essential to an iterative design approach, where a user experience is created, evaluated, and refined until the desired performance or usability is achieved. An ideal way of understanding the potential as well as the difficulties of development and scope of the interactive solution.

Random access: The ability to access any screen, event, or frame of program material almost instantaneously using the personal computer's multimedia capablilities.

Rehearsal: The stage of the writing process when the media writer focuses on how best to adapt content to meet audience or user needs to present content using the chosen medium. (Brainstorming and incubation are often used to stimulate concept development.) Typically, the rehearsal phase results in the media treatment, high-level design document, and/or flowchart, based on the needs of the project.

Revision: Literally, to "see again." This writing phase generally incorporates feedback from client, content experts, producer, director, and others involved in script development. The writer's ability to revise is often enhanced by setting first-draft work aside for a period of time.

Rollover: A type of computer program functionality in which an event occurs whenever the user places the cursor in a particular screen area. For instance, a line of text appears whenever the user rolls the cursor over a specific graphic element.

Script: A chronological sequence of events describing sounds, pictures, and ideas in media-production terminology. Can also be thought of as the scriptwriter's instructions to the production team on how to make the media presentation.

Segue: (Pronounced seg-way.) Originally a smooth transition between musical numbers, it generally involves an overlap or cross-fade of audio. Today, the term is used more loosely to describe transitions that involve overlapping audio and visual cues.

Storyboard: A series of simplified drawings, sketches, or computer graphics assembled to illustrate what happens visually on screen as synchronized to audio cues.

Style: The writer's (or client's or character's) viewpoint toward the content expressed through tone, word choice, music, sound effects, graphics, and visual special effects and use of on- and off-camera participants.

Structure: A planned framework for revealing the chronological sequence of events on screen.

Subject-matter expert (SME): (Also, "content expert.") The individual or group providing the technical input for script development and reviewing draft scripts for accuracy of content.

Subtext: Usually used in dramatization to suggest the character traits or relationships that are implied or known to the writer but that do not play a major storytelling or instructional role. Subtext gives drama a sense of reality, as well as rich, full character development.

Super: Term used to indicate the superimposition of text or graphics over another picture, often live video. Most frequently used to indicate titles or text to be superimposed over another video image.

Teleconference: A television program produced using conventional television technologies and techniques during which elements of the program originate live. The program is transmitted to one or more places, via satellite, where it is usually viewed by groups gathered specifically for the occasion. Sometimes viewers have opportunities to place telephone calls to the originating location to ask questions or make statements on-air or have their questions or statements noted and addressed later in the program.

Time code: The signal encoded on videotape to provide a readout of elapsed time on the reel expressed in minutes, seconds, and frame numbers. The Society of Motion Picture and Television Engineers (SMPTE) has set a standard for recording such signals on videotape. Time codes are useful to the scriptwriter for identifying content from production footage (such as interview material) to incorporate into a script.

Transitional effects: Media production terms used to describe the way in which one scene, screen or event is joined to another. Scriptwriters frequently use the following terms to describe a transitional effect in a media production script:

> FADE UP/FADE TO BLACK—All film and television programs begin and end in black. The very first image FADES UP from a black screen. The final image FADES TO BLACK. A momentary FADE TO BLACK can be used as a transition between major program segments.
> CUT—An instantaneous change between two shots or scenes.
> DISSOLVE—A momentary overlapping of two scenes or images. The tail end of Scene 1 fades out as the first image of the next scene fades up. The two images overlap for a moment, creating a fluid transition that signals shifts in locale, time, or content.
> WIPE—A visual effect as though Scene 1 is being wiped off the screen by the appearance of Scene 2. Wipes can take a variety of formats: horizontal, vertical, diagonal, etcetera.

Treatment: The writer's verbal description of sights and sounds imagined as a result of rehearsal and concept development. A treatment for a linear-media presentation expresses the concept *chronologically*, describing how action will unfold on the screen from beginning to end. The treatment is written as a result of the rehearsal stage of the writing process.

Videowall: Use of several video monitors (typically 16 in rows of four) arranged together to create a large video "billboard" for which videotape can be programmed to appear on monitors in various configurations.

Voice: As defined by Donald Murray, voice is the "illusion of individual writer speaking to individual reader (viewer)." It is the element of narration that gives a program its emotional force. A scriptwriter may choose from a range of human emotions when using voice: sad, detached, angry, amused, bewildered, etcetera. Voice is similar to tone or style.

BIBLIOGRAPHY

Brady, John Joseph, *The Craft of the Screenwriter* (New York, NY: Simon & Schuster, Publishers, 1981).

Brooks, Paul, *Rachel Carson at Work—The House of Life* (Boston, MA: G.K. Hall & Company, 1985).

Campbell, Joseph, with Moyers, Bill, *The Power of Myth* (New York, NY: Doubleday, 1988).

Cartwright, Steve R., *Training with Video* (White Plains, NY: Knowledge Industry Publications, Inc., 1986).

Davenport, Thomas H., and Prusak, Laurence, *Working Knowledge: How Organizations Manage What They Know* (Boston, MA: Harvard Business School Press, 1998).

Davis, Shelia, *The Craft of Lyric Writing* (Cincinnati, OH: Writer's Digest Books, 1985).

Dreyfuss, Henry, *Symbol Sourcebook* (New York, NY: McGraw-Hill Book Company, 1972).

Edison, Thomas A., *The Diary and Sundry Observations of Thomas Alva Edison* (New York, NY: Philosophical Library, 1948).

Elbow, Peter, *Writing with Power: Techniques for Mastering the Writing Process* (New York, NY: Oxford University Press, 1981).

Gardner, Howard, *Art, Mind and Brain* (New York, NY: Basic Books, Inc., 1982).

Gardner, John, *On Becoming a Novelist* (New York, NY: Harper & Row, Publishers, 1983).

Gery, Gloria, *Making CBT Happen* (Tolland, MA: Gery Performance Press, 1987).

Goldberg, Natalie, *Writing Down the Bones* (Boston, MA: Shambhala, 1986).

Goldman, William, *Adventures in the Screen Trade* (New York, NY: Warner Books, Inc., 1983).

Hilliard, Robert L., *Writing for Television and Radio* (New York, NY: Hastings House, Publishers, third edition, 1976).

Iuppa, Nicholas V., *A Practical Guide to Interactive Video Design* (White Plains, NY: Knowledge Industry Publications, Inc., 1984).

John-Steiner, Vera, *Notebooks of the Mind* (New York, NY: Harper & Row, Publishers, 1985).

Kirkpatrick, Donald L., *Evaluating Training Programs: The Four Levels.* (San Francisco: Berrett-Koehler Publishers, 1994).

Langer, Suzanne K., *Philosophy in a New Key* (Cambridge, MA: Harvard University Press, 1956).

Mager, Robert, *Preparing Instructional Objectives*, second edition (Belmont, CA: Pitman Learning, Inc., 1975).

May, Rollo, *The Courage to Create* (New York, NY: Bantam Books, 1975).

Matrazzo, Donna, *The Corporate Scriptwriting Book* (Philadelphia, PA: Media Concepts Press, 1980).

McLuhan, Marshall, *Understanding Media: The Extensions of Man* (New York, NY: McGraw-Hill Book Company, 1964).

Murray, Donald, *A Writer Teaches Writing*, second edition (Boston, MA: Houghton Mifflin Company, 1985).

Murray, Donald, *Writing for Your Readers* (Chester, CT: The Globe Pequot Press, 1983).

Negroponte, Nicholas, *Being Digital* (New York: Alfred A. Knopf, 1995).

Noble, William, *"Shut Up!" He Explained* (Middlebury, VT: Paul S. Eriksson, Publisher, 1987).

Peck, Robert Newton, *Fiction Is Folks* (Cincinnati, OH: Writer's Digest Books, 1983).

Perkins, D.N., *The Mind's Best Work* (Cambridge, MA: Harvard University Press, 1981).

Postman, Neil, *Amusing Ourselves to Death: Public Discourse in the Age of Show Business* (New York: Penguin Books, 1985).

Reeves, Byron, and Nass, Clifford, *The Media Equation: How People Treat Computers, Television and New Media Like Real People and Places* (Cambridge, England: Cambridge University Press, 1996).

Richardson, Alan Red., *Corporate and Organizational Video* (New York, NY: McGraw-Hill, Inc., 1992).

Rico, Gabriele Lusser, *Writing the Natural Way* (Los Angeles, CA: J.P. Tarcher, Inc., 1983).

Schlossberg, Edwin, *Interactive Excellence* (New York, NY: The Ballentine Publishing Group, 1998).

Seabrook, John, *Deeper: My Two-Year Odyssey in Cyberspace* (New York, NY: Simon & Schuster, 1997).

Sheehan, George A., M.D., *Running and Being, the Total Experience* (New York, NY: Warner Books, 1978).

Sterne, Jim, *What Makes People Click: Advertising on the Web* (Indianapolis, IN: Que Corporation, 1997).

Stoll, Clifford, *Silicon Snake Oil: Second Thoughts on the Information Highway* (New York, NY: Doubleday, 1995).

Swann, Brian, ed., *Smoothing the Ground: Essays on Native American Oral Literature* (Berkeley, CA: University of California Press, 1983).

Van Nostran, William, *The Nonbroadcast Television Writer's Handbook* (White Plains, NY: Knowledge Industry Publications, 1983).

von Oech, Roger, *A Kick in the Seat of the Pants* (New York, NY: Harper & Row, Publishers, 1986).

von Oech, Roger, *A Whack on the Side of the Head* (New York, NY: Warner Books, 1988).

Whittlesey, Marietta, *The New Freelancer's Handbook* (New York, NY: Simon & Schuster, Inc., 1982, 1988).

Widner, Doug, *Teleguide: A Handbook on Teleconferencing* (Washington, DC: Public Service Satellite Consortium, 1986).

Zinsser, William, *On Writing Well: An Informal Guide to Writing Nonfiction* (New York, NY: Harper & Row, Publishers, second edition, 1980).

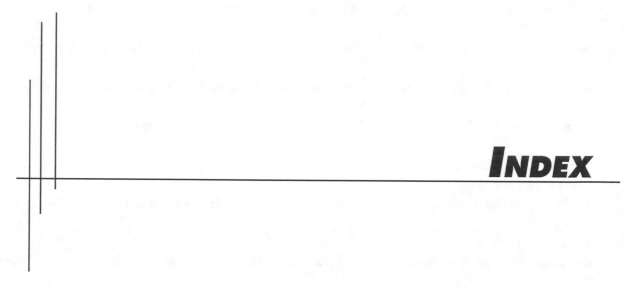